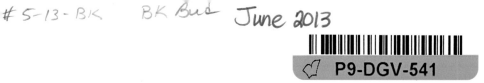

The Garage Sale Millionaire

*Make Money with Hidden Finds
from Garage Sales to Storage
Unit Auctions and Everything
in Between*

REVISED AND UPDATED

Aaron LaPedis
with **Jeffrey D. Kern**

WILEY
John Wiley & Sons, Inc.

Published by John Wiley & Sons, Inc., Hoboken, New Jersey.
Published simultaneously in Canada.

First edition published in 2010 by A Beautiful Media Publications.

For general information on our other products and services or for technical support, please
contact our Customer Care Department within the United States at (800) 762-2974, outside
the United States at (317) 572-3993 or fax (317) 572-4002.

Wiley also publishes its books in a variety of electronic formats. Some content that appears in
print may not be available in electronic books. For more information about Wiley products,
visit our web site at www.wiley.com.

Library of Congress Cataloging-in-Publication Data:

LaPedis, Aaron.
    The garage sale millionaire : make money with hidden finds from garage sales
to storage unit auctions and everything in-between / Aaron LaPedis with
Jeffrey D. Kern.—Rev. and updated.
        p.   cm.
    ISBN 978-1-118-37054-4 (cloth); 978-1-118-40800-1 (ebk);
978-1-118-40801-8 (ebk); 978-1-118-40802-5 (ebk)
    1. Garage sales.   2. Secondhand trade.   3. Selling—Collectibles.
I. Kern, Jeffrey D.   II. Title.
HF5482.3.L37   2012
381'.195—dc23

                                                                2012015378

Printed in the United States of America
10 9 8 7 6 5 4 3 2 1

Contents

Foreword

With this book, Aaron LaPedis has proven true the old adage, "One man's trash is another man's treasure." Aaron teaches us all about the main ways that exist for generating income from collectibles.

As the author of a bestselling book, international business consultant and cash flow expert, I have always taught in the world of business that marketing is one of the most fundamental things at which you must become proficient. That still holds true, but now I want to clearly make the point that there is another way to make millions! It's simply known as *hunting*. Hunting for great deals or hidden treasures and even unknown fortunes out there, waiting in someone's garage or storage facility; just waiting to be discovered by YOU!

How can you find them? Where are they? What do they look like? How can you plug into this cash-generating business? What do you need to do to locate these buried treasures, these valuable finds that can make you tens, even hundreds of thousands of dollars?

The answers are contained here in this easy, informative and fun-to-read book. Aaron shows you how to locate, identify and acquire treasures that can make you huge profits! He also tells you what NOT to buy so you don't waste your money on common junk. This unique book is a fabulous resource and will assist you in your quest to make a lot of money.

Read it NOW and become a real life hunter of treasure!

Jack M. Zufelt
Author of the bestselling book,
The DNA of Success

Preface

I Am a Garage Sale Millionaire!

That has a rather nice ring to it, wouldn't you say? Actually, there are many Garage Sale Millionaires out in the marketplace. You'll find them at garage sales, in secondhand stores and attending auctions. As you read these very words, many collectors and treasure hunters just like you are looking for and finding the next amazing deal that will make them a tidy profit.

You too, can become a successful Garage Sale Millionaire. All it takes is a little effort and some collecting know-how, and in no time at all you'll be on your way. It really isn't as difficult as you might think. With this book, you will have me to show you the ways to success as a savvy collector.

So what exactly is a Garage Sale Millionaire? A Garage Sale Millionaire is any individual who searches out those hard-to-find items, hidden gems or buried treasures (as I like to call them) and turns those found items into a profit. From my experience, not only do Garage Sale Millionaires make money reselling a few random items, they usually make very substantial residual profits over time.

Before I even begin to discuss the many ways you can become a successful Garage Sale Millionaire, one of the most essential elements on your new journey is the ability to have FUN.

What's the point of doing something if you're not totally enjoying yourself? In *The Garage Sale Millionaire*, I have taken all the mystery and guesswork out of this process as I show you how to turn everyday items into cold hard cash. Not only will you make some serious money, you'll reap a great deal of satisfaction in the process of doing so!

Leave behind the boring and mundane at your 9-to-5 job (or jobs) and let's spend some quality time together as I teach you the ins-and-outs of collecting, the know-how on where to find the best collectibles to sell for the most profits and all the vital information you need to know, so that you too, can strike it rich by buying and selling collectibles. With the assistance of my co-author, Jeffrey Kern, you'll gain valuable insider knowledge based on our 60+ years of combined treasure hunting experience.

By the time you've finished reading *The Garage Sale Millionaire*, you'll be well-equipped in this money-making journey and you will have the confidence to know exactly where to look for those hidden gems and buried treasures as you strike out on your own to claim your treasure-hunting fortune.

A Treasure Hunter? Is That Really What I Am?

The answer to that question is a definite "Yes." One of the key characteristics of any successful Garage Sale Millionaire is that you must begin to consider yourself an actual treasure hunter. It takes a treasure hunter's stealth mentality, along with a healthy dose of curiosity, to actively seek out and find that one hidden, never-thought-to-ever-be-seen-again item that you will be able to turn around and resell (or flip) for much more than you paid for it.

What is This Book All About?

Within the pages of *The Garage Sale Millionaire*, collectible-savvy experts will help you navigate the often friendly, yet sometimes quite unfriendly, terrain of treasure hunting.

I will personally lead you in the right direction and guide you along the best avenues to travel, so that you too, can turn the pursuit of finding often-overlooked items into money in your pocket. Throughout the pages of *The Garage Sale Millionaire* you will gain specific knowledge and tremendous insight that can only be gleaned from seasoned collectors like me, who are willing to share decades of collecting experience.

Remember, even in a bad, down or downright awful economy, there are definite riches to be made!

The Garage Sale Millionaire is geared specifically to giving you the ability to gain an advantageous jump on the competition by learning how to recognize and bargain for rare, hidden items that are actually authentic, treasured finds. Although the collectibles market is highly competitive, I will carefully guide you in your efforts to turn your newfound items into very healthy profits. I'll give you that ultimate edge and the advantage of the expertise and experience the most successful treasure hunters use to make their money. Never before in the highly diverse world of collecting has one book contained so many valuable topics along with an abundance of insider secrets, tips and tricks for successful treasure hunting. This book is meant to be used not only as an informative, educational tool but also as a guide that will direct you in your quest for an optimal treasure-hunting and collecting experience.

Additionally, it is my goal to make this book the official go-to-guide and the ultimate whenever-you-need-it reference you will use for many years to come. The information presented here is timeless and will never become outdated. How can that be? *The Garage Sale Millionaire* is based upon solid treasure-hunting principles acquired from many decades of proven experience.

I offer the proverbial no-stone-unturned approach for you to use in your quest, giving you as much information as possible as you travel down your personal path to becoming a seasoned treasure hunter and guiding you directly to the unique areas you should seek out when hunting for those hidden treasures. Throughout the years, I've experienced my own share of battles associated with getting those special pieces I just had to have. Like yourselves, I've struggled in the trenches common to most treasure hunters and I want to share that wealth of knowledge I've acquired with you now.

> **Million $ Tip**
>
> While you can't expect to become an expert overnight, you can begin becoming more knowledgeable over time by reading this book. As you gain more experience, you will become one of the more knowledgeable treasure hunters around!

My Pledge to You . . .

I want you to enjoy this book. So, if you ever have a collection of different items you need help with, feel free to contact me. Whether it's buying or selling, let me know and I will try to assist you. If you need a good reference for companies to insure, appraise or even auction items for you, I'm more than happy to help.

Please e-mail me at thegaragesalemillionaire@gmail.com or visit my website at www.thegaragesalemillionaire.com. I look forward to hearing from you!

Acknowledgments

Aaron LaPedis
I would like to give special thanks to Cindy Dunston Quirk, Jeffrey Zimmerman, Donna Sanford, Rich Kylberg, Jack Zufelt, Eron Johnson, Don and Judy Oglevie, Katherine Phelps, Paul Suter, Dan Gibson, Masten Hamlin, Rod Reece, Brian Neville, Mark Hewlette of Channel 12 KBDI in Denver, Colorado and Carolyn MacRossie.

Jeffrey D. Kern
I would like to thank Katherine Phelps from Beautiful Media Publications and Melanie Fischer from Reed Photo. Katherine, your guidance throughout this project has helped me become a better writer. Melanie, you've done a wonderful job in putting this book together and, as a result, have made it look fantastic. The hard work, patience, dedication and professionalism you've both shown has made a tremendous difference. Thank you both very much.

CHAPTER 1

Your Garage Sale Millionaire Journey Begins Now!

Even in difficult times, finding consistent monetary success as a treasure hunter is an attainable reality. So, how do you get from Point A to Point B? Point A, being where you are now, to Point B, reaching a point where you're successful at generating income from your treasure hunting exploits.

Although I was never particularly talented at playing sports, I discovered at an early age how to become exceptional at collecting different items from my favorite athletes. As a kid, I loved reading comic books and in fact, I still read them today. Due to my great love for these collectibles, I have added valuable comic books to my personal collections. Co-author Jeffrey was really big into collecting coins as a kid and therefore he has amassed an excellent coin collection. He has had a life-long love affair with television and the movies and as a result, has a very detailed collection of television and movie memorabilia.

What to collect? Start with something you really like and have a strong interest in. This

> **Million $ Tip**
>
> After figuring out what type of collectible you want to specialize in, go to the bookstore and start reading up on that particular item or set of items. Most collectible categories have numerous books or magazine articles written about them. Even if the collectible seems rare or of very little interest, there's probably a book written on the topic.

An autographed photo of Thomas Edison that was given to my
grandfather and then given to me. This was my very first collectible, and
I still treasure it to this day.

will ensure that the treasure hunting process will be much more fulfilling, as well as more profitable for you. Both authors of *The Garage Sale Millionaire* found specific areas of interest to focus on—certain collectibles we really liked a great deal when we were young. This helped set us off on the path to becoming lifelong collectors.

The Necessities

Before you begin your treasure hunt, you'll need a definite plan of action to maximize the profits you're attempting to make. If you're merely collecting items for fun, a serious plan is not important. When you add the goal of making money to the equation, a definite action plan is necessary.

There are some basic needs and necessities to consider before you can seriously begin your quest to become a Garage Sale Millionaire. By having all the proper tools at your immediate disposal, you can expedite the process and decrease the amount of time spent on pursuing your success. Now, let's discuss those basics and exactly what weapons you'll need to include in your money-making, Garage Sale Millionaire arsenal.

Computer

An essential component for Garage Sale Millionaire success is having your own computer. You really need to have a good desktop computer or mobile laptop computer to excel in this endeavor. Accessing a computer at a library, community recreation center, Apple Store or some other public location really isn't a viable option.

As a Garage Sale Millionaire, you're going to be conducting very personal business with bank accounts, credit cards and other electronic forms of commerce. Having your own computer is a

Million $ Tip

After setting up your e-mail account(s), access the Internet and search out local auction listings, then subscribe to as many auction e-mail lists as possible in your area. For starters, enter "How to find local auction lists" into Google (www.google.com) for a listing of auction websites. By taking advantage of various internet search engines, you can sign up and be constantly notified about many auctions in your area. Another fantastic place to find auctions searchable by zip code and distance is at AuctionZip (www.auctionzip.com).

necessity for keeping private matters private, especially since you'll be dealing with money. By owning your own computer, you will have complete freedom and total privacy to access the Internet, check e-mails and do business online where much of the treasure hunting business is conducted.

E-mail

E-mail accounts are extremely easy to establish and having your own separate e-mail account for your Garage Sale Millionaire activities is another necessity. E-mail accounts can be acquired free of charge through your **Internet Service Provider (ISP)**. **Windows Live, Windows Live Hotmail, GMail, Yahoo! Mail** and **Microsoft Office Outlook** are all very good e-mail tools for PC users. Mail is a great e-mail application for those individuals using Apple computers. If you plan on making this endeavor a serious business venture, you may want to consider having two e-mail accounts. That way you can better separate your business affairs from your personal affairs.

Software Packages

Having effective antivirus and firewall protection programs along with a solid financial accounting software program is another necessity for any prospective Garage Sale Millionaire. Treasure hunters in the wild need to be protected and organized during their adventures and expeditions. Every treasure hunter requires protection from all sorts of nasty computer viruses like worms and Trojan horses, not to mention spyware, phishing scams and professional hackers who prey on innocent e-commerce buyers and sellers, hoping to steal their hard-earned cash. These thieves can take a huge chunk out of your bottom line if you let them.

When it comes to the financial end of things, you'll need a good accounting software program such as **Peachtree by Sage Accounting (www.peachtree.com), Quicken (http://quicken.intuit .com)** or **IntuitQuickBooks (http://quickbooks.intuit.com)**. These programs will help you keep track of what you're buying and selling as well as any other expenses, large or small, you might incur as a result of your treasure-hunting business. You need to document everything for legal and tax purposes and to help you more effectively monitor your bottom line. Business software programs these days are quite intuitive for those of you who are not yet already accustomed to working with them.

To keep your personal identity and all your financial activities safe, you'll also need to get an efficient antivirus and firewall program installed on your computer. Programs such as **Norton AntiVirus from Symantec (www.symantec .com), Kaspersky Lab (www .kaspersky.com) and McAfee AntiVirus (www.mcafee.com)** have solid reputations, excellent track records and are very effective tools for keeping you and your private information safe while you're online.

Million $ Tip

If you can't afford to pay for an antivirus and firewall program, there are some wonderful free online alternatives. Two excellent free programs to use are AVG (http://free.avg.com) and Ad-Aware (www.lavasoft.com). Because I am talking about your hard-earned money, you definitely need to protect yourself online with antivirus and firewall programs.

Million $ Tip

To date, the safest computer you can buy is an Apple computer. Rarely (if ever), have viruses been created for the Apple platform. Almost every virus that has been unleashed onto the Internet to date has been targeted at computers running on the Microsoft Windows Operating System.

Digital Camera

You'll also need a good digital camera to take decent pictures of your valuable finds. On websites such as **Craigslist** and **eBay**, displaying really good pictures of the items you want to sell is an essential part of helping to make great sales. A picture of an item that does not look good online or one that makes your products look cheap or inferior due to poor picture quality will be a deal breaker.

Reliable digital cameras with excellent image quality can be purchased for surprisingly low prices. A few start as low as $50. Your digital camera doesn't need to be an expensive professional grade model to get the job done. All you really need in order to have fantastic pictures is a solid digital camera that takes a decent, good-looking picture at 300 pixels or higher. Two good brands to look into are Nikon and Sony. Check with **Walmart (www.walmart.com), Best Buy (www.bestbuy.com) or BrandsMart USA (www.brandsmartusa.com)** for affordable options. If the item you're trying to sell is accompanied with pictures that look appealing to potential customers, your chances to sell that item greatly increase.

Newspapers

Local newspapers and their classified sections offer a fantastic way for you to remain consistently informed about local flea markets, estate auctions, storage unit auctions, garage sales and anything else going on in your area that might be beneficial to your treasure-hunting activities. If someone is trying to sell something in your area, the sale will usually be listed in your local newspaper. You need to subscribe to all the local newspapers in your area as well as newspapers from nearby major metropolitan areas. Also, pick up all the local freebie publications in your area that you find in racks at various locations. This is the best way to monitor what's being sold and what's going on close to where you live on a day-to-day basis.

Although I've covered the basics of what is needed as you begin your journey in becoming a successful Garage Sale Millionaire, there are some other important tools that will benefit you greatly as well. The following are recommended to give you the best advantage possible to make a profit from the buying and selling of items.

eBay, PayPal and Craigslist: The Go-To Websites for Buying and Selling Items

eBay and PayPal.   If you don't already know what eBay and PayPal are, you are about to be introduced to the most innovative and effective 1-2 combination on the Internet when it comes to making money from buying and selling your collectibles. Getting registered with these two websites is an absolute necessity for any serious Garage Sale Millionaire. What follows are the need-to-know basics about eBay and PayPal. In Chapter 6, I will discuss eBay and PayPal in much greater detail.

eBay (www.ebay.com) is the number one website to make money from your treasure-hunting finds on the Internet. It is as close as you can get to a full-fledged, one-stop buying and selling destination. eBay has been tagged by many as "The Biggest Garage Sale of Them All," and I really can't argue with that observation. With billions of dollars in sales every year and millions of registered users, eBay is probably the most highly recognized, most popular and most effective website you can use to turn a profit.

When considering the best way to conduct your business on eBay, you need look no further than PayPal. **PayPal (www.paypal .com)** is the official electronic payment website and preferred payment method for all of the eBay user's financial transactions. The signup process for both websites takes approximately twenty minutes and is free of charge.

Because you're going to be using eBay and PayPal for buying and selling items, you will need to register a credit card along with your account. Users who just want to buy items and not sell anything, only need to provide payment information when they have won an auction.

> **Million $ Tip**
>
> Most vendors do not take American Express Credit Cards due to the additional fees charged to process each sale.

When selling items on eBay, it's very important to understand exactly what the fees are so you can price items accordingly. This allows you to gain the highest profit margin possible from any sale. On eBay, the two basic fees include an initial listing fee and a percentage paid to the website from every sale that takes place. The buyer does not pay any fees, but as a seller you can adjust the asking price to make up for any charges you may incur. When doing business with PayPal, understand that PayPal takes approximately 1.99% to 2.9% of the sale price plus 30¢ as their fee for processing each transaction. PayPal has a high level of security and protection for of all its buyers and sellers, and the fees charged by the website help keep activities safe and secure. Even though the fees associated with using eBay and PayPal cost a little, the positives (profits) certainly far outweigh the negatives (nominal costs).

Craigslist. Craigslist (www.craigslist.org) is another online marketplace where you can buy and sell goods from toys and coins to computers, cars and art. On Craigslist, there are no registration fees or selling fees, so it is completely free to use. Because of the tremendous profit potential Craigslist offers, this website needs to be on your short list of important places for making money. Craigslist is full of fantastic bargains. When you're buying and selling on Craigslist, you must always be aware of the possibility of potential scams that fraudulent users enact to try and separate you from your money. Always make sure you receive certified funds, use PayPal or accept cash for anything you sell. Always remember to get a receipt in writing.

Craigslist is in all 50 states and in over 60 countries, so you can list your items for sale or buy items locally, nationally or internationally. I will cover Craigslist in more detail in Chapter 5.

Separate Shipping Address and Shipping Account

One of the benefits of having a *separate shipping address* for conducting your treasure-hunting business is that you can effectively separate your collectible dealings from your personal dealings. Although getting a separate shipping address is optional and may cost you a nominal fee, it might be the best way to do business.

> **Million $ Tip**
>
> Do all your own packing. Never pay people to pack items for you, as this unnecessary expense will take a big bite out of your profits.

A separate shipping address involves renting a mailbox at an established business such as **The UPS Store (www.theupsstore.com)**. You will also have a physical location away from your home to use for shipping items to customers and also a place that signs for and receives all your packages. One of the best perks that comes with owning a separate mailing address is that you don't have to be present to receive your packages. The store's staff will sign for any shipment and store it securely for you until you come to pick it up. There are, however, a couple of negatives involved with having this type of arrangement. There is a semiannual or annual rental fee for the mailbox and you have to travel back and forth to pick up items you've purchased or ship items you've sold.

Another option to consider is shipping directly from your home to save money on overhead. If you decide on this option, you need to know that major carriers such as FedEx and UPS normally require physical signatures upon delivery for anything of value. Many times shipping companies will not deliver items if someone is not on hand to provide a signature. You will need to be present at your home every time a shipment arrives. This could become an issue for those individuals who have full-time jobs outside of their homes.

The United States Post Office (USPS) (www.usps.com), Federal Express (FedEx) (www.fedex.com) and **United Parcel Service (UPS) (www.ups.com)** are three of the best companies to consider when securing a shipping account. Signing up for a shipping account is free of charge and it will help you better manage and keep your records organized. All the information you'll need to get a shipping account can be found on the company websites or at any location where they conduct business.

The USPS is very reliable and is usually your most economical option. The best shipping company to choose for high-dollar items is UPS. FedEx is a very good company, but the insurance limit on collectibles, especially art, is only $1,000.

> **Million $ Tip**
>
> When you take out insurance on whatever you may be shipping and something unfortunate happens to it, the **United States Postal Service (USPS)** has never, in my experience, paid off on any of my claims. This is sad but true.

Cash

Last, but not least, we come to the subject of money . . . cold, hard cash. Any new venture needs some startup capital and the business of buying and selling collectibles is no different. The more cash you have access to means the more collectibles you can afford to buy. The math is quite simple: more items to sell equals more profit.

If you don't have much upfront cash set aside for getting started, no problem. There are several other ways to get startup capital together for beginning your new venture. One option is using some of your personal savings and another is to look around your home to see if you have anything appropriate that you can easily afford to part with. Be on the lookout for items you're not using any more such as old stereo equipment, unwanted gold or silver jewelry, baby items, used books and videos, computers, coins and furniture. All of these items can be sold to generate some immediate start up capital. Whatever you have on hand and don't need can be sold or auctioned off to help increase your bankroll.

Your Journey to Garage Sale Millionaire Success is Much Closer than You Think

In this chapter, I've introduced you to some of the basic Garage Sale Millionaire concepts and philosophies. As we take our journey together throughout this book, I will delve much more deeply into what is needed to become a very successful Garage Sale Millionaire. The necessary tools for consistent Garage Sale Millionaire success are out there for the taking.

The best is yet to come, so let's get to it!

CH**A**PTER

To Buy or Not to Buy:
The First Big Question Answered

There's an endless array of items to search for when you're ready to set out on your treasure hunt. For everything that's either manufactured or found in nature, there's usually someone who has a desire to collect that particular item. Who knows what will intrigue someone to the point they say, "I just have to have that!" No matter how odd the item might seem, there is indeed someone who is feverishly trying to collect it.

Of course, there are plenty of obstacles that could get in your way and possibly derail your express journey to Garage Sale Millionaire nirvana. For every item deemed highly collectible, there is another item that is not even close. With literally thousands of collectibles available today, how does someone begin to target an item? What to buy and sell? What not to buy and sell? Which collectibles will make a larger profit for you? More succinctly, how do you find what is valuable and, in turn, what's not?

To give you a jump on your treasure hunting competition, I've compiled the following list of items that continue to increase in value over the years and will most likely make you the sizable profits you're seeking upon resale (*What to Buy*). I have also included those items that have no substantial monetary resale value whatsoever so you know what to stay away from (*What Not to Buy*).

As you can see, there are many areas from which to collect and many areas that—trust me—you should avoid. As you read through this chapter, I will highlight many of the items found on the list so

A Civil War diary from a soldier who was killed in battle (circa 1867).

What to Buy	What Not to Buy
• Animation Production Cels	• Beanie Babies
• Antiques	• Bibles *(Family)*
• Barbie Dolls	• Comics and Comic Books *(Post-1970)*
• Baseball Cards *(Pre-1970)*	• Furs *(Old)*
• Beatles Memorabilia	• Magazines *(Old)*
• Books *(Antique or First Edition)*	• Movie Memorabilia *(Signed)*
• Civil War Memorabilia	• Newspapers *(Old)*
• Coins	• Pokémon Cards
• Comics *(Pre-1970)*	• Rugs *(Antique)*
• Depression Glass	• Silverware *(Antique)*
• Disney Collectibles	• Sports Memorabilia *(Signed)*
• Fine Art	• Stamps *(Foreign)*
• Firearms *(Antique)*	
• Maps *(Pre-1700)*	
• Military Memorabilia *(Pre-World War II)*	
• Motorcycles *(Pre-1960 Old Harley-Davidsons, Original Indians and Military)*	
• Muscle Cars *(Pre-1971)*	
• Posters *(Pre-1977, Movie and Music)*	
• Presidential Memorabilia	
• Sports Memorabilia *(Certified Game Used)*	
• Stamps *(Pre-1920, Not Cancelled)*	
• Toy Trains	
• Toys *(Antique or Tin)*	
• Toys *(Pre-1970)*	
• Vinyl Records *(Pre-1977)*	
• War Medals *(Pre-1940)*	

you can get a leg up on your competition in maximizing the profits from your treasure-hunting adventures.

What to Buy

I'll let you in on a little secret of mine so you don't get off track or overly excited when you find something you believe to be of value. Don't be fooled if an item is old or looks expensive. Just because an item is old, doesn't necessarily mean it has any real value. An item that looks expensive very well could be a lesser-valued reproduction or replica.

Many people see something old and don't understand that there's a lot more to be considered than age when determining an item's value. Of course, sometimes older items are indeed worth money, but age is not the primary determining factor in assessing a collectible's level of value. For example, a newspaper from July, 1969, when American astronauts first landed on the moon, has no real value. A 200-year old family bible, although having an emotional value attached to it, also has no market value. By comparison, however, an empty liquor or spirits bottle that is 150 years old, could actually be worth $30,000.

Animation Production Cels

This is a Disney production cel with a production background, valued between $3,500 and $4,500. Bought at a garage sale for $150.

An original animation production cel is a transparent sheet on which objects are drawn to create an animated cartoon. Animation production cels are currently hand-painted from behind onto celluloid acetate. In the early years of animation, these cels were made out of a thin plastic or nitrate, with paint on the back or front of a cel. Each cel represents one frame of a character's movement on film. The animation production cels that have high collectible resale value are from the 1930s to the 1960s. One of the main characteristics to observe in determining an animation production cel's value is to verify whether or not the paint is flaking off. A pristine cel will be intact, exhibiting no signs of degradation to the paint. Additionally, animation production cels can be restored with little value lost. The other main determinant in verifying the value of an animation cel is to check and see which cartoon character was painted on the cel. Animation production cels worth the most money upon resale will feature Mickey Mouse, Donald Duck, Bugs Bunny or any other main or famous cartoon character painted on the cel. Secondary characters such as Minnie Mouse, Daisy Duck and

Elmer Fudd will not fetch as much money upon resale as their main character counterparts. Additionally, do not let mini-framed prints from **Disney (www.disney.com)** or **Warner Bros. (www.warnerbros.com)** confuse you into believing that they are authentic animation production cels.

A fantastic resource for learning more about cels and their value is *Tomart's Value Guide to Disney Animation Art: An Easy-To-Use Compilation of over 40 Animation Art Auctions Organized by Film, Character, and Art Type* by Thomas E. Tumbusch and Bob Welbaum. This book organizes all Disney animation art sold at major auctions since 1993 by film, character and type of art.

Antiques

Antiques are a huge business. How huge? When I Googled the terms "Antique Stores + Denver, Colorado" on **Google (www.google.com)**, approximately 4,950,000 search results were returned. The same search for "Antique Stores +" "Chicago, Illinois," "New York,

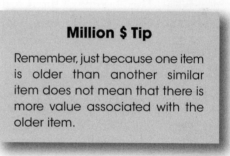

Million $ Tip

Remember, just because one item is older than another similar item does not mean that there is more value associated with the older item.

New York" and "Los Angeles, California" resulted in about 7,680,000; 25,000,000; and 11,400,000 search results, respectively.

When looking at any type of antique furniture, be it desks, chairs, dressers or sofas, it is extremely important to verify exactly how the item was put together. If the item is a desk or a dresser, check the drawers. Do the drawers match the desk or dresser or are they additions made well after the original manufacturing of that item? Also, make it a point to check the underneath and underside portions of furniture. This will tell you a great deal about the quality of the item and if it is an authentic antique, a restoration or a newly manufactured replica. I cover all of this and more, including how you can tell the difference between authentic antiques, fakes, replicas and restorations in much greater detail in Chapter 4.

Barbie Dolls

The Barbie doll was created in 1959 by inventor Ruth Handler. Since the toy's debut at the American International Toy Fair in New

York City, New York in 1959, the Barbie doll has been a collectible phenomenon with tremendous staying power. Barbie doll conventions are held in every major state in the United States, but not in any one state more than once every twenty years.

Barbie dolls made prior to 1980 have the most collectible resale value of any Barbie doll. As it is with pretty much every known collectible, the main component of value in a Barbie doll is its condition. Value is enhanced even more if the original packaging is included with the doll and it has not been played with very much. The most valuable among all the Barbies are the pre-1980 dolls that are still in their original packaging and have never been opened. When collecting Barbie dolls—especially the older pre-1980 dolls—you will want to make sure the doll comes with all its accessories and the original box is in good condition. The absence of the box does not eliminate the value of the piece, but it plays a huge role in retaining or increasing value.

There are several good price guides available to the Garage Sale Millionaire looking to turn a profit buying and selling Barbies. Over the years, I have found eBay, Craigslist and, at times, garage sales are all great places for finding those Barbie dolls that can be bought and sold for excellent profits.

Bonus trivia: The Ken doll was created in 1961 and was named after Ruth Handler's son.

Baseball Cards

Even though baseball cards are a highly sought-after collectible item, many of these collectibles have little or no real value. What will increase the value for any baseball card is the condition of the card, the card's age and the historical significance of the player featured on the baseball card. If the baseball card is a rookie card of a great player, that baseball card will be worth more money. Baseball cards that have increased in value over the past few years either have a player's signature included on the card or have a piece of the player's jersey in the card. A great way to enhance or increase a card's value would be to have the baseball card

> **Million $ Tip**
>
> Many collectibles from the 1950s through the 1970s have huge collectible value. If you have an item from that time period in good condition with its original packaging, you will have a better than average chance to make more money off of that item.

professionally graded. A professional grade on a baseball card could add up to 40% to its value and the fee for such a service only costs approximately $15 to $20 per card. There are several certified companies that professionally grade cards. I talk in great detail about grading baseball and trading cards in Chapter 7.

Beatles Memorabilia

Beatles memorabilia has been a popular item to collect since the early 1960s and is a fantastic collectible area in which to do business for excellent profits! As each year passes, finding authentic Beatles items from the 1960s and 1970s is becoming increasingly difficult. Some Beatles items to look for are old concert tickets, production cels from the

> **Million $ Tip**
>
> Unfortunately, for some reason many items from The Beatles were never taken care of properly over the years. So, if you do find an authentic item from The Beatles in great shape, you will more than likely obtain very good money for the item.

Beatles cartoon *Yellow Submarine,* posters, figurines, lunch boxes and vinyl records. To ensure the highest value upon resale, make sure concert tickets are not ripped or torn. One of the most collectible items from the Beatles catalog includes the "Butcher Block" album cover with its accompanying vinyl record. Even small posters that promoted many of the Beatles' concerts will net you big money. With regard to tickets and posters, always be wary and keep an eye out for fakes and replicas. You can find Beatles memorabilia on eBay, Craigslist, estate auctions and from time to time, at garage sales.

Books (Antique or First Edition)

Antique books and first edition books are what you should look for in this collectible category to maximize your profits. **Dictionary.com (www.diction ary.com)** defines the word *antique* as, "Any work of art, piece of furniture, decorative object or the like, created or produced in a former

> **Million $ Tip**
>
> Always buy books in the best condition you can afford. Actually, this advice could be applied to any collectible.

period or according to U.S. customs laws, 100 years before date of purchase." A first edition book refers to the first commercial publication of a work.

Why are first editions of a book so important? First of all, there may have been only one edition ever published. Secondly, there are normally many changes made to a book between the first and second editions. At times, corrections are made that many authors do not acknowledge in subsequent editions. Most importantly, the author may have signed the first edition when promoting the book. So, if you are able to find a first edition that has been signed, this is a huge coup. Buy it and revel in your good fortune! How valuable are signed first editions? On October 11, 2002, **Christie's (www.christies.com)** auctioned off first editions of the three *The Lord of the Rings* books by J. R. R. Tolkien, which were inscribed by the author to his son, Michael. These three first edition books, *The Fellowship of the Ring* (1954), *The Two Towers* (1954) and *The Return of the King* (1955) sold for $152,500 (Lot 373/Sale 1098).

Condition also plays a major role in determining the value of antique books. In first edition books published earlier than the 1800s, book covers were made of leather and were hand sewn. The better the sewing remains intact on the leather cover, the more valuable the book becomes. Many people collect antique books for years, yet still do not understand everything there is to know about this type of collectible. There are numerous reference books written on the topic, so before you jump into collecting antique books, I would strongly recommend you read a few books on the subject. Always match the reference books you're considering purchasing with several price guides that cover the same material.

Antique books and first edition books can be found at garage sales all the time. Estate sales, estate auctions and eBay are also great places to find antique books. Luckily for you, most sellers will not know the actual or true value of the antique books they are selling. Finding an antique book is actually like finding a diamond in the rough. This is a collectible you could easily find on any given day that could be worth hundreds if not many thousands of dollars.

Civil War Memorabilia

I love the subject of history and I especially love historical memorabilia. Historical memorabilia does not get any better than Civil War memorabilia. There are literally hundreds and thousands of items to collect from the American Civil War. If you ever visit Gettysburg, Pennsylvania you will be amazed at how much Civil War memorabilia is on display and for sale. From this particular conflict, you can collect presidential memorabilia and signed military memorabilia from the likes of Robert E. Lee, Ulysses S. Grant, George Pickett, Joshua Chamberlain, James Longstreet and autographs from numerous well-known and not-so-well-known soldiers. There is also an abundance of Union and Confederate coins and currency, as well as flags, swords, canteens, knapsacks, bottles, pottery, photographs, rifles, guns, artillery, belt buckles, clothes, plates and drums.

One of my favorite items to collect from the Civil War has been diaries. From an historical perspective, diaries are very important because each one includes the personal accounts, thoughts and actions of that diary's owner. The diary could be from a private, general, sergeant, doctor or nurse. If this person played a prominent role during the Civil War, the diary has increased value, as well as the added advantage of containing a lot of human history within its pages. These diaries will not be cheap—that is, *if* you can find them. Collectors are beginning to realize how highly valuable these diaries really are. Therefore, these types of items become more scarce every day. A fantastic source for determining the value of Civil War collectibles is *Warman's Civil War Collectibles: Identification and Price Guide* by John F. Graf.

Nearly any item from the Civil War era is highly sought after and very collectible. Most people truly don't know what they have when they put these items up for sale. Look for these historical treasures at estate sales and on eBay and Craigslist.

Coins

Coins are the number one collectible in the United States today. Collectors are always on the lookout for great coin finds. Condition is the most important thing to consider with this collectible. If a gold or silver coin is in poor condition, then the coin is only worth the gold or silver contained in the alloys of the coin. Also, stay away from foreign coins unless they're made of gold or silver. Overall, foreign coins are only a valuable collectible if you are knowledgeable in that field. I explain in much greater detail about coins and their valuation in Chapter 7.

But first, there are a few key resources you should seek out to gain a better understanding of coins and coin values.

The Professional Coin Grading Service (PCGS) offers invaluable numismatic information on their main company website at **www .pcgs.com** as well as a fantastic online reference for coins at **PCGS Coin Facts at www.pcgscoinfacts.com**. The two best books on coins and coin values, in my opinion, are *The Official Blackbook Price Guide to United States Coins 2013, 51st edition* by Thomas E. Hudgeons Jr. and *The Official Red Book: A Guide Book of United States Coins 2013* by R.S. Yeoman and Kenneth Bressett. Both books can be found at your local bookstore or on Amazon.com.

Comic Books (Pre-1970)

With pre-1970 comic books, there are a lot more that have value than those that don't. Unfortunately, the condition of most of these comic books is very poor. Because the majority of older, pre-1970 comic books are very valuable, some have been restored to enhance their quality and ultimately their potential resale value. If comics are restored properly, they will retain value quite well. Be mindful and ask about restorations when you find a comic book you want to purchase. Condition is everything, especially when dealing in the buying and selling of comics.

If you find an original comic book illustrated by a famous comic book artist, that particular book will definitely be worth more money. For this very reason, there are a few comic books made in the last thirty years that have great value. Even so, every one comic book that is valuable, I would say there are hundreds more that have no value whatsoever. For a fantastic resource on the Internet to gain a better understanding for which comic book artists are the best in their field based on each artist's technique, storytelling ability, accomplishments and longevity, visit the "The Top 100 Artists of American Comic Books," sponsored by Atlas Comics (www .acomics.com/best.htm).

Depression Glass

Depression glass refers to glass manufactured between the late 1920s and the early 1940s. From About.com Antiques, hosted by antiques guide Pamela Wiggins (http://antiques.about.com):

> Manufacturers such as Federal Glass, MacBeth-Evans Glass Co. and Hocking Glass brought a little cheer into some very dreary days by manufacturing the product we now know as Depression glass. This

mass-produced molded glassware was of relatively poor quality, often exhibiting air bubbles, heavy mold marks and other flaws in the glass; yet, it came in beautiful colors and patterns to suit every taste. The most popular colors with collectors today are pink, cobalt blue and green. It was made in amber, iridescent, opaque white known as "Monax" and several other colors. Some of the most popular patterns buyers seek are Cameo, Mayfair, American Sweetheart, Princess and Royal Lace. Even the pattern names alluded to better times and a longing for the glamorous lifestyles of the 1920s.

Depression glass also is an important collectible for reasons you may not even be aware of. Since the 1960s, this collectible has become much scarcer the older it becomes. An eBay search on "Depression Glass" turned up approximately 32,000 search results for this collectible with auction prices ranging from $0.99 for an "Amber Creamer" to $15,000 for a "RARE-Delphite 29oz Canisters-Delfite-ALL FIVE-McKee." This $15,000 listing is for a very rare complete set of all five 29-ounce canisters (cereal, flour, tea, coffee, sugar) made by *McKee Glass Company* during the Depression in delphite blue.

According to **Antique Milk Glass at http://antique-milk-glass .com/category/depression-glass**,

> One of the most sought after of all types of Depression glass is Jeanette Glass Company's Cherry Blossom pattern in the green color. The pattern is distinguished by having cherry blossoms and cherry clusters worked into the glass, and by having a delicate green shade. Jeanette Glass's Cherry Blossom is also extremely popular in pink.

When looking at Depression glass, always use a black light to determine authenticity. A black light or UV light is a lamp that emits small levels of electromagnetic radiation as well as very little visible light. When American Depression glass is held under a black light, the piece will cast a fluorescent glow. Reproductions of Depression glass, however, will not display any fluorescent glowing properties.

Million $ Tip

A black light is a potent weapon for any Garage Sale Millionaire to use. So, if you are planning on being in this business for a while, a black light is a tool you should invest in sooner rather than later.

Certain elements within Depression glass absorb invisible light and then discharge that light. When this discharge occurs, the fluorescent glowing effect will be observed. Black lights can be purchased via the Internet with pricing ranging from as little as $15 up to $125.

Disney Collectibles

In 1928, Walt Disney created his iconic animated masterpiece, Mickey Mouse. From Mickey's humble beginnings, **The Walt Disney Company (http://thewaltdisneycompany.com)** has evolved into a multi-billion dollar company with theme parks and resorts located all over the world, live action and animated motion pictures, television shows, stage productions, music industry acts, video games, an amazing amount of consumer products and the Disney Channel television network. Because of the Walt Disney Company's amazing popularity throughout the decades, anything produced by Disney has usually been worth very good money. But, since the late 1980s, many items released by Disney have become less than desirable to knowledgeable collectors. Nowadays, just because an item includes the Disney name, there is no automatic guarantee that there will be a lasting value associated with the item. I've seen many people who think because there is a Disney stamp on an item it is a genuine, properly licensed product from the company. Due to this common misconception, you'll need to do some research before buying any Disney collectible.

So what are some valuable collectible items from Disney? Pre-1960 animation products from Disney are worth a great deal of money. Many of the classics produced by Disney before 1960 introduced characters beloved around the world like Mickey and Minnie Mouse, Donald Duck, Pluto and Goofy. Other valuable items from Disney are pieces from the Walt Disney Classics Collection, or WDCC. The WDCC consists of a set of porcelain sculptures which were first released in the early 1990s. These sculptures have grown in value since they were first released, but have recently lost value due to their being sold in mass quantities on eBay. Old Disney watches and toys, with their original boxes, from the 1940s, 1950s and the early 1960s also have great value. But, here again, condition is the essential factor.

Disney collectibles can easily be found at many garage sales and estate sales and can also be found online for sale on eBay and Craigslist. When you are looking for Disney collectibles, always be aware there are a great number of people selling these items. You need to know what these items are worth before buying anything. To get an idea of the current value of Walt Disney Classics Collection items, please visit **www.disneyclassics.net**. Also, there are many great books available on the subject of collecting Disney paraphernalia. They can be found at your local bookstores and from sources on the Internet.

If you want to buy and sell Disney collectibles for a profit in your Garage Sale Millionaire endeavors, always make sure you do your research first.

Fine Art

Because I own a fine art gallery, you could say fine art is my true love. I have a passion for dealing in fine art, animation cels and sports and entertainment memorabilia and I work closely with popular artists who consistently have meet-and-greet events at my gallery. I'm not recommending you use my gallery, Fascination St. Fine Art, as your fine art gallery, but if you're looking to buy art, do find a reputable gallery in your area where you can develop a rapport with the owners and feel comfortable as a customer.

> **Million $ Tip**
>
> When buying art from a fine art gallery, always give the gallery a chance to earn your business. If you like something and feel the price is too high, make them an offer. It never hurts to try. All fair offers made in my gallery are accepted.

I really want you to understand that art is a great investment and is a great collectible either to own or resell for future profits. Most art you will find is framed. Although the frame may look very nice, it might be hiding many problems. Framing can hide a multitude of flaws on any piece of art. These can include physical damage to the piece of art, an incorrectly trimmed edge or color fading near the edges. Any of these defects will greatly diminish the value of the artwork.

Before you spend money on a piece of art, separate the actual artwork from the frame. I will guarantee you that for every 30 pieces you buy and take apart, at least one of those items will have flaws that have been hidden by the frame. Dry mounting the art to a piece of cardboard, foam board or foam core will eliminate the value of the piece as well unless it was an archival mount. An archival mount uses a dry mounting adhesive that consists of an acid-free tissue coated on both sides of the item you're getting mounted with a low temperature, acid-free adhesive. The acid-free tissue contains an alkaline buffering agent, which neutralizes environmental degradation. A qualified framer can tell you if your art has been mounted using archival standards.

Million $ Tip

Always remove art from a frame before you buy. Art could be damaged and the frame can hide it.

When you're looking for art, whether it's on Craigslist or eBay, in an art gallery or at a local garage sale, it's important to know the difference between original art, limited edition prints and a poster of an original piece of art. Unless you're an expert or until you have the piece removed from the frame, it is not always easy to tell the difference. An original is a piece of art that was completed entirely by the artist. Nothing on the canvas or piece's surface was added by anyone other than the artist. A limited edition print is any work of art that has a fixed number of copies or examples and may or may not be signed. A poster of an original piece of art is simply a poster with the image of an art piece and has very little real value.

It is also a good idea to look at the art without any sort of barrier such as glass. Also, ask to see the original Certificate of Authenticity or COA from the publisher. A Certificate of Authenticity is a document a gallery or collectibles store gives to the client, which comes from the publisher, guaranteeing the authenticity of the item you want to purchase. Do not accept a COA originated by the gallery or collectibles store and definitely do not accept a COA from someone who just sold you the piece (unless they are the artist's publisher); you must have an original COA from the artist's publisher. This certificate will tell you everything you need to know about the item. Furthermore, make sure you match the number on the COA with the number on the piece of art. If the numbers don't match, then ask the fine art gallery for the matching certificate. If they cannot provide one, you may have to rethink your purchase decision and pass on the item. When buying from a non-gallery venue such as a collectibles store, the process is still the same. *Always* make certain to ask for the original COA. If the retailer does not have the original certificate, either rethink your purchase or have your local gallery advise you on the item in question (just as you would in dealing with a fine art gallery). A local fine art gallery will usually appraise or certify a piece for a nominal fee or even for free if they are going to re-frame the item for you. I discuss Certificates of Authenticity in Chapter 4 in greater detail.

If your piece of art is damaged and the artist is still alive, there is a chance you can have your local gallery call the publisher directly so that they can replace the piece of art for a small fee. If you picked up the art piece for a really cheap price and it's damaged, there is a good chance you can get that piece of art replaced. What actually happens when it's replaced? The publisher takes your damaged piece of art, destroys it, reprints it and re-numbers it with the exact number you originally had. He or she then has the artist sign the new item. This common practice is completely legitimate, totally acceptable and is not considered fraud. What you've actually just done is purchase a brand new piece of art for one-tenth of what that same piece would have cost when it was brand new. Of course this does not work if the item you have is an original, as an original work of art can never be duplicated. You should always be absolutely certain that there is no damage to the original you are interested in prior to purchasing the item.

When you walk into a gallery and purchase an item, you're paying a premium to buy from that gallery. Although you're paying a premium price to purchase a piece of fine art from a gallery, there are tremendous benefits to be derived from the process of doing so. Perhaps you only want to buy one piece from them or you could have them do all of your framing. There's a lot you can learn from a fine art gallery owner about the art business. By doing business with a gallery, no matter how small the item you purchase, a smart owner will do whatever is necessary to keep you as a client. The gallery owner or the staff can also help you by answering questions. They can become a valuable resource for you in the future.

Firearms (Antique)

This is an incredible collectible with which to become familiar. There is a better-than-average chance you will not see antique firearms being sold at your local garage sale, but there are numerous antique firearm auctions held across the country throughout the year. For firearm auctions in your area, investigate listings in your local newspaper.

Savvy collectors know that when an antique firearm is not in working order its value will decrease slightly, but that particular firearm may still be a very collectible item and could net an excellent profit upon resale. Condition is another factor in determining an antique firearm's market value. Does the firearm have any rust? Is it corroded? If a gun is heavily rusted, noticeably corroded or if the wood on the gun is seriously marred, this will reduce the value substantially.

It is important to know that the buying and selling of firearms fall under the rules of the **Bureau of Alcohol, Tobacco, Firearms and Explosives (ATF) (www.atf.gov)**. What does this mean to you? When you purchase an antique firearm—or any firearm for that matter—is illegal for you to transport that firearm across state lines. So you need to be very cautious when you are buying or selling any weapon. I do need to clarify something, however, with regard to antique firearms. If a firearm doesn't use a type of ammunition that's currently available and instead, for example, uses black powder, you will be able to transport and ship the gun yourself. It is only when a firearm takes ammunition that is currently on the market that you cannot ship or transport these items across state lines.

If you find a modern gun you really want to purchase, you need to locate an authorized gun dealer in the area where the sale is taking place and have them transport the piece across state lines. Whenever you're buying a firearm, there is also a better-than-average chance you will have to apply for either a gun permit and/ or obtain clearance by the state in which you legally reside allowing you to possess a gun. If you are unsure of your state's gun laws, contact the ATF or your local police department. Yes, there are certain hurdles you must overcome when you want to own a firearm, but benefits in the form of potential profits (if you want to resell an antique firearm) certainly make it worth your while.

In antique firearms, the biggest and most recognizable names are **Winchester Ammunition (www.winchester.com)** and **Colt Manufacturing (www.coltsmfg.com)**. Weapons made by Colt have played a part in every war involving the United States since the mid-1800s. The Colt revolver, invented by company founder Samuel Colt, is known by many historians as the "gun that won the west."

The most valuable Colts were manufactured between the mid-1800s and the turn of the 19th century. The value of a particular Colt firearm may also be dependent upon the role it played in any given conflict.

The best Winchesters to deal in for profit are from the late-1800s when the western United States was the Wild West. These antique guns have considerable value if they are in very good to excellent condition. Once again, the condition of any particular collectible item plays a huge role in determining proper value. Actually, anything pre-1893 in terms of antique firearms will have a higher value and will be easier to buy and sell. When purchasing antique firearms, always be cognizant there are a lot of replicas that intricately resemble and copy old rifles and hand guns. If it looks like the condition of an antique firearm is too good to be true, this is a pretty good sign the item may be a replica or a reproduction.

> **Million $ Tip**
>
> The entertainment industry produces many replica guns for movies and television shows. Many of these fake weapons are available for sale alongside actual firearms in some stores. A word to the wise…always know your weapons before you purchase.

There are many great books on this topic available at your local library or from your local bookstore. The Internet is also a great resource to tap into for learning more about this subject. I definitely recommend you become as knowledgeable as possible about this collectible before you attempt to buy any antique firearm.

Military Memorabilia (Pre-World War II)

Military memorabilia prior to World War II will make you the most profit in this area of collectibles. World War II, the Korean War and Vietnam-era items have less overall value due to the fact that, from a historical perspective, these wars are considered too recent. I say this solely from a monetary viewpoint. There is, of course, an unbelievable amount of emotional value and emotional currency placed on memorabilia from these conflicts, as these wars were unquestionably important to many individuals and to the United States of America and American history.

The hierarchy of military memorabilia acquisitions solely based on value is, first, the Civil War, followed by the Revolutionary War,

World War I and World War II. Any collectible dealing with the Nazis is difficult to address due to the psychological wounds and deep social resonance that still affects an amazing number of individuals worldwide. Although you may be able to find Nazi memorabilia being sold by private dealers, this type of collectible is not allowed on eBay or in the classified sections of many newspapers. If you come across any authentic Nazi items to purchase, they will indeed be collectible, but you may have a difficult time trying to make a return on your investment for the foreseeable future.

As I discussed earlier in this chapter, Civil War memorabilia is extremely collectible. A few specific items I would seek out are Civil War diaries, weapons, uniforms and flags. All of these items are highly sought after by collectors. If you come across a good deal, you might want to purchase a few pieces. With Civil War movies such as *Gettysburg, Gods and Generals* and *Glory,* as well as the many Civil War reenactments which take place throughout different parts of the United States, there are many Civil War replicas available for sale. Most memorabilia dealers and individuals selling these types of items acknowledge the fact that some items are replicas, but many people are not so forthcoming with that information. Oftentime it is difficult to tell the real thing from the fake. Pre-1893 military weapons are also highly collectible. Guns from Winchester Ammunition, called Winchesters, which were used during the Civil War or to tame the Wild West are very valuable. Muskets, as well as handguns from the Civil War and the Revolutionary War are highly sought after as well.

You could easily overpay for many of these items, so be very aware of what you are purchasing. There are a multitude of books written on this topic in addition to extensive information available on the Internet. So, before you dive into this collectible, make sure you thoroughly research the topic.

Motorcycles (Pre-1960 Old Harley-Davidsons, Original Indians and Military)

Even though I personally enjoy motorcycles, my wife does not allow me to ride them anymore. Of course, the next best thing to riding motorcycles is collecting them. Motorcycles manufactured prior to 1960, including models from historied American motorcycle manufacturing companies such as **Harley-Davidson USA (www.harley-davidson.com)** and **Indian Motorcycles (www .indianmotorcycle.com)**, as well as military motorcycles, are the most desirable for collectors to buy. The number one name in motorcycles is, hands down, Harley-Davidson, with original Indian Motorcycles following as a close second. The maker of Indian Motorcycles has gone bankrupt several times since their founding in 1901, but in the late 1940s and 1950s they were a very serious player in the motorcycle manufacturing business. Unfortunately, there are not many Indian Motorcycles surviving today. They were not manufactured in large quantities due to the numerous financial problems and bankruptcies throughout the years. Because finding a vintage Indian Motorcycle is a rare occurrence, they are extremely valuable to collectors. Early Harley-Davidson or old military motorcycles from the 1930s and 1940s are also a very big deal. Many of these older motorcycles will be badly rusted and in poor to very poor condition when/if you come across them. If you do manage to find an old Harley, Indian or military motorcycle in a deteriorated state of condition, don't worry. The condition really doesn't matter that much. The rarity of finding just one of these types of collectibles more than makes up for much of the deteriorated condition the motorcycles may exhibit. Anytime you find one of these types of motorcycles, it will be a *very* valuable find.

When you visit a prospective seller's home and speak with them about their collectibles, always ask about motorcycles. If people have an old barn or garage that looks like no one has gone through it in a while, make sure to inquire (politely) about what might be stored inside. You could just be the one person to find that missing original Indian Motorcycle or that one hard-to-find classic Harley-Davidson no one has been able to discover over the decades. The worst anyone can say is, "No." If you do happen across one of these bikes, quickly think of a way to get this valuable find off their hands. Negotiate a fair purchase price, buy the item and have it moved immediately before someone else does. Congratulations! You have just put yourself in a prime position to potentially make a lot of money when you resell. Believe me when I tell you that scenario occurs every day with real Garage Sale Millionaires across the country. With a little curiosity and perseverance, it could also happen to you!

Muscle Cars (Pre-1971)

When searching for muscle cars during your many collectible trea-sure hunts, you will most likely not see these kinds of cars at your local garage sale. But, with the **Barrett-Jackson Car Auction (www .barrett-jackson.com), Mecum Auto Auctions (www.mecum.com)** and **The Speed Channel Cable Network (www.speedtv.com)** acquir-ing muscle cars has come onto the forefront of the American col-lecting scene. Muscle cars are defined as American, mid-size cars manufactured from 1964 to 1972 that were enhanced with large, powerful V8 engines, superchargers and special exhaust systems. The first true muscle car was the 1964 Pontiac GTO, a car immor-talized forever with the release of the mega-hit record "Little GTO" by Ronny & the Daytonas. The most valuable muscle cars to buy and sell for profit were those manufactured before 1971.

Because we're discussing the subject of cars and more specifically, muscle cars, I'm sure you understand that golden oldies like these cannot be purchased for $50, $100 or even $1000. Muscle cars are going to cost you much more! I want you to keep an open mind about this type of collectible. Why? Because you can make substantial sums of money buying and selling muscle cars. Pre-1971 muscle cars are generating huge sales and an enormous return on investment. Muscle cars, which carry an extremely high value, are Fords, Buicks, Corvettes (with big block engines) or anything with a Hemi. A Hemi, if you're wondering, is an extremely powerful, internal-combustion engine.

Most people underestimate the money-making potential involved in buying and selling muscle cars. For example, a 1965 Mustang Custom Convertible recently sold for $31,900 at the 2009 Barrett-Jackson Auto Auction in Las Vegas, Nevada. According to the Ford Mustang's entry on **The Henry Ford Museum Website (www.hfmgv .org/exhibits/showroom/1965/mustang.html)**, when the 1965 Ford Mustang was originally sold, the vehicle cost approximately $3,334. This single 2009 sale accounted for a profit of over $28,500. This is just one example. Many muscle cars sell for tens and hundreds of thou-sands of dollars at high-profile auctions held across the United States.

The overall condition of any muscle car is very important to consider if you want to resell it with the least amount of effort and for the most profit possible. To determine a muscle car's condi-tion, check to see if there is rust or corrosion on the vehicle, verify if all the parts on the car are original and ensure that the Vehicle Identification Numbers (VIN) on the car's engine block match the VIN on the main frame of the car. Also, try to get all the information you can from the current owner of the car. If you ever find a vehicle that has only had one owner and he or she has documentation to accompany the car, this adds huge value to the vehicle.

When gathering information on any muscle car you have a strong interest in purchasing, try to find out where the vehicle was primarily operated or housed geographically. If the muscle car came from the middle portion of the United States, the Midwest, the vehicle will more than likely have greater value. This is because of salt anywhere in the environment. Salt is the arch enemy of muscle cars. The reason for being careful purchasing a muscle car from the states bordering the Atlantic and Pacific Oceans, as well as the Gulf of Mexico, is due to the salt in the air originating from these expansive bodies of water. Over time, salt in the air can cause a great deal of damage to a car. This type of damage is one you may or may not be able to see. Salt will destroy anything metallic on a car from its exterior finish to any part under the hood. Even though I have identified salt as being a prevalent problem for the states bordering massive bodies of water, there is also possible trouble from the use of salt in the Midwest because salt is widely used on roads to help melt snow. If a muscle car was driven at any time during the harsh Midwestern winters, there may also be salt corrosion and rust on the vehicle.

If a muscle car has all of its original parts intact, as well as the original interior upholstery and original external paint, then the resale value of this vehicle will be much higher. If you find a car that has been restored and re-painted, it will not diminish the value of the car if that restoration has been done properly. Many muscle cars that sell at auto auctions such as the Barrett-Jackson Car Auctions and Mecum Auto Auctions have been meticulously restored or have had a full rotisserie restoration. A rotisserie restoration is when a car is completely disassembled and the body is taken off the vehicle's frame. Next, the body of the vehicle is placed on a rotisserie, which can be turned to show any area of the car. From this point, the car's body can be sandblasted to bare metal, have any body work completed and be primed, painted and reassembled in exactly the same way the vehicle was originally manufactured at the factory. Just remember, if an automobile restoration has been rendered, make sure that restoration was done properly.

Dealing in muscle cars offers any Garage Sale Millionaire the chance to make much more money than with many other collectibles. Always do your research either from books, magazines or the Internet before you make any purchase decisions and you'll be ahead of your competitors when it comes to buying and selling muscle cars for substantial profit.

Posters (Pre-1977, Movie and Music)

If you love to collect movie and music posters, don't pay extra for the authentic signatures unless the signatures are verified as legitimate and authentic through a regulated agency such as James Spence Authentication (www.spenceloa.com). I talk about James Spence Authentication, or JSA, in more detail in Chapter 4. Signatures verified through JSA have already been certified as genuine, so you're not just taking a store owner's word that the signature is authentic. This is very important when you're ready to spend a sizable amount of money on that one poster you believe to be very valuable. Pre-1977 posters from the movie and music business are the most collectible.

> ### Million $ Tip
>
> Signed movie and music posters are two of the most often and most easily faked items in the history of memorabilia collecting. It is extremely difficult to verify and/or document that the actual movie stars or musicians signed the posters. My recommendation is not to collect these items. They are fun to have, but don't pay big money for them unless you have them certified as being authentic.

I traded Claude Lemieux his game-worn Stanley Cup Jersey for a box of Cuban Cigars. It's great when you have a trade that's a win-win for both parties.

Sports Memorabilia (Certified Game Used)

To be placed in the game-used category, a sports memorabilia item must have been used in an actual sporting event. With game-used sports memorabilia, the treasure needs to be properly documented with a Certificate of Authenticity, which could come from the team, the player who used the item during the game or from a certifying agency. This certification is very important, because without it this item is just a piece of used sports equipment with no importance attached to it. If the game-used item does not come from a famous athlete or was not used during an important game such as the Super Bowl, World Series or Stanley Cup Finals, then the item will be worth less money. With game-used sports memorabilia, condition is not as important as the player who used the item, so long as it is documented through proper certification of authenticity.

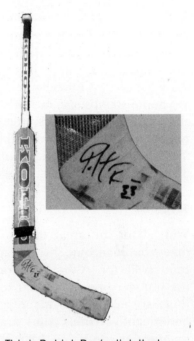

Stamps (Pre-1920, Not Cancelled)

I distinctly remember collecting stamps and coins when I was a child. But to me, stamps were far more fun than coins. With stamps, there was always a cool color picture and every stamp had a different story to tell. I've had great fun collecting stamps over the years,

This is Patrick Roy's stick that he broke in the last game he ever played in the National Hockey League for the Colorado Avalanche. I got him to sign it about six months later. Since Hall-of-Famer Patrick Roy, is probably the greatest goalie of all time, this stick could easily fetch $5,000 to $8,000 at auction.

but I have to share that stamp collecting is actually the worst collectible you can be involved in. Why? Because there have been millions upon millions of stamps manufactured over the years and as a result, many stamps retain no collectible value. Another reason for stamps being an undesired collectible is, if stamps are cancelled, that post office stamp (yes, a stamp on a stamp) eliminates any kind of value the stamp may have had. In addition to cancelled stamps, first-day stamp covers have very little value.

I know what you're thinking: "Why, then, did you list stamps as something in the What to Buy column when you believe they are the worst collectible you can be involved in?" Although many stamps have no true value, as previously mentioned, stamps that originated before 1920 and have no cancellation stamp from the United States Post Office are actually quite collectable. The only exception to the non-cancellation rule is if the stamp is dated pre-1800. With these early stamps, any cancellation will not harm the value.

Some stamps are, indeed, quite valuable. If you decide to begin the treasure hunt for this type of collectible, you really need to thoroughly understand how to value stamps. I suggest you get a copy of *The Official Blackbook Price Guide to United States Postage Stamps 2013, 35th edition* by Thomas E. Hudgeons, Jr.

Toy Trains

With all of the great toy trains manufactured over the decades, many have become highly valuable to the model train and toy train collector. Although **Lionel Trains (www.lionel.com)** will be the number one brand you recognize as you search for toy trains, there are many other manufacturers such as **American Flyer (www.americanflyertrains.com)** and **Bachmann Industries (www.bachmanntrains.com)** that have made classic and collectible toy trains over the years. Toy trains are a very entertaining collectible to become involved with. They have a very rich history and have proven to be an extremely profitable collectible item to trade in. Individual toy train cars, complete locomotive sets and entire toy train villages are consistently being resold for amounts ranging from just a few cents to tens of thousands of dollars.

Condition and packaging are extremely important factors in determining the value of any collectible and toy trains are no different. The better condition a train is in, along with its original packaging, the more money the train will generate upon resale. Additionally, some toy trains and toy train sets may have been restored. If restoration has taken place, the value will drop. When you buy a toy train that's very old, examine it closely to make certain your item hasn't been restored and isn't missing parts.

Vinyl Records (Pre-1977)

For vinyl records and vinyl record album covers to have any real value, they need to be packaged together. If you're looking to make any serious money from these collectibles, you simply cannot have one without the other. For example, if you have a record without its associated album cover, there will be no value attached to that vinyl record. Likewise, if you have an album cover without its associated record, little to no value will be connected with that item. Although vinyl record album covers made prior to 1977 retain the highest value, this doesn't necessarily mean vinyl records have to be from this era to have value.

Certain pre-1977 vinyl record album covers are substantially collectible with or without any of the signatures from the band or music group who made the particular record. The condition of these items is considerably important in determining value. With regard to old album covers, it is commonly known that some of these covers have been restored. Many Beatles, Rolling Stones and other album covers may be deemed highly collectible if they are the original album covers. However, do watch out for restored covers! If an album cover has been restored, it loses some of its value and loses *ALL* value if done poorly. This type of item is well worth collecting, but you must be highly observant and knowledgeable on the subject in order to make a profit.

Although compact discs and digital downloads have taken over the lion's share of today's audio market, vinyl records are slowly starting to make a bit of a comeback. According to Nielsen SoundScan in the *New York Times* (December 6, 2009), "Sales of vinyl albums have been climbing steadily for several years, dispelling the notion that the rebound was just a fad. Through late November, more than 2.1 million vinyl records were sold in 2009 . . . an increase of more than 35 percent in less than a year."

Vinyl records may still be considered a niche market, but those who continue to invest in turntables and stereo equipment costing thousands, tens of thousands, even hundreds of thousands of dollars are extremely passionate about their hobby. These impassioned collectors spare no expense in seeking out and buying the best vinyl available to play on their tricked out, two-channel audio systems. It's a point of contention among those who enjoy listening to music in a digital format, as in digital downloads and compact discs, to those who prefer to listen to their music in analogue format via vinyl records, as to which sounds better and more authentic.

On vinyl record auction results websites such as **Popsike (www .popsike.com)**, there are tens of thousands of vinyl record auction results listed. Vinyl records from groups and individuals ranging from the Beatles to Beethoven, Bob Dylan to Elvis Presley and from

Queen to the Velvet Underground can fetch upwards of $20,000 to $25,000 (or more) per album. Although the majority of vinyl records may not have a lot of resale value, older vinyl records from important ground-breaking individuals or groups in the music industry have great value and command substantial amounts of money upon resale.

Thrift stores are great places to look for vinyl records, as are second-hand stores, vinyl record stores and, of course, garage sales. When you find an old vinyl record, you need to check the condition of the record to see that no scratches are present. You'll also want to make sure the sleeve is intact and undamaged. Most importantly, check price guides to see if what you're holding is valuable. Websites like eBay and Popsike, as well as books such as *The Official Price Guide to Records, 18th edition* by Jerry Osborne and *Goldmine Record Album Price Guide: The Ultimate Guide to Valuing Your Vinyl* by Tim Neely are valuable tools in determining if the record you hold in your hands will be worth any money upon resale.

What Not to Buy

We now transition to those collectibles that are not so good and should be avoided at all costs. Sir Isaac Newton once said, "For every action there is an equal and opposite reaction." This quote directly relates to the following section of the book. As great as the previously mentioned collectibles are with regard to money-making potential, what follows is a detailed description of the equal and opposite collectibles that are not worth your time. Dealing with the following collectibles will do one thing and *one thing only*: waste your time and money.

> **Million $ Tip**
>
> Fad collectibles are the types of collectibles that are really hot one moment and really cold the next. With fad collectibles the excitement of a new collectible skyrockets and the price shoots up almost immediately. Then, when the collectible falls out of favor, the value plummets, never to be worth much again.

Beanie Babies

The number one fad collectible of all time, and an item that may be the worst collectible of all time is, in my opinion, the Beanie Baby.

A fad collectible is an item which when released for sale is extremely popular. A better description would be that the popularity of most fad collectibles starts out off the charts and the masses go absolutely crazy for them upon their release. Because of the overwhelming initial interest they create, fads attract a large number of collectors who assume interest guarantees lasting value. After the initial excitement subsides, the collectible eventually loses almost all of its importance and is left with no real value. I can't tell you the number of people, including seasoned businessmen, who hopped on the Beanie Baby bandwagon and started collecting them when they were first introduced by **Ty Warner Inc.** (now **Ty, Inc.** at **http://world.ty.com**) in 1993; some even spending tens of thousands of dollars. Beanie Baby collectors were obsessed with amassing these pellet-filled, stuffed animal toys that are virtually worthless in today's collectibles market. To this day, Beanie Babies are one collectible that had everybody fooled.

Experience has shown me that whenever there is a collectible that soars quickly, the chances are equally good it will plummet just as fast.

Bibles (Family)

There is absolutely no opportunity for financial gain in buying or selling family bibles unless the bible comes from a famous family. The average family bible does not have any resale value. Although a family bible may have personal importance to your own family, it will not mean anything to someone else's. Once again, unless the item originates from a famous family, you should not invest in bibles as viable money-making collectibles.

Comics and Comic Books (Post-1970)

Comic books are a lot of fun to read and, even more fun as a collectible to buy and sell for profit. As a matter of fact, I have a comic book collection myself.

Unfortunately, you'll have to search far and wide to find a comic book made after 1970 that has any resale value. Because comic books produced after 1970 were printed in such large quantities, the value of these items has diminished significantly. The large printing runs have hurt that value and the chances of that value ever increasing. Are there comics from 1970 and later that have value?

Of course! Comic book websites such as **Nostomania (www.nostomania .com/servlets/com.nostomania.CatPage?name=Top100ComicsMain)** and **Diamond Comic Distributors (www.diamondcomics.com)**, as well as local comic book stores, are great places to start looking for those exceptions to the rule.

When seeking comic books that have resale value, don't spend much time on comics produced after 1970. For the best possible profits, search out and acquire older comics made before 1970 that are in great condition.

Magazines (Old)

I know many people who collect old magazines. My mom actually saves old *National Geographic* magazines and believes with all her heart that her stash of Nat Geos is going to set me up for life if I ever need to sell them. With old magazines such as *National Geographic, Time, Life* and *The New Yorker,* it's difficult to find any true value. The only collectible value would be from a magazine's premier issue. There are, however, a few exceptions to the rule. *Playboy* has a few issues, in addition to its first edition, that have true lasting value. The very first issue of Playboy published in December of 1953 with Marilyn Monroe on the cover is the most valuable of any *Playboy* and can command sales of several thousand dollars. Many issues that originated in the 1950s and 1960s are also valuable collector's items, particularly if the copies are in pristine condition. With *National Geographic, Time* and *Life,* among others, there may be something on the cover that makes an issue very rare, but looking for these magazines is like finding a needle in the haystack. I would stay far away from this collectible because any upside opportunities are quite limited.

Movie Memorabilia (Signed)

Movie memorabilia is wonderful to collect, but you need to be aware that signed movie memorabilia is associated with a great deal of fraud. Many of the signatures and autographs used to sell this kind of movie memorabilia are often verified as fakes. When you're buying a signed piece of movie memorabilia from that famous movie star you absolutely adore, do be aware that the chances of the item actually having been signed by that particular person are basically slim to none. Signatures on movie memorabilia are extremely hard to verify unless you take your item to a company such as James Spence Authentication (**www.spenceloa.com**) to professionally certify your item as being authentic. I cover the topic of movie memorabilia in more detail in Chapter 4.

Newspapers (Old)

Whenever I speak to audiences or when I'm interviewed on the radio or television, people always ask about old newspapers. Unfortunately, the value of old newspapers is similar to stamps. Because there were tens of thousands, if not millions of newspapers printed over the years, many have very little value. Another strong negative component dictating a newspaper's lack of value is that they tend to yellow very quickly. Storing them together increases the yellowing process, so finding a newspaper in good to pristine condition is extremely difficult. If you want to talk about newspapers that may have considerable value, you'll need to go back to those printed in the 1800s. Try to look for newspapers dating historically close to the time when President Abraham Lincoln was assassinated (1865). If you find a newspaper you think has value, you definitely want to take care of it right away by placing it in a protective plastic cover. Like old magazines, this collectible has very little upside.

Pokémon Cards

Pokémon cards are another example of a fad collectible. The desire to collect this item was driven by kids between the ages of 4 and 18 years. This age group got so caught up in these cards that they gave this collectible a huge initial interest and a large initial resale value. As with any fad collectible, what goes up must come down. Eventually, the value of Pokémon cards came crashing down just as quickly as its interest skyrocketed. Many millions of dollars were spent on this collectible in the years following its 1998 introduction in the United States, but eventually, Pokémon card sales slowed. As a result, Pokémon cards currently have very little to no value at all.

Once again, always be very careful if you're interested in collecting something that could be considered a fad such as Pokémon cards or Beanie Babies.

Rugs (Antique)

Authentic antique rugs have great value, but this is another specialized collectible arena in which you have to be an absolute expert if you are to determine what's valuable and what's not. This collectible item also demands that you have an expert in your corner. You need someone with experience, someone you can completely trust to actually buy your rugs for you. Even if you work with professional, experienced rug dealers, you can still be misled with antique rugs because there are a great many replica rugs manufactured, easily posing as authentic, real and antique.

This collectible can be very expensive and if you're not an expert yourself, or you don't work with a reputable expert, I can almost guarantee you're going to lose a lot of money. Antique rugs are a difficult-to-learn collectible that takes a great deal of time to understand.

> **Million $ Tip**
>
> When verifying authenticity, look at the knots that hold the rug together. If the knots are uneven and the pattern is off center, this is storng evidence that it is hand-made. Carpets made after 1920 were usually made by machines. Take a few small pieces of that rug's fabric and light them on fire. Then, look at the color of the flame. If there is a color in the flame (other than the color of a normal flame, that is), then you know you have a newer carpet and not an authentic handmade. Also, if the carpet is made of real silk, when you light a small piece of it on fire, it will melt and smell like burnt hair. If it turns brittle and breaks off, it is something else. High-end carpets have 500 knots per square inch. Of course, always use the utmost caution when working with fire to avoid any accidents!

Silverware (Antique)

Pure silver was never used in antique silverware because it is actually too soft of a compound unless mixed with other alloys. All antique silverware was produced with different types of metals along with the pure silver. Antique silverware is collectible, but now it's mainly only desirable for the potential amount of silver these items physically contain.

Throughout the years there were a few early manufacturers such as Gorham Whiting, Towle, Dominick & Haff, Reed and Barton, R. Blackinton & Co., Tiffany, Unger Bros. and Wallace who created silverware that has maintained some lasting value. Finding antique silverware may pose challenges due to the rarity of the more valuable pieces. You really want to become very knowledgeable about antique silver before you buy.

> **Million $ Tip**
>
> As a rule, antique silverware will always be worth no less than the amount of actual silver each piece contains. If you are only interested in an item for its silver content, you will need to find out that information on the item before buying anything in this area of collectibles.

Don't get overly excited when you find some antique silver at an antique store or a garage sale that you think is undervalued. Do your homework before you make any purchase. Make sure you verify whether the piece of silverware is sterling silver or silver-plated. Many times people think just because a piece is old it's going to be sterling silver. Silver-plating was actually used more commonly than most people think, so be mindful of this before you buy. Also, look for the hallmark maker's mark or stamp on the underside of the item. All stamps on silver are usually on the backside of the silverware. Look for these marks on the neck, where the sharp edge meets the handle of a fork, knife or spoon.

> **Million $ Tip**
>
> Sterling silver is 92.5% pure silver. The remaining percentage is an alloy that is combined with silver to make the metal stronger. Most items that are sterling silver will have a stamp or hallmark on the bottom of the item.

With tea sets, these marks are always on the underside of the pieces. Most of the pieces should have some form of markings on them. These marks will tell you who manufactured the item as well as the percentage of silver it contains. This is a good way to tell if what you have is truly silver as well as if it is from a well-known maker.

If you don't have the proper knowledge of what's collectible and what isn't, that pricey antique tea set you're thinking of purchasing for its potential resale value, may not be worth as much as you think.

Sports Memorabilia (Signed)

Having been in the sports memorabilia business, I still enjoy buying and selling the occasional piece of authentic sports memorabilia. Recently, I had a yellow jersey from the Tour de France worn by Lance Armstrong during his last tour for sale in my animation art and collectibles gallery. This piece eventually sold for $10,000.

Sports memorabilia can really be as exciting and challenging as the sport itself, but like anything else in the world of collectibles, you must always be cautious when verifying to ensure an item is authentic. When you're thinking of purchasing a piece of sports memorabilia, always ascertain that the item has been certified by one of the major certification companies such as **James Spence Authentication (www .spenceloa.com)**, **The Upper Deck (www.upperdeck.com)**, **Steiner Sports (www.steinersports.com)** or **Mounted Memories (www.mount edmemories.com)**. Additionally, due to the popularity of eBay, there are many well-done fakes and forgeries. These items are mass produced by a skilled cadre of sellers in order to make a quick buck. I estimate that for every one authentic signature, there are probably two that are forged. For a piece to have any true value, you need to have it certified by a well-known certification company such as those mentioned previously in this section. This topic is covered in more detail in Chapter 4.

Stamps (Foreign)

You should stay as far away as possible from foreign stamps. Yes, like everything else in this world, there will always be a few exceptions to the rule. You could possibly find a few foreign stamps with some value, but from my experience, there aren't many out there. Even if someone is selling one hundred thousand stamps on eBay for just $100, it will take you an incredibly long time to find that one stamp that is worth a few dollars. It takes too much time and effort

> **Million $ Tip**
>
> Never buy international stamps if you're hoping to make money. Their only value is to people who are experts in this field.

to discover even a few stamps that might eventually have some sort of value. Again, this is one collectible I recommend staying away from altogether. When you're offered a great deal on foreign stamps, although the deal may be tempting, I'm telling you, by all means, trust me on this: run as fast as you can in the opposite direction!

"To Buy or Not to Buy? That is the Question!"

In this chapter, I described many categories of items you will encounter on a daily basis as you foray out on your adventurous treasure hunts. When you come across a piece that interests you, you'll need to determine if it falls under the category of What to Buy, or if it falls under the category of What Not to Buy.

Eventually, you'll find one particular item that intrigues you so much you're moved to start collecting it. When you find one collectible that's right for you and you want to start buying and selling, read everything you can about that item. Strive to become an expert in that collectible. Thoroughly research your interests and re-read this book. And always remember, there is much to learn and great fun to be had in educating yourself about your particular collectible.

Often, when you first begin collecting one item, such as antiques or fine art, you will most likely become interested in collecting other items in different genres. You may eventually pursue something far different in an area you never imagined could hold your attention. When you become a Garage Sale Millionaire, you need to be knowledgeable in several different collectibles. Why? So, when you go to garage sales, auctions, storage unit auctions and estate sales or when you buy and sell items via the Internet, you'll be prepared to purchase items to sell for a profit.

In this chapter, when I say a collectible has no value, please understand that I am generalizing. For every Beanie Baby, Pokémon card or recently created comic book, there will be a few items that will still have a value to some buyer somewhere. Also, no matter how often I say an item is something you should not buy, there usually exists a collector who will be looking feverishly to collect that exact item.

Most importantly, be careful throughout the course of your Garage Sale Millionaire adventures. I would rather you err on the side of caution, sometimes because the overall collectible category either has a bad reputation or, at other times, it may be that you're trying to purchase that one hard-to-find item in an entire collectible category that simply has no value. For all of the details I've shared in this chapter, I have merely scratched the surface with the information regarding the collectibles I recommend you buy as well as the ones I suggest you stay away from. As always, there are many great collectibles to be bought and sold for substantial profits!

Negotiating Like a Pro

In the first two chapters of this book, I suggested which items are best to look for and also those items it's best to distance yourself from. The next step in becoming a successful Garage Sale Millionaire is learning the proper way to negotiate the best deals for your treasured finds.

The Art of the Deal

To master the art of the deal, you'll need to understand a few different techniques for becoming the greatest buyer you can possibly be. Even though you won't become an expert negotiator overnight, the more you deal with items at garage sales, secondhand stores, estate auctions, storage unit auctions and on eBay and Craigslist, the closer you'll come to achieving expert Garage Sale Millionaire status. Being successful at negotiating is not based solely on how aggressive you are as a buyer. A more important skill is knowing how to talk someone down on their price in order to achieve the greatest deal possible. There are three ways to buy an item: face to face, over the phone or through e-mail. Of course, there are different tricks to employ for each of these methods that will yield the highest rate of success.

Dealing with Someone Face to Face

When dealing with someone in person, the seller will be able to look at you in real time and make lasting judgements regarding what your financial status might be. This is accomplished largely in

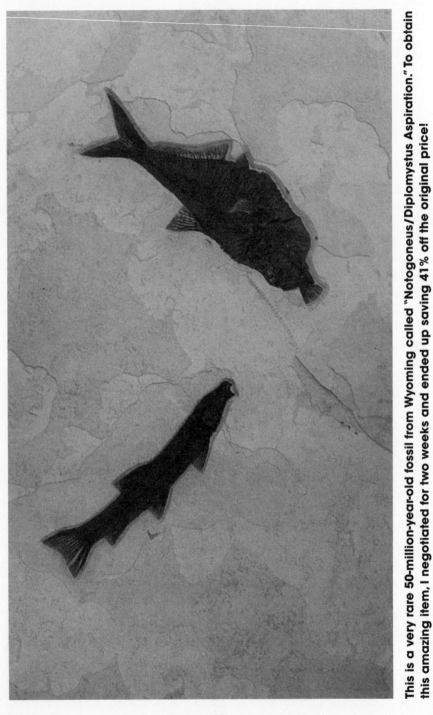

This is a very rare 50-million-year-old fossil from Wyoming called "Notogoneus/Diplomystus Aspiration." To obtain this amazing item, I negotiated for two weeks and ended up saving 41% off the original price!

part by the way you're dressed. Whatever you intend to purchase, whether it is jewelry, art, cars or pretty much anything else, a salesperson will always size you up by giving you the once-over. I'm not saying this practice is fair or that I agree with it, but it is a reality.

I know what you're thinking: People don't look at or even take the time to notice these types of personal details. I can guarantee you this happens all the time! Attention to detail and observations help us as salespeople to better understand our buyer, meaning YOU. Three to five years ago, the probability of someone actually asking for a deal when they walked through my gallery doors was about 50/50. Due to the poor economic climate we are currently experiencing, I estimate that easily 80% of my customers will ask for some kind of a deal.

When you participate in any type of sale, be it a garage sale, at an antique shop, art gallery or a collectibles store, you will want to dress appropriately. Don't get all dolled up for the occasion. Don't wear an expensive watch, never wear big, gaudy rings and always leave the designer clothes and shoes at home. When you're shopping for any item that is going to require negotiation, you'll definitely want to dress appropriately for the experience. Looking the part, especially in the way you're dressed, is one of the main considerations that will help you become a master negotiator and a successful Garage Sale Millionaire.

Personally, I like to wear something simple like a pair of jeans and a shirt. Button-down shirts are fine, and a plain pair of tennis shoes are also an option. The only acceptable piece of jewelry to wear would be a wedding ring. If you have a big diamond ring, leave it at home and instead wear a simple gold band if you have one. Also, an inexpensive or casual watch is acceptable. When salespeople see that you can easily afford the finer things, it's much harder to negotiate any kind of bargain with them. Another dead giveaway that you are

> ### Million $ Tip
>
> One way salespeople size you up as a potential customer, is by what you're wearing . . . your jewelry and shoes. Always leave the expensive accessories at home. People usually forget to dumb down these two personal items and they are a dead giveaway in revealing you have more money to spend. This means less leverage for you, the buyer, in any bargaining or negotiation.

too well off is if you drive a high-end car. If you don't have access to a clunker and you arrive at the store in your nice flashy vehicle, never park in front of the store where the salesperson can see what you're driving. Leave it down the street and walk a block.

As you walk around the store, always be cordial and pleasant. Never act aloof or be rude towards the salesperson. As soon as you're deemed to be discourteous or difficult, your chances of getting a better deal go right out the window. Salespeople will literally jump through hoops and be more accommodating to a potential customer who is polite and affable.

When you find something you like, you don't have to pretend you didn't see the item or don't want it and then ask for a deal on the item. You should always examine the piece closely and make sure it's something you have a strong desire to buy. If you need to leave the store to do your research and return at a later time, this is always considered an acceptable practice. Traveling back and forth to the store once or twice is fine, but if you start coming back three, four or even five times and to look at the same item, you will definitely hurt your chances of making a good deal. In the best-case scenario, you'll want to leave only once, then come back and make the appropriate offer. Enter a store, browse to your heart's content, find the items that interest you, make notes if necessary and then perhaps go home for a while and do some research on your computer. Then, when you feel confident you are armed with all the knowledge you need to make an informed assessment, go back to the store and make your best offer.

If you're completely certain you want to make a purchase, take a good look at the item and confirm that it's in a condition to your liking. Ensure the item has not been restored and it has all the original packaging. If the original packaging is not included, you'll need to make a decision as to whether or not this is something you really want to buy. I will discuss the importance of having original packaging and how this directly affects resale value in Chapter 7. If your item requires accessories (a set of keys, for example), you need to make certain that everything is included before negotiating a price.

When you're ready to make a purchase, ask if there is an owner available so you can speak to someone in charge to start the negotiation process. When speaking to the owner, always be friendly and civil. Never be critical of the item you want to purchase. It's always amazing to me how many people will insult the very items they want to buy. What constitutes an insult? If the item is an antique, don't begin the conversation by stating the item is heavily over-priced or in bad condition.

Never try to find fault with the item in hope of getting a better deal. Remember, the owner has been in this game for quite a while and probably for much longer than you have. The person standing in front of you fully understands that when you're trying to find the less attractive points relative to an item, you're really trying to

> ## Million $ Tip
>
> The owner of a store will always make you the best deal. The store manager and the art gallery director will only make you an average deal. The reason store managers and gallery directors will not offer any type of deep discount is because the money you save on any item comes directly out of their pocket. I also guarantee that in most stores, salespeople are on a commission-only pay basis and will not make you a deal on much of anything. If you have your sights set on something that is a high-dollar item and you want to get the best deal possible, you will need to get in contact with the owner of the business.

position it at a lesser price. In simple words, this is just an obvious and blatant negotiation tool being played out poorly, and in bad taste, on your part. The store owner has heard it all before and he or she will be less willing to make a deal if you employ this type of unsophisticated bargaining strategy!

Now, if you point out scratches or dents that are not so obvious, that is fantastic and considered fair game. When you do this, always acknowledge that the item in question is nonetheless a nice piece. Remember, never be too negative. Begin your dialog with the store owner by saying you're looking at the piece and the item is of genuine interest to you. Also, take time to make the usual small talk. There's nothing wrong with asking how long the store owner has been in business or pointing out that it's unfortunate he or she has to work on the weekend or on such a nice day. You should definitely try to find some common ground to discuss. By finding something in common, the owner will look at you more as a person than a client and more as a friend than a mark. It's very important to have a good working relationship with the owner or whoever is in charge when you start the dealing process on an item of interest to you. If you do this, there's a better-than-average chance he or she will like you, take an interest in you and give you a much better deal.

Dealing with Someone Over the Telephone or by E-mail

Now that you understand a few of the tricks used to negotiate a better deal when working with someone face to face, let's discuss how to handle other forms of negotiation. These types of transactions take place over the telephone or via e-mail. Using methods other than the face-to-face approach to negotiate the best possible deal are a bit trickier, but with some experience they can be mastered. Because you're not dealing with someone face to face, you don't have to worry about your looks, and you don't need to speak any differently than you normally would or put on airs to make your point. You will, however, have to pay extra careful attention to what's being said. With the evolution of technology in recent years, the average person relies heavily on using the Internet and e-mail to get the best deals on a broad range of merchandise. Prior to the current popularity of the Internet (and people's increasing dependence upon it), high-speed technology meant using the telephone to negotiate a deal. Using the phone to negotiate deals and buy items is still a potent weapon in any Garage Sale Millionaire's arsenal, but the Internet makes doing a great deal quickly and efficiently that much easier.

Let's turn our focus to transacting business by e-mail. Many businesses have items available for sale on the Internet. In antique stores, art galleries and secondhand stores, there is usually a designated person who places items for sale on the company website. A good website operated by a proficient company is updated regularly by removing information about items that have already sold and posting new items as soon as they become available. Because the Internet is such an important sales weapon for these stores, much of their overall business is transacted across state lines or even worldwide. If you find an item you're interested in buying on a website, the best thing to do is to e-mail the owner directly. In your message, identify and describe the item you are interested in (be sure to include the item number associated with a posting) and make it very clear (in a nice way, of course), that you have a limited budget. You are a serious buyer and want to purchase something right away, but you need the very best deal he or she is willing to offer. In your e-mail, you need to emphasize that your decision to buy an item is all about price and that you are shopping around. In the current down-state of the economy, people are always looking for the best deal they can find. When you discuss price with a store owner, you'll want to let them know right away that if he or she wants your business, you will need to be offered their best price, immediately.

The majority of shop owners, art gallery directors and store managers prefer communicating by e-mail because they know they'll have one or two shots to get you to buy. The impetus for convincing you to buy is contingent upon these individuals making you the right (best) offer. If they are unsuccessful at getting you to make a purchase in their first or second e-mail, there's a good chance you will have obtained the item elsewhere. If you're contacting the seller from another state, you'll want to make your location known so you are recognized as being exempt from sales tax. This will make the transaction a bit easier for the seller as well. Also, let the seller know you will accept the easiest and least expensive method for shipping the item. You definitely do not want to incur costly overnight charges for shipping. Always inquire about getting insurance on your shipment to protect it while it's in transit to your location.

Making any kind of deal over the telephone is, in my opinion, the toughest way to negotiate. Why? There's no real sense of bonding between the seller and the customer or vice versa on a cold call. Many store owners don't feel as though they have a reason to give you a better deal because they don't know you or anything about you. At the very the least, with e-mail correspondence there's usually a sender's name, a personal greeting and some sort of contact information listed prior to the first contact between you and the store owner. Usually, a telephone number is listed in the signature portion of an e-mail. Even with the smallest amount of information provided in an e-mail there is some level of trust built into that first actual moment of contact.

> ### Million $ Tip
>
> Always be aware that the negotiation of any item or multiple items, is not a speed contest. Take your time and listen carefully to the other person as he or she negotiates their end of the deal so you can get the best price possible.

If you're calling about an item you saw on the store's website, you will want to start a dialog with the owner immediately to find some sort of common ground so the seller will begin to feel comfortable with you. Once you've found your common ground, it's time to begin to negotiate.

The Basics of Negotiation

In this chapter, I have discussed the best way to work with people in person as well as remotely through telephone or e-mail. I've also made you aware of how sellers instantly size up buyers and what they're thinking of during every aspect of the sales process. I've given you the essential information about what goes into a sale and now it is time to discuss how to properly negotiate a sale to get the best deal possible.

When you begin discussion about an item you want to buy, you'll definitely want to ask questions specific to that item. Once again, always make sure the item you're interested in is the exact item you want to purchase. Ask everything you want to know about the item, even if you're positive it's the piece for you. Even if you're 100% certain you know everything there is to know about the item, there's nothing wrong with asking the seller for more information. You never know what additional information might be divulged as you discuss specifics about an item. Remember, nothing is final until you spend your hard-earned money, so why not try to find out as much information as possible?

After you've spoken for a few moments about the item you want to buy, it's time to mention the fact that although you're really interested, you have a limited budget to spend. Let the seller know how much you like the item, but also that you don't know if you can afford the asking price. Now is the time to ask if something can be done to help you out on the price. The seller will then probably begin to tell you about their free layaway policy.

A layaway is basically a way of paying for items in installments. You put a small amount of money down on the item as a first payment and then continue to make small payments every month until the item is paid in full. Your purchase will remain in the store until all the layaway payments are made. A layaway payment plan simply makes it much easier for you to pay for the item by allowing you to make smaller payments spread across a set period of time instead of having to pay for the item in full all at once. Let the seller know you appreciate knowing about their layaway policy and that you might eventually want to use this as a means of payment. By mentioning you may possibly accept some sort of layaway agreement to purchase an item, you could get an immediate break on the price. Usually, shop owners, gallery directors and managers will decrease the price up to 10% knowing the item will soon be out of the store. Store owners would rather take a percentage hit on the item to accelerate immediate cash flow and free up space in their store right away. Believe it or not, this is a common practice within the industry.

But, you're not looking for a meager 10% off on items you have a serious interest in. You did not buy this book so you could find a way of getting a better deal that only amounts to a 10% discount.

Now you're going to say to the person you are negotiating with, "Thanks, but a 10% discount really isn't such a great price for me. There's a store closer to where I live that will offer more than 10% on the exact item you have in your store. However, I do prefer to conduct all of my business out of state so I don't have to pay any sales tax." By making this statement, you could receive an immediate price drop on the item you want to buy, but you will also help the seller better relate to you. This lets the person you're dealing with know that you will be a serious buyer in the future.

All sellers love to hear, "I'm starting my collection and I need many more of these kinds of collectibles." They absolutely love finding out that they've come across someone new to work with, both now and in the future. This is the point where you say, "You know, right now we're at 10% and I really appreciate the discount, but I was thinking more of a number closer to 25% or 30% off."

Now's the right moment to reference whatever discount you're comfortable with discussing and ask if you can have the item at the seller's maximum discount. If you ask for more than a 50% discount over the telephone, more than likely you're going to hear a dial tone very quickly. Furthermore, if you're asking for more than a 50% discount in person, you may get the cold shoulder and whoever you are dealing with may shut the door on future business dealings forever.

I recommend you go to a percentage somewhere between 15% and 45%. You should realize that whatever final sales price you agree upon, the seller is going to offer a final sales price higher than your lowest proposal. If you try to get a discount between 40% and 45%, the seller will more than likely offer a discount that is half of your offer.

If you truly love the item and know it's a great find, be careful not to lose it no matter what the final price may end up being. You should always be ready to concede the final price and possibly accept something for much less of a deal than you originally wanted. I can't tell you how many times I wanted the best deal in the world and I ended up losing out on the deal altogether because I wouldn't accept a final sales price barely 5% over my final offer. I walked away from the sale after standing my ground thinking the seller would call or e-mail me to accept my final offer. A day or two later, I usually found the item was sold to someone else. I could have made a huge profit from reselling the item, but I got greedy and blew the deal.

After you've agreed on a price, you should be willing to make your payment arrangements over the phone with the store owner or manager. There are two ways to proceed. You can offer to come in and pay cash for the item or you can offer to pay with a credit card. If you don't live in the city or state where the business you're dealing with is located, then it's best to pay by credit card. In this case, you also would want to make sure the seller offers free shipping.

One of the benefits of negotiating for the best price on an item over the phone is that if you're still unhappy with the price, you have the option of leaving your name and number for a call back. Tell the person you are negotiating with, "If you're interested in the price I offered, please give me a call. I'm going to consider your offer for the next few days (or a week . . . whatever time frame you are comfortable using) and then I'll make up my mind." The reason you have to give the seller a set number of days is that you don't want this cat-and-mouse game to continue on for an indefinite period of time. Your decisiveness and commitment in offering a set time limit will entice and motivate the seller to make the deal or forever hold his peace by not making you a better deal. There's always a very good chance if the counter price you offered is fair, the seller will call you back to make the sale.

If you're impatient (try not to be), if you need this piece as a gift or if you're afraid of losing the item, then you need to make the deal right then and there on the phone.

If time is on your side and it's acceptable to lose out on the item, try to bluff the seller by proposing a very deep discount with the hope he or she will call you back to accept your lowball offer. It never hurts to try a bluff with the owner as long as you're prepared to lose out in the end. I have a 70% success rate when I bluff. Sometimes, the seller will call you back to apologize that they won't be

Million $ Tip

It is never a good deal if you cannot get the deal completed. This is one of the best tips I can ever give you regarding mastering the art of the deal. As a Garage Sale Millionaire, you are buying a particular item because you know there is a substantial profit awaiting you upon its resale. In the end, you may lose out on a large financial windfall from the resale of any item by asking for too deep of a discount and eventually losing the item. You most certainly cannot make any money from the sale of an item that you do not actually own!

able to make the deal at the low price you offered. He or she may ask, once again, if there's any way you might still want to buy the item at a higher price than your final offer. Depending on what you really wanted to spend, you can discuss another final price and see if the seller is intent on working with you to move the item out of their store and into your possession.

Expert Negotiating Strategies

I would love to give you a detailed look at and talk you through the negotiation process based on my decades of professional and personal experience. I've worked in the art field for over 25 years. I've also been a memorabilia and art collector for most of my life. The following example perfectly illustrates what the negotiation process is all about. Let's take an item originally marked at $500 and let's negotiate this treasure down to something a bit more affordable!

You'll want to start by offering the seller a little more than half the original sales price. That means a little less than a 50% discount.

If you go under $250, you'll basically insult the seller. This is not a very good strategy to use, but if you have no problem losing your chances of getting a good deal, you can always try it. Remember our bluff example earlier in this chapter. Of course, if you're serious about acquiring the item, I strongly recommend against this strategy! When people offer me less than half the price on any item I'm selling, I am personally insulted. I never price items in my own gallery too high, but rather at a fair price where I can make an honest living. So, be forewarned. If you were to use that tactic on me, maybe one time in 50 I would bite and make the deal. If it's worth it to you to try to get the best deal in the world and you believe this sort of tactic works, then by all means give it your best shot. Don't be surprised if you're asked to leave many stores if you choose to employ this tactic. When you really like the store, shop or gallery and want to come back in the future, the goal is not to insult people. Remember, sellers need to earn a living as well!

I recommend offering a little bit above half of the original sales price, perhaps using $275 to $300 (based on the $500 price tag of our example) as an appropriate starting point. The seller will always counter higher and he or she will never say okay to your first offer. So whatever you do, you don't want to give your best dollar offer knowing the counteroffer will be much higher. You could start by offering $450, which is quite high for a first offer, but I guarantee the counteroffer will come back at $475. Starting your negotiations with the sales person by making a lower initial offer, you'll leave room for both of you to meet in the middle and eventually come to an acceptable final sales price.

For fun, let's go bare bones and offer a very low starting price of $275. (This first offer is to buy the item at a 45% discount. Good for you!) The seller will probably counter your offer at $400. Pay careful attention here. At this point during the negotiation, you will want to be holding the item in your hands if it's not too large . . . an old clock, an antique or collectible toy, a coin, a vase, etc. This action shows the seller a seemingly sincere and emotional attachment to the item. You are actually sending a signal that you have marked the item as your own and are making a statement by literally holding onto it. Now, as you stand with the item in your hands, having offered $275, the seller counteroffers $425. This is $25 more than you expected the counteroffer to be. If the seller does this, look him straight in the eye, then glance at the item in your hands and shake your head back and forth. Put on your best sad face and place the item back on the shelf.

You may not think this is going to accomplish anything, but right there the seller just got really scared! He or she may have just felt a little twinge or a funny feeling and are thinking he or she may have just lost you as a customer. It has also just occurred to the person you're dealing with that their commission on the item you were holding is about to leave the store right along with you. While placing the item back where you found it, you should be shaking your head and muttering under your breath, "Yeah, that price is more than I can spend . . . it's too much," using a very disheartened tone. At this moment, it's almost a guarantee the person who was assisting you is going to come after you, magically dropping their price. Let the tried and true psychological maneuver known as the *put back* work for you.

Let's go back to the seller's $425 counteroffer. Usually, after an initial counteroffer of $425 is made, the next best counteroffer will be somewhere near $375. When you make your counter to their counteroffer and come up a little bit in your new price, but do not touch the item again. Never touch the item until you both are a little closer to agreeing on a final sales price. If the seller offers $375 (and the seller usually will), you counter the offer with $325. The goal will be to stand pat at $325, which is a 35% discount off of the original $500 price!

If you are so sure the seller is not going to budge any lower than the $375 he or she offers you, then you will have two options. The first is holding firm at $325, saying, "I'm sorry, but I just can't accept that price. Thanks anyway for your time." Always wish the seller a good day and then leave the store. There's a very good chance this will rattle the seller's cage and he or she may agree to your $325 price. I have to tell you that this strategy works like a charm, seven out of ten times for me.

OK now, if this course of action hasn't worked for you and you get to the door without making the deal, you may want to turn around and nicely say, "Is it okay to leave my name and telephone number with you? If you change your mind on my offer, and I hope you do, please call me right away." At this point in the negotiation process, write down your name and telephone number and leave the information with the proprietor. Another option is to counteroffer once again with a final acceptable price of $350. This final price is $25 more than your $325 offer, but still $25 below the top counteroffer of $375. Tell the seller you will take it at $350 and that is the best you can do. There is still a good chance the seller will accept your final offer because it is so close to the middle point of your negotiations. There is always a middle point in all negotiations and usually people will accept the middle ground. The seller might hem and haw a bit, but he or she will usually accept.

This is the best example I can give to you, my future Garage Sale Millionaire, to show you how proper negotiation is performed in any situation in any sales venue. This kind of negotiation should be employed at art galleries, garage sales, antique shops, collectibles stores or any place where a customer, salesperson and merchandise are involved. I have had an 80% success rate when I enact this negotiation strategy and have made some good money over the years by implementing these tactics. Good luck!

As an art gallery owner, if I'm given contact information during the negotiation process, I will start thinking about accepting the lowest price the customer has offered. Then I find myself thinking, "Well, maybe the price the customer offered was not too bad and the offer was not all that low." If I've had a week when sales were a little lower than expected and I don't have anyone else interested in the piece, I'll call every one of my customers to see who might be interested in this item. If I still don't have any takers after making all my calls, there's a good chance I will call back the customer who gave me the offer and accept it.

Another negotiating ploy or strategy that works to save you 2% to 3% on items is offering to pay for an item with cash. Now that you have the item you want at a price you can live with, it's time to inform the seller you'll be paying by credit card. The seller will say, "Okay," because you already know the seller takes credit cards, just not American Express. Remember what I said in the Chapter 1: American Express charges the seller a higher per-transaction percentage than all the other credit card companies. Once the seller accepts the idea that you'll be paying by credit card, you have one final way you might be able to get an additional 2–3% more off the price of the item. After you make it known you will be paying by credit card, simply ask, "I can use my credit card, but I also

> ### Million $ Tip
>
> Never send checks or money orders in the mail. Don't wire money if you haven't previously worked with the seller. Using checks, money orders or wire transfers is not the optimal way to get the best deals on the items you want to purchase. Once you send money in any of the aforementioned methods, you have no recourse if events don't go well and there is a dispute with your transaction. Also, never use a debit card. With a VISA or MasterCard debit card, money is taken directly out of your account and recourse of any kind is almost impossible.

have cash. If I pay with cash, will you be willing to take off another 3%?" Not many sellers will say no to that. Why? The first and most important reason is that they're going to have to pay the credit card companies for processing each credit card transaction. If the merchant accepts cold, hard cash, there will be no additional processing fees. Secondly, when you pay with a credit card, the merchant doesn't receive payment at the time the transaction takes place. On average, it takes from two to five days to have the money from each credit card sale deposited into the seller's bank account from the respective credit card company. So with every deal, you will want to have cash as a backup whenever possible. Cash will always leverage the deal. When you agree on a price, always ask for 3% less than the final sale price if you pay for the item entirely in cash. If the store owner offers only 2%, you should immediately counter with, "No, then it's not worth it." Usually, that's enough to get the merchant to let you have the item at the full 3% discount. Cash really is and always will be, king!

Once your offer has been accepted, you've paid for your purchase in cash and the item is all wrapped up and ready to go, make sure the seller has your complete contact information. By having your name, telephone number and e-mail address on file, store personnel can call you if anything interesting arrives that may be on your wish list or could perhaps pique your interest. You've also made an informal announcement to the store that you want to continue to do business with them. As a result of your actions, you've made a valuable ally who will go to battle for you in the collectibles business and be there to give you a heads up regarding great finds that come through their vast information pipeline or databases. Store personnel will search out new items for you. They'll be available to answer any questions you may have about items that may be of special interest to you and they'll be happy to do so. Additionally, now you will have someone to share announcements and provide expert recommendations concerning expos, events and gatherings you should attend to further your knowledge. By establishing an on-going relationship with an established collectibles businesses, you'll be privy to any future store sales, VIP and invite-only events and over time, if you continue to spend more money with them, you will get even greater deals on items you want to buy in the future.

Once you've made your best deal and you were able to negotiate a perfect sales price, be kind. Don't ever gloat or do an "I got the best deal" dance in front of the seller. The merchant already understands your good deal, so be nice and cordial. Leave on a good note so you can comfortably visit the store again in the future. Remember when you come back, the seller has your number and he or she will already have a feel for how you do business. The second and subsequent visits should be a bit easier than your initial visit. When you want to visit a store or gallery again, don't call ahead and say you're dropping by to look at certain items. If you do this and store personnel know what you usually buy, believe it or not, some unscrupulous establishments (a small minority within the industry) will raise prices on specific items knowing full well you have an interest, before you arrive at the store! Then they will lower prices on those same items when you leave the store.

To get even deeper discounts, try the following strategy. When a seller offers you a discount of 10% or 15%, counter with 10% more than what they offer. If they offer 15%, you should counteroffer a discount of 25%. There is a better-than-average chance they will say they can't go that deep, but once again, you're going to agree on an amount in the middle of both your offers. If the seller is at a 15% discount on an item and you've offered 25%, try to come to an agreement on a final discount of 20% (once again, right in the middle of his or her 15% and your 25%). Once you've secured a 20% discount, this is a fantastic time to consider whether or not you'd like to purchase a second piece from the store. Perhaps it could be another chair or a decorative vase to place alongside your antique dining room table. Be sure to ask the seller what discount he or she can offer if you purchase two or even three pieces?

This is where your discount can grow exponentially. Never put all your cards on the table by telling the seller you want to buy more than one piece at the beginning of your negotiations. If you do, you will lose the leverage you had. The key to negotiating this way is to bring the seller into your negotiations at a very gradual pace at a time when you have the optimal vantage point. Start to reel in the seller with the initial concept that you are only going to buy one item. Once you agree on a price for that one item, you then drop the hammer and let the seller know you are actually thinking about two or three additional pieces. The seller should instantly give you the original discount, plus maybe a little bit more. You want the best deal possible and from my experience, you're more than likely to get it!

Are You a Garage Sale Millionaire?

Mastering the art of the deal takes a little practice, but if you follow the personal strategies I've outlined in this chapter, you should move to the head of the class very quickly. Any successful Garage Sale Millionaire will eventually master and consistently be proficient in the art of the deal. One of your main objectives in trying to achieve Garage Sale Millionaire status is to become a Donald Trump in the fine art of negotiating. Take your time, be knowledgeable, understand the process, remember to have fun, be cordial and respectful and know that by implementing what you've learned in this chapter, you're going to have a better opportunity for purchasing the item you want at the price you want.

By following these few simple steps, you'll become a master of the art of the deal in no time!

Fakes, Replicas and Restorations: How Not to Get "Taken"

For every great collectible, there's a fake or replica made of that same item. If you have a collectible you love and it's worth money, someone, somewhere has already realized how they can make more money from that same collectible by creating an authentic-looking fake. Whether the item is an autographed piece of sports memorabilia, a Civil War-era item, a piece of American presidential memorabilia, a signed movie poster or a 125-year-old antique, there's always someone working diligently to forge and replicate that item so they can make a quick buck from you. *That, dear reader, is a guarantee.*

When you finish reading this chapter, you'll have a thorough understanding of how to keep one step ahead of the people who create the frauds, fakes and restorations so that when you place your hard-earned money down, you won't be bilked or ripped off. The way to protect yourself from being taken by these nefarious individuals is to acquire as much information as possible about the collecting process. In the following pages, I will personally share the secret tips that have protected me throughout my 30-plus years of collecting.

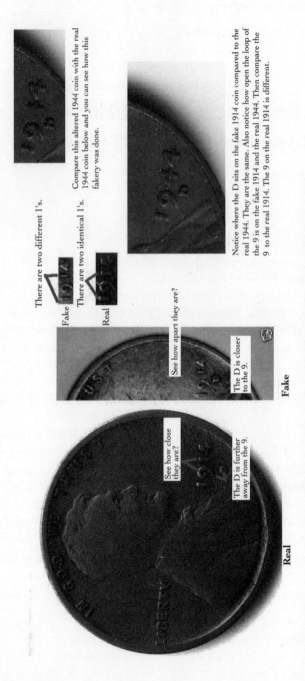

There are two different 1's.

There are two identical 1's.

Fake

Real

Compare this altered 1944 coin with the real 1944 coin below and you can see how this fakery was done.

Notice where the D sits on the fake 1914 coin compared to the real 1944. They are the same. Also notice how open the loop of the 9 is on the fake 1914 and the real 1944. Then compare the 9 to the real 1914. The 9 on the real 1914 is different.

See how apart they are?

The D is closer to the 9.

Fake

See how close they are?

The D is further away from the 9.

Real

This is a good example of what can happen if a coin is not looked at carefully.

How to Protect Yourself

With all the rules, regulations and laws our society has in place, how can people blatantly continue to produce products that mimic authentic items? More importantly, how in the world can these individuals make such consistently good money and evade the law time after time? I know the idea may come as a shock to you, but the practice of perpetrating this type of fraud is commonplace. This is one of the main reasons why I decided to write *The Garage Sale Millionaire.* I want to show you how to protect yourself from these unscrupulous individuals and to provide you with knowledge that will prevent you from becoming another rip-off statistic.

The practice of creating and passing off fakes, replicas and restorations was far more difficult to accomplish in the past when people dealt with others in a more personal, one-on-one manner. Since the emergence of eBay, Craigslist, e-mail and the Internet, this sort of criminal activity has become increasingly easier to pull off.

Protecting yourself against fraud, like many other processes detailed in this book, is easy enough to accomplish. All it takes is the understanding of some basic information and the implementation of your new-found knowledge. After that, you can safely proceed with your Garage Sale Millionaire activities knowing that you won't get cheated. In 1537 Francis Bacon said, "Knowledge is power," but today, it's what you do with your knowledge that is the power. This is what Chapter 4 is all about: helping you gain understanding and awareness about fakes, replicas and restorations so you don't get cheated.

As stated earlier, any item manufactured today can be duplicated. My goal here is to discuss what collectibles are the most lucrative and most often replicated by crooks as well as where you are most likely to encounter fraudulent documentation, fakes and replicas.

Presidential Memorabilia

Collecting presidential memorabilia is one of the most problematic areas collectors encounter. Why? As far back as 1789, when President George Washington was in office, there were certain individuals who were authorized to sign the president's name for him.

> **Million $ Tip**
>
> Autographs from Presidents are very valuable and are among some of the most-often forged collectibles.

Yes, you read that correctly. Often, a signature from a president is actually signed by a secretary, another staff member, even a friend or family member, rather than the president himself. If the signature you have on your document is not signed directly by a particular president, the value of the item decreases by 75% or more. There are also other items used by presidents such as clothes, blotters or even dentures, that are very collectible, but these items must have a verifiable certificate and/or auction record where the item sold.

Unless you're an expert in the art of collecting signed presidential memorabilia, it's very difficult to determine which signatures are authentic and which are not. This is one collectible you don't want to gamble on because even the experts tend to get fooled. You need to be very careful when buying authentic signed historical documents, especially when it involves presidential signatures.

Sports and Entertainment Memorabilia

People are buying and selling fake autographs 24/7. The only way you can fully protect yourself against fraud is to verify the authenticity or source of the autograph. It's a known fact that for every actor, director and professional athlete who lends their signature to an item, there are probably two signatures from the same celebrity verified as fakes. The Emmy award-winning CBS News program *60 Minutes* recently broadcast a segment about the potential pitfalls of collecting signed sports memorabilia. After speaking with numerous experts in the field of collecting, *60 Minutes* concluded that roughly half of all signatures on the market are fakes.

Many people selling autographs will claim that they were actually present with the person who signed an item and witnessed the person attaching his or her signature to the item. One of my very good friends, a well-known professional in the autograph and collectibles business, has always said, "It doesn't matter how good the seller's story is if the buyer can't personally back it up." Basically, what he meant was, if the signature is not real, then whatever story is being told to prove the authenticity of that autograph doesn't even remotely matter.

It's astonishing to me (and keep in mind that I am actually in the art and collectibles business) just how many times over the years I've heard similar stories from almost every autograph seller. They proudly say, "I was there and watched (fill in the famous person's name) actually sign it." Then, I'll take that signature to the back room of my gallery and compare the seller's so-called original to a signature I know to be verifiably authentic. I almost always find that the so-called authentic is not even close to being a match. Only when I advise the seller that their signature isn't authentic, do they admit, "We actually didn't watch him sign it. A secretary took the paper to another room, came back and handed it to us."

> **Million $ Tip**
>
> If you want to make money dealing in the buying and selling of signatures, you'd better know your signature. Astronauts, movie stars, entertainment moguls, Presidents, athletes, business leaders—anyone who is or was famous, as well as infamous, may very likely have had a secretary or assistant signing for them.

Regardless of various stories coming from the seller of the autograph, you definitely want to have a Certificate of Authenticity or COA to accompany the item you want to purchase. As I mentioned in Chapter 2, a COA is a document the seller issues which guarantees the item being purchased as authentic. Of course, a COA can always be faked by a seller and many people will tell you a COA is not worth the paper it's printed on. Almost anyone can print out a COA. It's as easy as printing out a generic certificate generated from any number of inexpensive computer desktop publishing software programs. To make sure your COA will be recognized as representing an authentic item, always do business with a reputable art and collectibles dealer and always ask for a money-back guarantee on the item you want to buy. For example, over the last decade, co-author Jeffrey Kern has done business with several art and collectibles companies including Antiquities International (Las Vegas, Nevada) and my own Fascination Street Gallery (Denver, Colorado). Both companies have stellar reputations and have been in the art and collectibles business for over 25 years. Jeffrey knows that when he buys art and collectibles from these two companies, the COA they include with each purchase is going to be authentic and will be recognized as such in the future.

Page signatures are obtained when stores or agents contract with an athlete or celebrity to autograph multiple memorabilia pieces in exchange for a set fee. This type of arrangement usually occurs with sports figures, movie stars, former presidents or anyone whose signature has an assigned value. When this is the case, there should be a contract for the page signature signing that can be produced upon request for your examination, as well as actual photos of the celebrity signing the item(s). If the store where you're shopping is a reputable establishment, there's a good chance that the signature is legitimate.

Stores such as The Upper Deck, Mounted Memories and Latitude Sports, as well as many other memorabilia businesses, contract for these types of signings many times throughout the year. But, if the COA states only the location where the signing took place without an address, phone number or working website, then the COA is most likely junk and you should steer clear. Most signatures from individuals in the entertainment industry, both film and television, are usually acquired at public events, on the set, through private meetings or from autograph companies or individuals who have direct access to these types of celebrities. When collectible merchandise and memorabilia is professionally graded, the agency verifying an item's authenticity will affix a sticker that displays a one-of-a-kind image in the form of a hologram, proving the item is deemed to be authentic.

Before you buy any item with a verified-as-authentic signature, you should always know what the signature you're attempting to collect really looks like. There are many resources available to the autograph and memorabilia collector that include photographs of authentic signatures of famous individuals so you can look and compare what *may be* real and authentic to what actually *is* real and authentic.

One fantastic company for self-verifying and self-authenticating celebrity signatures in both the sports and entertainment industries is **StarTiger (www.startiger.com)**. As of October 2010, StarTiger.com has an exhaustive database of over 323,000 scanned celebrity autographs, 342,000+ celebrities listed in their database (with addresses and contact information), 511,000+ test results and over 657,000 forum posts from members. There are multiple scans and numerous examples of almost every signature on the website so you can compare the variations in a personal signature every time a celebrity has signed an item. Although you can do a basic website search free-of-charge, a membership fee is required to enjoy full access to the website.

> **Million $ Tip**
>
> When you are serious about getting into the business of buying and selling autographs, you should buy *Collecting Autographs and Manuscripts* by Charles Hamilton as well as *The Standard Guide to Collecting Autographs: A Reference & Value Guide* by Mark Allen Baker. Because this is such a diverse topic, you can never learn enough on the subject.

Antiques

A whole generation of new furniture has entered the marketplace and it was created to look exactly like the true antiques. There are companies located in every part of the world whose sole purpose is to replicate antiques. What do I mean by replicate? This type of antique furniture is built from newly-sourced, raw materials and is then roughed up, distressed and placed in the weather to fade or to rust. Basically, these manufacturing companies will try anything they can to make their product

> **Million $ Tip**
>
> Antiques are a great collectible on which to make money. To gain an advantage in your Garage Sale Millionaire competition, proactively search out and make friends with several of your local antique dealers and store owners. Not only will these individuals help advise you about the antique business, but they will also make you great deals when they know you are in the business of buying and selling antiques.

look old and worn. To the untrained eye, these newly made antiques look convincingly like authentic antiques. Of course, the result of this unscrupulous business practice is that good people often wind up paying for fraudulent products.

Fortunately, most conscientious shops know the difference between a genuine antique and a replica. There are, however, a few less-than-honest stores that won't tell you the difference and will charge you as if the item were an authentic antique. They will even go so far as to say it *is* an antique! But the good news is there are ways you can look at a piece to determine if what you're seeing is or is not genuine.

The first thing you need to do is to flip the item over and look at its underside. If the piece you're looking at is a table, get down on your hands and knees and examine the underside of the table. Look at the way the item is put together. Were any screws used? How about nails? What specific kind of screws and nails were used? Certain types of nails indicate an item is newly manufactured. For example, if you see the flathead nails we use today in furniture manufacturing, that is a dead giveaway that what you're looking at is a newly made item. In fact, nails used to build furniture over 100 years ago were very long, skinny, sort of lumpy and had heads that were not perfectly round. This was due to the fact that blacksmiths of that era made every single nail by hand.

If glue or staples were used on the piece you're inspecting, you need to stay away; you are most likely looking at a restoration or a fake. Many times antiques are restored incorrectly. If restorations are completed properly, they can be performed without damaging the item and the process will usually bring the piece back to its original state. Many collectors agree that the cleaning and restoration of antique items is an acceptable practice. I will cover restored antiques in more detail later on in this chapter.

The easiest way to find out if there is any glue present on an item or to verify that a restoration was done properly, is to use a black light. Whether the item is furniture or pottery, if glue has been used incorrectly in the restoration process, the added glue marks will stand out visibly with the use of a black light. What makes these marks so obvious are the compounds used in making the glue. When glue is present, the object in question will emit a glowing characteristic when held under the black light.

If possible, go into a room where you can control the lighting and use a hand-held black light device. Certain colors and pigments, such as those found in glue compounds, absorb the invisible light and then discharge that light. When this discharge occurs, a glowing effect will be observed. While the room is darkened, turn on your black light and carefully inspect the item in question. Hopefully you won't encounter any tell-tale traces of glue and nothing else you observe will have any glowing properties.

Black lights are extremely helpful in determining if an item has been improperly restored or if it truly is a genuine antique. The difference between an improperly restored item and an unrestored antique item is big money.

> **Million $ Tip**
>
> A black light will determine if a piece of art has been restored and can even identify a missing signature. What do I mean by a missing signature? When some pieces of art were originally created, the item's artist may never have placed their signature on that particular piece. A black light will properly identify if a signature was added after the fact by a collector. If this has occurred, then the piece you coveted for its resale potential loses almost all its value.

Jewelry

When purchasing jewelry, I want to strongly warn you that counterfeiting diamonds is big business. Additionally, when someone is trying to sell a fake diamond, more than likely they will present you with a counterfeit grading report to support their claim that the diamond they want to sell you is verifiably authentic. To make matters worse, even authentic diamonds are not

> **Million $ Tip**
>
> If a diamond has been graded by the GIA, the seller will have GIA-certified papers to accompany the stone. If the diamond does not come with certified grading papers from the GIA and a jeweler grades the diamond, chances are good that an error in grading will occur. By buying a diamond that has been misgraded, you may very well pay a substantial amount of money for a diamond of lesser quality and value.

always thoroughly and carefully examined during the grading process. What exactly do I mean by this? If a jeweler personally examines and grades the diamond or stone, he or she could be off, misjudging the diamond by several different grades or colors. These discrepancies directly affect the value of the jewel and the retail sales price. To protect yourself, you'll always want to have a diamond graded by the **Gemological Institute of America (GIA) (www.gia.edu)**. The diamond grading set by the GIA is the preferred, nationally accepted standard. Here is a quote taken directly from the GIA website: "Because diamonds are so valuable, it is essential to have a universal grading system for comparing their quality. In the 1940s and 1950s, GIA developed the 4Cs and the GIA International Diamond Grading System™ to objectively compare and evaluate diamonds."

The 4Cs include:

Carat—Diamonds and other gemstones are weighed and categorized in metric carats. One metric carat is equal to 0.2 grams.

Color—Diamonds are valued by how closely they approach colorlessness. The less color a diamond has, the higher its value.

Clarity—An indication of a diamond's purity. Diamonds without faults, inclusions or blemishes are rare. Of course, the more rare a diamond, the higher it will be valued. Diamonds are assigned a clarity grade which ranges from Flawless (FL) on the top end of the grade range, to Obvious Inclusions (I3) on the lowest end of the grade range.

Cut—The verifiable level of craftsmanship applied in cutting the symmetry, shape, proportions and polish into a stone. The better the cut of a diamond, the higher its value.

This grading methodology also applies to gold. Just because gold is stamped 14K or 18K, does not mean the carat grading is correct. If you buy gold or silver outside of the United States, even if it's marked with an authentic-looking stamp, chances are good you're not purchasing the real thing. If you don't trust your seller—buyer beware! Always know your grader and always make sure any piece of jewelry you purchase is certified by a respected organization, the same way GIA is respected throughout the gemological industry.

Also, make sure you receive a money-back guarantee and always use your credit card to make any jewelry purchase. By using a credit card you will have the most recourse regarding any transaction, just in case you need to exchange or return an item for a refund. Jewelry is one of the areas where most people get taken

> **Million $ Tip**
>
> 14 karat gold is only 58.33% gold; 18 karat gold is 75% gold; 24 karat gold is pure gold. If the jewelry is gold, a stamp will appear somewhere on the item noting the purity of the gold in the item. However, just because an item is stamped 10K, 14K or 18K, it doesn't mean it is real gold. Some fraudulent companies will stamp gold-plated items as real. The same goes for all silver items (i.e., rings, necklaces, silverware, etc.).

because they never realize they've been duped until it's too late. Again, when buying jewelry, remember to be extremely careful.

Restorations and Replicas . . . Not as Advertised!

I have talked a bit in this chapter regarding restoration and I haven't had a lot of good things to say about the practice. But believe it or not, restorations are not all bad. If you know you're buying something that has been restored and the item is exactly what you want at a price point you find reasonable, then good for you! By all means, enjoy your purchase. When I speak badly about restorations, I'm referring to the term from the viewpoint of a Garage Sale Millionaire. I can't tell you how many times I've talked to individuals from across the United States who have been taken by buying from someone selling what they thought to be an authentic antique, only to discover later that what they've actually purchased is a newly manufactured and poorly completed restoration or replica.

As I stated at the beginning of this chapter, "For every great collectible item available today, there is also a fake or replica made of that item." If you have a collectible you love and it's worth money, someone, somewhere has realized how they can make money by creating an authentic-looking fake version of that same collectible. As a savvy Garage Sale Millionaire, you always need to be aware of this duplicitous practice. At any time you could be misled into buying something that is not as advertised. You not only have to be aware of restorations, but you also have to be aware of the way in which an item is restored. If the restoration is completed incorrectly, it can hurt the value of a piece.

Consider comic books, for instance. There are so many comic books available today in poor to extremely poor condition and in need of proper restoration. If you are a comic book collector and have an extensive collection, chances are one or two of your comic treasures have probably been restored at some time in the past. Restorations are not entirely bad when they involve comic books. It's only when a comic book restoration is completed improperly that the book's value is diminished. A restoration, when rendered properly, will decrease the value of your comic a little, but the subsequent value of your comic may be improved more than had it not been restored in the first place.

Many antiques are also improperly or properly cleaned and restored. As I suggested earlier in the chapter, if the restoration process on antiques is completed in a proper manner without hurting the original item, then that item will be brought back to its original vibrancy and value.

The restoration of antiques and comic books is acceptable, but cleaning coins is not. Period! If you clean coins, even just slightly, you will be wearing away the sides of the coins and causing very fine scratch marks. These scratch marks degrade the coin's overall quality and inevitably lower the collectible value of the coin. Because of this, I never recommend cleaning coins. In my professional opinion, you will always do more harm than good. There is a whole contingency of learned collectors and individuals who will argue both sides of this "to clean or not to clean" theory, but once again, you will probably want to leave your coins alone. By letting coins sit in their current state, even if they are a little rough and a bit dirty, you will always retain the value of the coin and will avoid permanently damaging the coin in any manner.

If the Deal Sounds too Good to Be True, It Probably Is

Whether you're looking to buy an item on eBay or Craigslist, at a thrift store or in a secondhand store, you'll need to do more investigation prior to making any purchase. As the saying goes, "If the deal sounds too good to be true, it probably is."

On eBay you have to ask detailed questions. Request specifics about the seller's return policy, ask for better pictures and always pay by credit card. Remember, using a credit card gives you better recourse if your purchase is not as it was represented in the seller's auction. With eBay in particular, it's a huge plus if the seller agrees to

> ### Million $ Tip
>
> Always get a money-back guar-antee in writing. Even when this guarantee is listed in an auction on eBay you should still print out a copy of the auction with the money-back guarantee for your records. This paper trail will help you prove your case in the event that you need to contact eBay's security department over a dis-pute with the seller.

refund your money if you're not completely satisfied. Learn to live by these words on eBay: money-back guarantee. Usually, you'll only have up to seven days to return an item. This seven-day return policy is the norm on eBay, so be aware of it. If you go beyond the seven days, the seller will most likely not honor your merchandise return, and you will be left keeping something you really don't want because you didn't keep better track of time.

Items obtained through Craigslist are handled in much the same way as items acquired on eBay, albeit with some minor differences. If you're buying an item from someone on Craigslist who's not in your area, implement the same strategies you do on eBay to verify the items. Ask detailed questions, ask for better pictures, ask about the seller's return policy and always pay by credit card (usually through PayPal, which I cover in greater detail in Chapter 6). As far as I know, there is rarely a seven-day return policy, or any return policy for that matter, for sales transacted on Craigslist. This is very important to know before buying something from someone on this website. One of the reasons why there is no return policy enacted on the site is because much of the buying and selling on Craigslist is completed in person or face to face, and almost every transaction is completed with cash. This is very similar to the way sales are transacted at garage sales, which I discuss in Chapter 5. When you buy an item from someone locally on Craigslist, the transaction typically goes like this: People meet at a designated location, the item is presented for the buyer to determine if it is worth buying, money is exchanged and both parties go their separate ways.

In secondhand stores, antique shops and thrift stores, once you leave the premises you own the item you just purchased. When you buy something and walk out the door, you immediately become the official owner of that item. In these stores, the owner is counting on you to know what you're buying. If fakes are sold or if items are misrepresented in an antique store, the owner will usually return your money. The proprietors of antique stores don't want the bad publicity generated by doing something unethical or in a worst case scenario, doing something illegal. Once again, for your financial protection, always pay with a credit card if you have a worry as to whether an item is real or if there is something that worries you about the item's authenticity. The best way to handle situations like this is to not make the purchase until you have done your research.

A Penny Saved

The most important element of this chapter and the point I want to emphasize most is: not everyone who sells memorabilia, antiques or collectibles is honest. On another level, there are a few people in the business who genuinely do not know exactly what they have to sell or do not know what the true worth of their items are when they place them in their stores, garage sales or estate sales. However, there is a third group of people selling collectibles who prove to be very honest and their items are represented as verifiably authentic or properly labeled as replicas and/or reproductions. When you shop with the last type of individual listed here, you can comfortably complete your transaction with the confidence that you know exactly what you're buying.

Unfortunately, it's always up to you to be at a heightened state of awareness regarding everything you're purchasing. You always need to make sure that what you think you are buying and what you're actually buying are exactly the same thing. If you make a hasty decision—if you don't do the proper research to verify and authenticate an item—there is a very good chance you may buy something that has very little value or no value whatsoever. The usual buyer beware adage applies, as always!

When Ben Franklin said, "A penny saved is a penny earned," he very well could have been referring to future Garage Sale Millionaires. As Garage Sale Millionaires, we fervently strive not to get "taken" because we know the subtle and not-so-subtle differences between what is truly authentic and what is fraudulent. We cut through the purposeful lies of unethical and unscrupulous shopkeepers and always complete the necessary research before even thinking about putting down our hard-earned money to purchase an item. By avoiding illegitimate or unauthentic items, we save our collective pennies and then use that money to purchase those hidden gems and buried treasures that will make us money in the future.

Remember that at all times you must be aware, be ready and have all your bases covered! We are informed Garage Sale Millionaires and we will not get taken by those individuals trying to sell us fakes, replicas and improperly completed restorations!

CHAPTER

Launching Your Own Treasure Hunt

Now it's time to launch your own great treasure-hunting adventure. In this chapter, you'll learn where to find those hidden gems, one-of-a-kind pieces and extremely valuable treasures. Take your chance at attaining fame and fortune by becoming the next Indiana Jones of urban tombs. Your adventures will lead you to Goodwill stores, Salvation Army thrift stores, estate sales, second-hand stores, antiques stores, auctions, storage units and the online marketplace. So, without further adieu, let's get started!

Tools of the Trade

Before you begin your quest for treasure-hunting immortality, you'll need some specific tools to ensure you have the best chance at success. By supplying yourself with the proper treasure-hunting tools from the start, you will be giving yourself the best opportunity to achieve financial success in your treasure-hunting activities.

Acquiring the right tools for your treasure-hunting adventures is simple. Let me start with a list of what you will need in order to venture off and make those great finds:

- A fanny pack
- A good magnifying glass (with at least 5X magnification)
- Sturdy gloves (strong work-type)
- White cotton gloves
- A pen

This Victrola (circa 1910) has not been restored and sits beautifully in my Presidents Room. I bought this item in a live TV auction for only $125.

- A small note pad
- A large, high-powered flashlight
- Extending pole (on the end of which a mirror can be affixed)
- Calculator
- Padlock (combination or keyed)
- Black light flashlight
- A box cutter or sturdy knife
- Magnet

Along with these tools, there are two more that could really help you out a lot in certain situations. The following treasure-hunting tools go above and beyond the scope of basic items listed above, but are very beneficial to have.

A trailer or any vehicle large enough to carry big loads—Having a large vehicle available is a huge asset, especially when you're looking to bid on the contents of a storage unit. I will cover storage units a little later in the chapter, but when you buy the contents of a storage unit, you'll usually need to move all the items within 24 hours after the purchase. Having a means of moving all those potential treasures without having to rent a truck will add to your efficiency and ability to get great deals.

Sales tax license—This license could save you thousands of dollars over time. A sales tax license allows you to avoid directly paying tax on items you've acquired from estate sales, auctions and storage unit sales since you'll be charging sales tax upon resale of your items. In most states, sales tax ranges from 6% to 14%, so for every $1,000 you spend, your savings will range from $60 to $90. This amount can add up substantially throughout the course of a year. Additionally, if you sell the items you buy in your own state, you must charge sales tax. At the time of publication of this book, if you sell your items across state lines you're not required to charge sales tax. Of course, there are different tax zones for every city and county, so

Million $ Tip

As a buyer, if you have a sales tax license or you are buying over state lines, you don't have to pay sales tax. Always check with your accountant, as rules may vary from state-to-state.

seek your accountant's advice on what to charge. A sales tax license will usually cost you approximately $25 to $100.

These two additional treasure-hunting tools will streamline your business activities and in the end will save you time and money. Now that you have all the necessary tools at your disposal, it's time to start hunting for goodies.

Where to Treasure Hunt

Always be alert! You never know when you might come across a buried treasure that could make you a substantial profit.

Secondhand Stores

When I talk about secondhand stores, I'm referring to places such as Salvation Army thrift stores, Goodwill Industry stores, AMVETS (American Veterans Thrift Stores), mom and pop secondhand stores and Consignment stores. These are all excellent locations to find some very valuable items.

People often ask me, "How can there possibly be treasures at secondhand stores?" Believe me when I tell you that people are making huge finds at these locations every day. In February 2009, a person found a piece of art at a secondhand store that was verified to be 150 years old. An appraiser friend of mine valued it and wouldn't you know it, that buried treasure was eventually auctioned at **Sotheby's (www.sothebys.com)** for $450,000!

That particular treasure was found at a Goodwill Industry store. The item was waiting in the store for what could have been days to weeks to months. One day, because someone knew what to look for, they found a treasure worth close to half a million dollars. It's an amazing story, and it's true!

Whether you're cleaning up your home or someone else's, you're bound to find items that could eventually be worth good money. Opportunities lie in wait in places you might never imagine: You could be helping a neighbor with spring cleaning. In an unfortunate, but almost inevitable situation, a family member may have just

> **Million $ Tip**
>
> You need to check secondhand stores on a regular basis since they restock items every day of the week.

passed away and you could find yourself with items that are no longer needed and must be disposed of. Perhaps a family friend might need help cleaning out their attic or garage.

After everything is gathered and cleaned, people usually just load their found items in a truck and try to help out their community by taking everything to a local thrift store. Unwanted belongings are usually taken to Goodwill Industry stores, Salvation Army thrift stores or AMVETS Thrift Stores. By choosing this easy way out as your first option and not taking into consideration the money that could be made from what you collected, you've made a huge mistake. This is how items like the previously mentioned 150-year-old piece of art, get discarded. *It happens every day in secondhand stores.*

I recommend you go to secondhand stores on a weekly basis and usually at the beginning of the week. I find Mondays or Tuesdays are the best days to visit and do your treasure hunting. These are the days of the week when shelves are completely restocked with new merchandise. Stores receive most of their goods over the weekend and the employees will work very hard to price everything for placement on their shelves early in the week. If you really want to be thorough and persistent, check back more often. The more you visit these businesses, the better chance you have of finding that item worth hundreds to thousands of dollars.

> **Million $ Tip**
>
> If you are close to a mountain resort town, you will definitely want to visit their second hand stores. You are guaranteed to find some wonderful and amazing things that were donated by the local residents.

Secondhand stores usually accept credit cards and a few of them even accept checks for payment. Unfortunately, the practice of accepting checks is becoming the exception to the rule because so many people have tried to pass bad checks. Many secondhand stores have limited budgets and closely monitor operating costs just to survive, so the practice of not accepting personal checks is becoming the norm. I suggest all of my customers bring credit cards or cash. As far as credit cards go, bring your Visa or MasterCard, but not your American Express. You can leave that card at home. Why? Credit card companies charge the retailer transaction fees every time a credit card is used. It costs the retailer from 2% up to 5% of the purchase price on every sale, and American Express is the most expensive with regard to fees.

When can you negotiate prices? If the secondhand store is a mom-and-pop type store, you can always try to negotiate the sales price. The worst thing the seller can say is no. The smaller the store, the more negotiating leeway seems to be allowed. From my experience, larger secondhand stores (for example Goodwill or Salvation Army) rarely, if ever negotiate. If you become friends with the manager and they see you all the time, then you might be able to negotiate.

Almost every major city has these types of secondhand stores—places packed with great items, valuable finds and hidden treasures. They're yours for the taking! To locate the closest mom-and-pop second-hand stores, check local listings in your telephone book, your local newspaper's classifieds section or try searching the Internet. To find some of the larger second-hand stores located near your community visit:

> **Million $ Tip**
>
> Become friends with the managers of secondhand stores. They will give you great little tips like when new shipments arrive and when the store will be restocked.

- Goodwill Industry Stores (http://locator.goodwill.org/)
- Salvation Army Thrift Stores (www.salvationarmyusa.org)
- AMVETS Thrift Stores (www.amvetsnsf.org/stores.html)

Some of the main things you'll want to look for in secondhand stores are art, books and china. For art items, check the walls, the back room or anywhere else art could possibly be placed in the store. Small-sized items such as books and china are usually scattered throughout the store. Many items considered valuable by the store owner are kept close to the front of the store in glass cases. But don't be fooled by their conspicuous placement; most of the items displayed in the cases have little value.

Many times, individuals will go into their parents' homes when they've recently passed away or moved into an assisted-living facility, taking anything and everything they can lay their hands on. Then it's off to the secondhand stores. Although the majority of the items you find in secondhand stores carry no value whatsoever, there are some items of value to be found. I constantly hear stories of people finding items worth a great deal of money this way.

> **Million $ Tip**
>
> Don't just go to your local secondhand stores. If you go to the ones in more expensive neighborhoods, there is a good chance you will find more valuable items.

Estate Auctions

Estate auctions might seem a bit intimidating to you since you're bidding against other people, but this fear is totally unfounded. Not only are estate auctions a great deal of fun to attend, but you can also find some real treasures that can net you serious cash.

> **Million $ Tip**
>
> Always be cautious about getting caught up in a bidding war. Most of the time if you're not careful, you'll pay more than you want to and you may actually pay more than the item is really worth.

When a crowd of very excited individuals sets the price for all the items being auctioned in a room, you can bet your bottom dollar it's going to be an exciting day. Whether you're in a bidding war against a group of people or just with one other person, it's important to know why people bid an item up so you can make sure you don't get caught up in the middle of an unnecessary bidding frenzy and wind up paying too much for an item. Consider the following possibilities:

- These bidders know the real value of the item and they're willing to pay whatever they think the actual value is on that item.

- They may have some sort of sentimental attachment to the item they're bidding on. Money is a secondary concern in these cases.
- They think there's big value for the item for sale but they have no clue whatsoever about it's true value.

Once you understand why people bid an item up, knowing as much as possible about the item is extremely important. If you truly do not understand what you're bidding on, you will get caught up in a bidding war with one of these people or a group of them and pay much more money than you should.

Knowing the way estate auctions work is also key. One of the best ways to understand how the process works is to attend as many estate auctions as possible before you start bidding on anything. A major benefit of attending multiple estate auctions is that you'll learn how to pick out the professional bidders—the elite group that you'll soon become a part of, once you know how the system works. These experienced bidders know exactly how to place the right bid at the right time and work the system, so that the final auction price stays as low as possible. Also, by attending a lot of estate auctions, you can see what these pros are bidding on so you can get an idea of what's valuable and what's not.

When you attend an auction, you'll need to be ready with the right method of payment and know in advance what the preferred method of payment is at that particular auction. Cash is best for items up to a few thousand dollars. If you're going to be buying something in the ten thousand dollar range and up, it's probably best to make good use of your credit card for the payment. But by paying cash when

---

Million $ Tip

Don't miss a chance to go to an auction if the weather is bad or if there's a big game on television. The fewer people who show up at an auction means a better chance for you to get the best deals!

Million $ Tip

One of the secrets for getting the best deal on items at an estate auction is to stay until the end. People tend to leave auctions early, so later is when some of the very best deals can be found.

you can for auction items, you'll save on credit card fees. (Some auction houses may charge you more if you use a credit card.) Auction houses usually do not take American Express and many do not accept Discover Cards either. If you stick with Visa or MasterCard, you'll be just fine. As mentioned earlier, many auction houses do not accept personal checks due to fraud issues associated with them. Again, it is imperative to call ahead to verify which payment options are accepted because every auction house is different.

Estate auctions can last just a couple of hours or be an all-day event. Set your schedule to afford yourself enough time in case the auction runs late. If the auction takes all day, make sure you bring extra food, snacks and water. This may sound funny and may feel awkward at first, but many auctions don't have any type of concession stand available for their customers. If they do have one, prices are exorbitant and can cost double what you might normally expect to pay. Also, check to see what the weather will be on the day of the auction. Some estate auctions are held outside or in warehouses that could be very hot or cold depending on the time of year. Dress accordingly.

Storage Unit Auctions

When I talk about the most exciting treasure hunting out there, I'm talking about going to storage unit auctions. You may be asking, "Storage unit auctions? Are you serious? How can they be exciting? They're just storage units, right?" Well, they really are great fun, as I will explain.

In every city, in every county and in every state in

> **Million $ Tip**
>
> With the exposure from television shows about storage unit auctions, there's a good chance there will be a large crowd at any auction. You should know that most of them are "lookie-lous," so you needn't be intimidated by the size of the crowd. Usually, there's only a handful of actual bidders at every auction.

the country, millions upon millions of people use storage units to hold some or most of their belongings due to a variety of circumstances. When people move, many times they need a place to store items. When they can't fit everything in their home or simply don't want to have their homes filled with clutter and unused items, they store their extra items at an external location.

Storage unit operators usually charge a monthly rental fee for the use of their space and many times offer discounts if the customer signs up for the rental on an annual basis. If a customer fails to remain current on rental payments, lapsing for a period of 90 days, and doesn't respond to repeated calls or letters from the storage unit operator or company, by law the contents of the unit can be auctioned off. Usually the owner or manager of that specific location will place auction advertisements in the local paper, list the auction on their website and continue making basic attempts to let the storage unit renter know that their contents are subject to a potential auction. Once a storage unit customer has reached the 90-day delinquent mark, an auction date is set, the auctioneer is called to the storage unit and the bidding commences.

Once the bidding starts, it's up to you to take a look at the contents to see if you want to bid on the items contained in the storage unit. You will only have one to three minutes to take a look, and as I explain a little later, you will not be allowed to enter the unit. There could be only you and a few other people bidding on the contents or there could be dozens of other individuals bidding. It's a crap shoot with regard to what you may end up buying and you really need to be prepared for any situation. Everyone at a storage unit auction is thinking the same thing: They're going to find that big treasure and huge payday. This is the point where the excitement begins. You really are going to have to put that excitement in check if you want to focus and score big at the auction.

> ### Million $ Tip
>
> When you're ready to bid at a storage unit auction, don't get caught up in the excitement of the bidding. Stay calm. Because you are not allowed to enter the unit, you can't see everything in inside, and most items you may not be able to see at all. Make mental notes about what you can see, and try to figure out what the value is based on what you're seeing. Then make the best educated guess on what the remaining contents of the unit may be worth.

Let's backtrack a bit to give you better insight into the storage unit auction process. As I mentioned before, you'll be given a short time to look at the contents. This is where the tools of the trade—those items I listed at the beginning of the chapter—come into play. The large, high-powered flashlight helps you get a good look at the contents tucked in the back of the unit. Of course, there's a catch to viewing the contents: You can't break the door jamb. What does that mean? Your head cannot cross the threshold of the door to the storage unit. As I've already said, this process is a real crap shoot! If your head crosses this line, the auctioneer will shout at you. Truth be told, I've been yelled at on more than one occasion!

This is where the extending pole with a mirror enters the fray. I like to rig a mirror on a long pole so I can get a good look at what is wedged way in the back of the storage unit. Have this pole-mirror arrangement set up in advance and practice with it so you can get a good look quickly.

When it comes to bidding on the contents, only about 10% of the crowd will make a bid. Usually, after the first couple of bids, most bidders will drop out. When it comes to the end of the bidding, usually it will be you and one other person. This is really when you have to put your emotions in check. If you don't, you could wind up paying much more than the contents are actually worth.

Additionally, you will need to calculate the time it will take to clear out the unit if you are the person with the winning bid. You need to consider not only the money you spend to win the auction, but also the total amount of time you'll need to spend throughout the entire process. It's really beneficial and a huge time saver if you can find someone to help you empty out the unit. Family members or good friends are the best helpers. Plus, they usually work cheap! For the price of a trip to Starbucks or McDonald's, you'll usually get all the help you need. Along with your helper(s), you need to have a trailer or large vehicle available so you can get all the goods you've just purchased removed quickly within the allotted time.

> ### Million $ Tip
>
> Antiques are HUGE money-makers! When people see antiques, they're going to start bidding the price up immediately. You have to consider your ability to sell what's in the unit. People will bid and push their bids high. Ultimately, you have to place a ceiling on what you're willing to spend.

If everything goes well and you've won the bid, now what? Usually, you'll have 24 to 48 hours to remove everything in the unit and leave it completely empty. If you feel you're unable to clean out the unit within this time span, then you'll need to rent the space for a month. I strongly recommend this course of action. By renting the space for just a month, you will save on having to pay the deposit money, which is usually between $50 and $75. There's nothing worse than knowing you are under the gun and cannot get the storage unit cleaned out in time. By renting the space for a month you'll have more time to find a place to permanently put all the new-found treasures you've just acquired.

Million $ Tip

If you don't have enough cash to pay for your storage unit auction winnings approximately thirty minutes after the auction closes, the storage unit operator will re-auction the unit, and you will lose your claim on all the items in the unit.

Million $ Tip

A quick warning about participating in storage unit auctions. Many of these units have never been gone through before the auction begins. From my experience, there could, and probably will be almost anything in there including knives, guns, drugs or even used needles. It is safe to say there are going to be items that could really injure you, so wear very thick, sturdy gloves and be mindful of how you are sifting through and opening all the items.

Don't buy the contents of the storage unit and then go home and think about it. You'll want to clean out the contents from the storage unit immediately. Get it done ASAP, as time could be of the essence if there are treasures that need to be resold promptly. You certainly don't want to miss your window of opportunity if a potential buyer for what you have goes elsewhere because you procrastinated.

Large plastic bags for trash are handy as well as a wheelbarrow, dolly, cart or something you can load items on and move them to your vehicle. Most times, you won't be able to back up to the storage unit. Many franchise storage facilities are located indoors. Obstacles may include elevators or stairs used to get to and from the unit. The easier you make it on yourself, the faster you can remove your new-found cache out of the unit.

When you're looking at items in storage units, you're going to see almost everything. In my many years of buying and selling storage unit auction items, I've seen items ranging from furniture and antiques to kitchenware and personal items such as clothing or personal paperwork, even food items. You name it: I've seen it! Many storage unit operators recommend that if you find something of a very personal nature such as a birth certificate, you should attempt

to return it to the unit operator and ask that he get it to
the rightful owner. I think
this is a great idea because
some of the personal items
discovered in these units are
of no value to you, but are
irreplaceable to the person
who lost them.

Also, be prepared to find
metal objects in a storage
unit. There may be items you
can sell for the metal weight

> **Million $ Tip**
>
> If you discover anything you
> believe is illegal, call the police
> right away. You do not want to be
> a part of any crime! Simply call the
> police and advise them you just
> bought the contents of the unit.
> They will completely understand
> and you will not be charged with
> anything criminal.

such as copper, silver or even gold. You'll find many tools as well.
Tools have a huge amount of resale value and many people will bid
on the unit if they see tools as part of the contents. Additional items
to seek out in a storage unit are televisions and computers. There's
a catch here though. Many of these items could be obsolete and
have little to no resale value. You should never place much value
on older computers and televisions. These items may not work or
newer versions have been produced at much cheaper prices. Don't
let obsolete electronics distract you when you're looking through a
unit.

You will likely find a lot of trash, so always be prepared for
that. You'll find many items in a storage unit have no real market
value and can be easily donated to Goodwill or the Salvation Army.
If you don't have need for an item, make a donation. You'll be helping families in need and in addition, you might be able to use your
donations as a tax write-off.

As I mentioned earlier, make sure to bring cash. Credit cards
and personal checks are almost never accepted. What happens
when you run out of cash and don't have the money to cover your
purchase? Hopefully you can leave for a few moments and run to an
ATM, your bank or call a friend or relative to bring you more cash.

Storage unit auctions move very quickly. I'll bet you anything,
if you put a stopwatch to it, from the time a unit is originally shown
to the time the auction for that unit ends is less than eight minutes. Storage unit operators want to move quickly to get the unit's
contents sold so they can make money from the next renter of the
space. Individual auctions can include a single unit to fifteen units
being auctioned off all at once. You'll want to make sure you have

the bankroll to bid on all of them because you never know what's in the next unit since only one is shown and auctioned at a time. You'll never get to look through all the units first to then bid on the one or ones you want.

To find out where the storage unit auctions are in your area, look to the Internet and search for storage unit auctions in your city. You can also find these auctions listed in the free newspapers in your town. Daily newspapers will have these sales in the classifieds. When you locate the auctions you want to do business with, get on their e-mail list so they can send you an alert when auctions will take place. This is the easiest way to get advance notice of the auction times and dates as well as locations and the number of units to be auctioned. In case you don't get the e-mails or your Internet connection is down, always double-check your local newspapers as suggested above.

Garage Sales

Attending garage and yard sales as a buyer and running them as a seller are how I got started in the collecting business a long time ago. With garage sales and yard sales being similar in nature, I will just refer to them from this point forward as garage sales.

> **Million $ Tip**
>
> If there's a garage sale you think is going to be a blockbuster, go to the house the night before and offer them $20 to get a look at what they'll be selling. This will save you time and effort for the next day. If you see something good, you might want to try negotiating right then and there.

Way back when, I was putting on garage sales with my mother, learning the value of the goodies we were putting out to sell. Frequent garage sale goers would tell us we should raise our prices on this or lower our prices on that. It was kind of those people to share their helpful pieces of information. If people were telling us that our prices were too low, imagine how many garage sales there are where people not only do not know what they are selling, but also do not know the best price to charge for their sale items? It happens all the time.

The main component of any garage sale, besides the buying and selling of items, of course, is negotiating every sale. As a buyer, you never want to pay the asking price. If you are not negotiating every sale, you are wasting your money.

I've run garage sales in the past where I put the sale sign up and someone was at my front door waiting for me before I got back from putting up the sign. People absolutely *love* going to garage sales because they usually go to find things they may need or want to own. As a Garage Sale Millionaire, you're going hunting with the express intent of finding items you believe to have a high resale value—items that will make you lots of money!

If your garage sale begins at 9:00 AM, you want to be there and ready to go at 8:30 AM. Don't be at all surprised if people, wanting to get a jump on the crowd, arrive at your sale before it's scheduled to begin.

When people hold a garage sale, there is a great deal of time and stress expended in the preparation. You have to make certain everything is laid out and displayed the way you like. Items need to be labeled and prices need to be set correctly to guarantee you're getting the maximum sale value possible. People often forget they have items they want to sell and forget to put them out. One of the keys to a successful garage sale is to take your time in the days before your sale and make sure everything is accounted for with regard to what you want to sell.

The old adage "the early bird gets the worm" applies perfectly to garage sales. By arriving early for a garage sale, the savvy garage sale buyer gets the jump on the competition by being able to see everything laid out and

> ### Million $ Tip
>
> To get the best deals at garage sales, go early and go often. Hit garage sales when they start and go to as many sales as possible.

ready to be sold before others arrive. The only reason you would show up at the end of a garage sale is if the seller had something really good at the onset of the sale, but the item was priced way too high. If you show up during the last moments of any sale and make a low ball offer on the items you're looking for, the seller may take your offer knowing he or she won't be getting any others. If you don't want to drive back to the garage sale as it nears completion, you could try and get the name and telephone number of the seller before you take off and call back at the end of the sale to see if they still have the item in which you were interested. Most sellers will gladly give out their name and telephone number.

Newspapers are a huge asset in finding local garage sales. Most newspapers have a separate garage sale section in their classifieds. Another way of locating garage sales is to drive around to as many neighborhoods as you can on Friday night or Saturday morning. People will begin putting out signs for their sales during this time. Another great way to view garage sales around your area is to use the Internet. By using specific search terms, there's a great chance a website will pop up listing sales in your area. A quick Google search for "Garage Sales + Denver, Colorado" netted 1,300,000 results. Another Google search of "Garage Sales + Los Angeles, California" yielded 3,350,000 results. It's truly amazing how popular garage sales really are!

Whenever you attend a garage sale, be prepared so that you don't pay more for an item than you should. If you have a smart phone, such as an iPhone, or Blackberry, you can search the Internet and track down an item's value. As I will discuss in detail later in the book, a good place for determining value is eBay.

When you're trying to research items very quickly, be very certain to take the extra few moments needed to match apples to apples. For example, if you just found an original Star Wars Kenner Darth Vader action figure in near mint condition from the 1970s at a neighbor-hood garage sale and it was being sold on eBay for $2,495, make sure the action figure at the garage sale matches the eBay listing exactly. You would hate to find out when you got home that the $375 cash you just spent on what you thought was valued at about $2,500 ended up being a "Star Wars ROTJ Darth Vader figure MOC KENNER" action fig-ure from 1983 valued on eBay at only $55.

> **Million $ Tip**
>
> When you are at a garage sale, just because an item is not out does not mean it is not for sale. You need to ask the seller about items you are specifically looking for—antique chairs, old photo-graphs, old baseball cards, pretty much anything in which you are interested. Ask them very politely and you never know what you may be able to get!

When buying at a garage sale, it's definitely caveat emp-tor: Buyer beware. You need to make sure you're happy with whatever item you buy. Try to do your due diligence, research on the spot, and of course, if you're not happy with the item at all, don't buy it. There is a no return, no refund policy at almost every garage sale. This is true even if you walk to your car, turn right back around and try to return your purchase immediately. You'll be stuck, because all sales are final. That's one of the main reasons why garage sales are operated on a cash-only basis. The Salvation Army Thrift Stores, Goodwill Industry stores and other secondhand stores will not refund the selling price either, but they may give you a store credit. Store policies may differ from location to location, so be sure to check those policies prior to making your purchase. You always have to buy things with the understanding that you are not going to be able to get your money back even if you decide to return an item.

There is no harm in bringing collectibles resource books along as well in order to help you make your decision at a garage sale. No one will say anything negative if you have a coin book in one hand and an antique book in the other. This is just what a smart and savvy Garage Sale Millionaire does: they arrive prepared!

Auctions

Auctions used to occur maybe a few times per month depending on the size of the auction house. Now that the current economic conditions have worsened, auctions occur much more frequently. Auction houses now hold multiple auctions on a weekly basis. They are easily found by looking in your local newspaper or searching online. In the business section of your newspaper classified ads, you'll find a section just for auctions.

Don't confuse regular auctions with estate auctions, as they are completely different. An auction is a public sale of property that is sold to whoever is the highest bidder. With an estate auction, all merchandise is valued by an appraiser, priced accordingly and sold on a first come, first serve basis. At auctions or estate auctions anything and everything could be auctioned off to a lucky high bidder. Items at a regular auction may include entire inventories from an auto parts store, valuable (and not so valuable) coins, used cooking equipment from a restaurant, television or movie memorabilia, old tractors, antiques, guns or home theater equipment. You personally need to determine what auction is interesting and potentially profitable.

Besides the crowd that sets the auction prices, the really interesting facet of the auction process is that an auction can be held anywhere. They can be held in the capital of your state or in the smallest rural towns. The auctions held in small remote areas are the ones you definitely want to frequent. If it's difficult for you to get there, likewise it's equally difficult for everyone else. The fewer people who attend an auction means the better chance there is for you to get a fantastic deal.

For every auction, there's usually an online listing for what's going to be auctioned off. Some auctions also hold preview days where you can show up at the auction location to look at everything that will be going up for sale. Preview days usually take place 48 to 72 hours before the start of the auction. Taking advantage of preview days and asking questions about the items on the auction block are very important components of the auction process. Why? Because you can get an in-depth idea and understanding of what is up for sale at an auction, make detailed notes about what's going to be auctioned and do valuable research before the auction begins to find out the actual value of the items being offered. By taking advantage of the preview days, you can also view any item, make sure it hasn't been damaged or poorly restored and ensure it has all the parts, packaging or whatever it takes to make the item worth the highest amount of money possible. If you can't attend the auction preview days in person, give the company holding the auction (usually an auction house) a call if you have any questions.

You need to set your top end price on items before the auction. If you do not complete your due diligence and research on the items you're interested in owning, you can easily overpay for them. I've seen so many people overpay for auction items over the years that I lost count decades ago. It doesn't happen once or twice; it happens at every single auction. I've seen people pay many times over the retail price for items being auctioned. However, the way to become a Garage Sale Millionaire is being able to find those hidden treasures and pay less than their values, so you can turn a profit when you resell them.

If you are bidding against someone or against a group of bidders, there are usually two reasons why people bid on an item:

1. **People think the item is more valuable than the current bid**.

    At some point during every auction, people believe they are way ahead of the curve and believe the current auction bid price on an item or set of items is undervalued. This usually occurs when the due diligence is not done prior to the beginning of an auction. You would be surprised at how many people believe they know what an item is really worth, when in reality, they have no clue. This happens all the time. These are the moments when you can really clean up as a Garage Sale Millionaire. If the bidding doesn't reach the actual value of an item, you can win the bid and make a fantastic profit upon resale. If the bidding goes way above the actual value of an item, by not bidding too high because you have done the proper research on the item, you won't overpay for something.

2. **The item has some kind of personal meaning to the bidder**.

When you're bidding against someone who has an emotional attachment to an item, it's definitely not about the money. These bidders want to have the item at any cost. They usually have the means and bankroll to buy any item they desire. You need to watch out for this kind of bidder because it will cost you big if you're not ready. You're thinking they know something about the item, when in reality, they know nothing about the item and just want it because it has some degree of personal meaning or importance to them. When you get caught up in the bidding war against this type of bidder, this is where you can go way upside down on an item and pay too much. How can you spot this type of person? Before an auction begins, people linger around the items they are interested in and are very chatty about what's going to be up for auction. Listen closely to what seems to be innocuous and innocent banter, as it could give you great insight and save you money when the bidding begins! During the bidding, also pay careful attention to how people are bidding and how emotionally attached they seem to be to certain items. Are they excited? Are their eyes wider than usual? Are they unusually attentive and does their posture—the way they carry themselves—appear as though they're excited about something that's happening? All these signs mean there's more than a passing interest involved in what is up for sale at the auction.

3. **They think there's big value in the item for sale but have no clue whatsoever about the item's true value.**

These are spur of the moment buyers who saw the item on eBay or in another auction and feel that they're experienced enough to bid on it. These bidders can be dangerous at an auction because they start quickly bidding up items without the knowledge to back up their numbers. This is why you must have a ceiling when bidding because these spur of the moment bidders could run the cost up to two or three times above the actual value of the item and won't realize their mistake until they get home and do their research.

If you do your research before the auction and place a mental ceiling on what you are willing to pay, you will always be protected.

I was at an auction a few years ago and wanted to win a particular item very badly. It was an old vase I saw that had very interesting markings. I found out about the auction at the last minute so unfortunately I did not have time to research the item, but I did place a ceiling on what I was willing to pay for it. A woman began bidding against me and the bidding quickly escalated. Everyone else but the two of us dropped out of the bidding for the vase. I made an exception to my own rule as I kept making bids above my ceiling. As I said, I really wanted this item! As a result, I got unnecessarily caught up in the heightened level of excitement! Unfortunately for me, she kept on making higher and higher bids. By this time, I was way above my ceiling and had to end my

---

Million $ Tip

Set maximums for yourself so you do not overpay or overbid on items that interest you. By setting maximums, you can also focus on the items you believe will make you the most money upon resale. If your maximum is to make at least $25 from any sale, let that amount be your guide. If your maximum is percentage-based for making at least 10% on an item, then that will be your guide. With that being said . . . do not always rely on maximums to get the best eventual profits. You need to always be aware and open to new possibilities if an opportunity presents itself. If you can buy something for $5,000 and you know you can sell it for at least $6,000 and this line of thinking goes completely against the way you have set up your maximums, then, by all means, go for it as you have just guaranteed yourself a darn good return on your money. At any possible moment, you could find that treasure that gives you a fantastic payday. Be on the alert for anything to happen in an auction. In the long run, you will reap the profits!

bidding and bow out. To my chagrin, she eventually ended up buying the item.

After the auction, I approached her and asked her what she thought was so important about this vase. She told me she actually knew nothing about the vase, but she had described it to her mother over the telephone and her mother was extremely interested in acquiring this piece. I further inquired as to why her mother was so interested in this particular item. It was because her mom had a similar vase at home which was irreparably damaged. Her mother quite simply thought that this vase could easily replace the broken one. She had no idea what the vase was worth and she didn't care. She just had to have the vase.

I guarantee you that once you begin attending auctions, you'll start seeing the same faces at almost every auction. Many people do this for a living and they attend auctions weekly, like clockwork. These are the people who will also drop out of the bidding quickly when the bidding goes too high. If you want an item more than they do, they see this and they will stop bidding when the price rises beyond their ceiling.

When I talk to my customers, I find out all the time that people are intimidated and afraid of the magical and mystical bidding process at an auction. Some people think, like they see in the movies, they have to do something very elaborate like tweak their nose or pull their ear to even take part in an auction. This couldn't be further from the truth. All you have to do is take your bid number, which is provided to you at the start of the auction, and raise it in the air. This is always the acceptable sign that you are bidding on an item. It's that simple.

Bidding and buying an item correctly at an auction separates the successful Garage Sale Millionaires from the wannabes and the money-earners from the money-losers.

Along with completing your due diligence and research in finding out what items to bid on and deciding what to buy based on the profit you want to make, you also need to consider your costs. Costs throughout this process include three factors:

> **Time**—Time is money. The time it takes you to research an item, determine how much to charge for an item, sell the item and collect payment all factor into the time equation. The more time you spend on something diminishes the

actual profit you will make. If you sell something for $4,500 that cost you $4,000 and it took you nearly 40 hours to sell it, that does not sound like it was a win-win. To me it sounds more like a lose-lose situation. You need to figure time into your bottom line because it directly affects profits.

Auction House Premiums—Whenever you win something at an auction, you're going to be charged a buyer's premium by the auction house. This buyer's premium is a fee that is charged in addition to your winning bid amount. In the higher-end auction houses such as Sotheby's and Christie's, there's a very good chance you will be charged a fee ranging anywhere between 12% and 24%. In smaller auction houses, the premiums are a little less than that. Unfortunately for the buyer, all auction houses have this buyer's premium as this is how these houses make their money and stay in business. Sellers also pay the same type of premium or fee called the seller's premium. These premiums are also steep and can range from 10% to 25%. If you ever wondered how auction houses stay profitable, now you know.

Sales Tax License—Earlier in the chapter, I discussed the benefits of having a sales tax license. Sales tax licenses are easily obtained and can potentially save you money. Again, the cost of acquiring a sales tax license is approximately $25 to $100.

Every auction house has slightly different rules regarding acceptable payment. As mentioned earlier, credit cards and cash are usually universally accepted forms of payment, whereas the practice of accepting personal checks is becoming rarer over time. Some auction houses take checks, but many do not. I recommend calling ahead and inquiring about the acceptable payment options.

Almost every auction house takes credit cards as a form of payment. By using a credit card to pay for your auction wins, you can keep track of financial activities in much greater detail than by solely using cash to make your purchases. Credit cards also have some level of theft protection, so if your card gets stolen you're usually going to be protected. Please check with your credit card issuer to determine and verify what level of protection you have, as every card is different. Many credit cards have some type of mileage rewards program, so after a long week of buying at auctions you will receive reward points as well. Visa and MasterCard are usually accepted, while American Express is typically not; sometimes Discover Card is not accepted either. So it pays to check out what is accepted in advance. Carrying a lot of cash around presents problems. I'm not talking about $50 or $60 in your wallet, but many hundreds or thousands of dollars in cash. Cash can be lost or it can be stolen and once it's gone, it's gone. If you don't have to carry cash, don't. Use your credit card.

For an exhaustive list of auctions, by category, visit **The Internet Auction List (www.internetauctionlist.com).** Please keep in mind that many times auction houses hold auctions covering many categories. For example, **Heritage Auction Galleries (www.ha.com, www.entertainment.ha.com)** holds multiple auctions in the areas of art, comics, currency, entertainment memorabilia, historical items, movie posters, natural history items, rare books and sports collectibles. Some of the major companies in the auction business are:

Type	Auctioneer	Internet Address
Art	G. B. Tate & Sons Fine Art	www.gbtate.com
	Lunds	www.lunds.com
	Phillips de Pury Company	www.phillipsdepury.com
	Swann Galleries	www.swanngalleries.com
Automotive	Gooding & Co.	www.goodingco.com
	Barrett-Jackson	www.barrettjackson.com
	Mecum Auto Auctions	www.mecum.com
	RM Auctions	www.rmauctions.com
	Russo and Steele	www.russoandsteele.com
Baseball/Trading Cards	Baseball-Cards.com	www.baseball-cards.com
	Greg Bussineau Sports Rarities	www.gregbussineau.com
	Memory Lane Inc.	www.memorylaneinc.com
Books	Americana Exchange	www.americanaexchange.com
	PBA Galleries	www.pbagalleries.com
	Quinn's Auction Galleries	www.quinnsauction.com
Coins	Stack's Bowers	www.stacksbowers.com
	Spink	www.spink.com
Comics	Comic Book Auctions Ltd.	www.compalcomics.com
	Mile High Comics	www.milehighcomics.com
Consumer Electronics	AudiogoN	www.audiogon.com
	VideogoN	www.videogon.com

(continued)

(*continued*)

Type	Auctioneer	Internet Address
Entertainment Memorabilia	Heritage Auction Galleries	www.entertainment.ha.com
	Premiere Props	www.premiereprops.com
	Profiles In History	www.profilesinhistory.com
Firearms	GunBroker.com	www.gunbroker.com
	International Bonhams	www.bonhams.com/us
	Christie's	www.christies.com
	Freeman's Auctioneers	www.freemansauction.com
	Heritage Auction Galleries	www.ha.com
	Neal Auction Company	www.nealauction.com
	Regency-Superior	www.regencystamps.com
	Sotheby's	www.sothebys.com
Online	eBay	www.ebay.com
	eBid	www.ebid.net
	uBid	www.ubid.com
Sports Memorabilia	Lelands	www.lelands.com
	Rob Edward Auctions	www.robertedwardauctions.com
	SCP Auctions	www.scpauctions.com
Toys	Smith House Toy & Auction Co.	www.smithhousetoys.com
	Theriault's	www.theriaults.com
	Toyzine	www.toyzine.com/sale.htm
Wine and Cigar	Acker Merrall & Condit	www.ackerwines.com
	Chicago Wine Company	www.tcwc.com
	Cigar Auctioneer	www.cigarauctioneer.com
	Hart Davis Hart Wine Co.	www.hdhwine.com
	Wine Bid	www.winebid.com
	Wine Commune	www.winecommune.com
	Zachys Wine Auctions	www.zachys.com/auctions

Antique Stores

Antique stores are fascinating to visit. There are thousands of these shops across the country and, in some locations, there are also huge conglomerates housing antique stores and antique booths in the same location. Each booth and/or store is usually owned or rented by a different individual or company.

I like to go to antique stores in small towns as well as big cities because there are wonderful treasures to be found in both. Even where you think there aren't many antique stores, like in the tourist cities of Santa Barbara, California or Gettysburg, Pennsylvania, there actually are many of these shops to browse and shop to your heart's content. When visiting any antique store, don't think just because there are seemingly knowledgeable people behind the front desk that proper research has been done on every item on the floor. People make mistakes all the time. Sometimes big mistakes can work in your favor. It's up to you to search out which items are priced incorrectly. When you find those mistakes, and hopefully it will be a big mistake in your favor, make an immediate offer on the item. You might go home with a gem of a find that will net you big money upon resale.

I've gone to some wonderful antique stores in my time and have seen some really tantalizing items being sold. Some of the antiques are fairly accurately priced; others not so much. If I befriend the manager or store owner while I'm in their store, I'll usually learn more from them (not to mention there's a better chance I can make a deal on any item I find). It doesn't hurt to ask questions. In fact, I highly recommend it.

Always make an offer on anything you're interested in buying. In these harder economic times, I've not seen a reasonable offer rejected at an antique store. Sellers need to make quick sales so their business will survive. When you go into an antique store,

> ### Million $ Tip
>
> Some antique furniture has been unscrupulously replicated and, as a result, people are paying more for some things they believe are labeled correctly as an authentic antique when they are not. Unfortunately, I see newly manufactured furniture being disguised as old and labeled as antique much more often at conglomerate warehouse antique stores. Overall, most vendors are honest and place a sign on the item advising it is indeed, a replica. Of course, there are always some vendors who are not so honest. Always be on the alert when you go to antique stores. It is extremely easy to make something look old and worth much more money than the item is truly worth.

look around and take your time. If you find an item you like, negotiate. Quite a few antique stores will take credit cards, but if you pay in cash, you might be able to get a better deal. Antique stores prefer taking cash for a sale because it saves them money by not having to pay any credit card transaction fees.

The Online Marketplace

There are many places online where you can find new or used items. The Internet is full of websites where people can buy and resell personal items for a profit. Since attending garage sales continues to be an increasingly popular activity, it's only natural that this garage sale–type of activity has evolved onto the Internet.

With so many places to buy and sell goods, it's an essential business strategy to choose the most successful from among all of the websites listed in this chapter. You have the best chance for success if you make the most money possible as a seller and save as much money as possible as a buyer when you do business online.

There are a couple of websites that have not only stood the test of time but are also still thriving in an extemely challenging economy. These two websites have been in business for many years and are considered the heavy-hitters of the online marketplace: Craigslist and eBay.

Craigslist

One of the websites that first comes to mind when discussing superior online marketplaces is **Craigslist (www.craigslist.org)**. Craigslist is the most amazing online shopping experience I could ever imagine. It began operations in 1995 and originated as a bulletin board–type message service to help people around San Francisco, California find things to do. Today, the company has grown into a global marketplace reaching all 50 United States (including Washington DC), as well as having a presence in over 60 countries.

The items offered on Craigslist change every minute of every day. The most recent listing is on the top of the webpage. In as short a time as 30 seconds, listings will dramatically change and brand new listings will be posted. If you want to find some great items that will make you money, it's very important to check the website often throughout the day. If you see something you want to purchase, e-mail the seller immediately. Business transactions on Craigslist happen extremely quickly. If you don't act in a very timely matter, which could be from minutes to hours, there's a strong possibility you'll lose out on an item because there are other individuals just like you, trying to make money on this website.

As with all online activities, don't let your guard down when it comes to conducting business. Always be on guard whenever you're thinking of parting with your money by making a purchase or when you're ready to accept payment on an item you're going to sell.

As a buyer, there are several ways to protect yourself when doing business on Craigslist. If you're conducting business with someone locally, don't send any money to the seller until you actually see the item of interest. Arrange to meet the seller in a public place to look at the item whenever possible. In my experience, a local coffee shop seems to be the best place to meet the seller.

If you do business with someone from another state or country, try to get as much background information as possible (i.e., a detailed description of the item, multiple pictures of the item and references of past business dealings). It is not that buying on Craigslist from a different part of the world is a bad thing; deals can be made. It's just a bit trickier. If you are the seller of an item, the ways to protect yourself when doing business on Craigslist are pretty much the same as they are for a buyer. This means when conducting business locally, always provide verification for the item in question and personally meet the buyer in a public place (preferably) to get payment on the item.

> **Million $ Tip**
>
> Use websites like **CraigsPal (www. craigspal.com)** to conduct a more thorough and time efficient search throughout multiple states and countries for your treasures on **Craigslist** at once!

The best payment option when conducting business on Craigslist is cash. Almost every time I've sold items on the website, the buyer pays in cash. Because people usually sell their items locally, people expect to pay cash for whatever they buy. Be wary of accepting cashier's checks or certified checks. They can easily be counterfeited. It's better to meet the person face to face and ask for cash for your item. If you sell to someone outside of your area, such as another state or country, make sure the payment you receive clears the bank and funds are verified before sending the merchandise. If you can't meet someone in person to exchange funds, use **PayPal (www.paypal.com).** I will discuss PayPal in much more detail in Chapter 6.

Remember, when looking for items on Craigslist, listings change very rapidly and there is always something of interest to buy. Also, do not limit your search to the state in which you live. As previously mentioned, there are Craigslists for areas all over the world. If you live in California, take a look at what's being sold in New York. Searching these lists can consume hours each day, but when you find that rare hidden treasure all your efforts will be worth it.

Many of my friends who buy items at secondhand stores, thrift stores, storage unit sales, estate auctions and garage sales will put those items on Craigslist to move them quickly, so they can get their cash back along with a profit as soon as possible. My friends also note that they'll list items for less on Craigslist than they would elsewhere because they want to move the items quickly. Don't ever be afraid to make a counteroffer on items you're interested in buying on the website. Talk to the seller, make the counteroffer and you never know what you might get for less money than you ever expected to spend!

eBay

Everyone who has a computer and even those who do not, know about eBay. Over the years, **eBay (www.ebay.com)** has managed to make its way into the popular vernacular as the default expression and term for selling and buying anything on the Internet. eBay is where more items are bought and sold than any other single location in the world with a reach spanning over 30 countries. I've dedicated Chapter 6 entirely to eBay in order to explore this website in greater detail.

I sell a lot of items on eBay each month. As a businessperson, eBay has opened up avenues I could never have even imagined for my art and collectibles gallery. The same opportunities I have as a gallery owner and private collector to sell my treaures globally is also easily afforded to you. With a simple and straightforward user interface, tens of millions of users with hundreds of millions of items listed for sale and a support community that helps buyers and sellers alike, eBay is the best place to get your items noticed and to make a handsome profit.

With the information provided to you in this chapter, you now have the necessary tools to launch your own grand treasure hunt. The rewards are too numerous to mention and the riches you can make are only limited by the strength of your desire to succeed. Think big, and in no time at all you will be on your way to becoming a Garage Sale Millionaire!

CHAPTER 6

eBay: Virtually Limitless Potential to Buy and Sell Collectibles for Great Money

For any potential Garage Sale Millionaire, one realm rises above all others for making amazing amounts of money. It's an arena where almost any object—baseball cards, toys, action figures, sports memorabilia, art, antiques, watches, DVDs, magazines and books, sporting goods, home and garden items, movie memorabilia, electronics and even cars—can easily be sought out, acquired, then flipped and sold for sizable profits. That province, conveniently located on the Internet, is known as **eBay (www.ebay.com)**.

By the time you've finished this chapter, you'll see eBay is a dynamic, multifaceted online community where almost anything can and is auctioned or sold to an enormously active and extremely loyal customer base. Endless streams of people continuously support eBay with their prodigious purchasing demand to buy items for sometimes serious amounts of money.

Never before in the long, illustrious history of collecting and treasure hunting has there been one singular resource that brings together so many people from around the world—people with diverse interests—the way eBay does. eBay has been described as the world's largest garage sale. The reason eBay has continued its momentous growth in popularity lies in the website's simple format—an environment that makes it extremely easy to conduct business. When you want to become a Garage Sale Millionaire, time

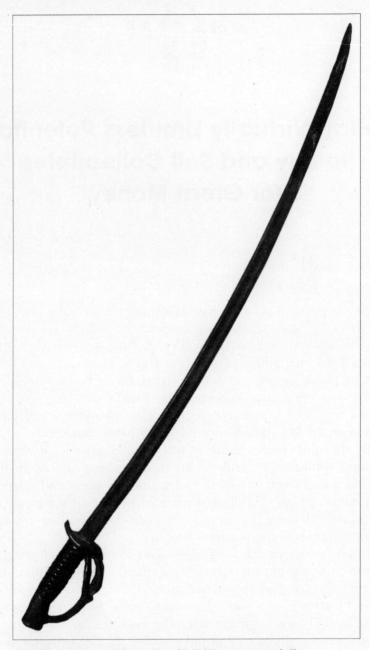

An officer's sword from the Civil War successfully purchased on eBay.

is money. Selling items on eBay offers maximum simplicity. We all know that time saved equals substantial profit making.

In this chapter, you'll learn many valuable insider tips gleaned from my own years of experience working on eBay that will allow you to amplify your quest to make money quickly. These are personal tips that you will absolutely not be able to find anywhere else. My main goal within this chapter is to show you how to make your eBay experience not only more gratifying and fulfilling, but exponentially more profitable.

The eBay Homepage—A Starting Point for Your Garage Sale Millionaire Treasure Hunt

As it is with most every corporate homepage on the Internet, the eBay homepage is the launching point for the entire website. eBay's homepage is divided into ten primary sections:

- **The Top Header**—This is the uppermost section of the eBay homepage which includes access to sign in to your account or register for a new (and of course, free) account. Also included on the top header section are links to buying and selling items, a link to your personal My eBay page where you will be able to monitor all the auctions you're involved in, a Contact Us link to approach eBay directly, a drop-down menu for over thirty different auction categories, links to their Motors and Stores sections, as well as a link to eBay's Security and Resolution Center.
- **eBay Website Advertising**—eBay lists promotional advertising in this space. Sometimes, links to the Daily Deal—great items to buy and items with deep discounts—will be located here.
- **Daily Deal/Cool Stuff**—This section of the homepage includes items eBay highlights for its bidders.
- **Welcome to eBay**—This is an additional area on the eBay homepage where you can either sign in to your account or register for a new eBay account.
- **Great Buys**—Here you will find links to items listed as the coolest, wildest and most watched.
- **My Recent Activities**—Whatever you have searched for recently on eBay is listed here.
- **Favorite Categories**—Links to over 35 categories of goods and services within the eBay website, as well as a Visit All Categories link.

- **More Fun Finds**—This section highlights additional areas to visit. Some of the items here can include promotional items from television show-sponsored auctions (e.g., Ellen/Oprah) or items for upcoming holidays (e.g., Mother's Day).
- **From Our Sellers**—This section highlights featured items up for auction throughout the website.
- **The Lower Tier**—The bottom of eBay's homepage contains links to many websites within the eBay system. This last section at the bottom of the homepage includes: links to all 30 international eBay websites from eBay Australia to eBay Vietnam; links to partner websites such as Half.com, PayPal, StubHub, Shopping.com; links to more than 15 additional eBay services such as Feedback Forum, Security Center, Resolution Center, Gift Cards & Gift Certificates and Announcements.

Note that eBay's website content and organization change frequently. The eBay homepage may be altered due to seasonal changes, such as the advertising for American holidays like Christmas, Chanukah, Kwanzaa, and so on or to promote a special addition to the website.

eBay and PayPal: Registration, Bidding and Buying

Registration

To take advantage of all the potential eBay has to offer, you must first register with eBay and PayPal. You might be asking yourself, "Why in the world would you have to register with PayPal to attain success on eBay?" Not only is **PayPal (www.paypal.com)** the official payment website for all of eBay's transactions, but it's also the easiest, most secure way to do business with the auction website.

The process of registration on both eBay and PayPal is a very simple and straight-forward fill-in-the-blanks process. Almost all the data fields that need to be filled out to register on eBay and PayPal are many of the usual data

> **Million $ Tip**
>
> A few credit cards give their customers some level of buyer protection against breakage and theft for the first 90 days of ownership. Call your credit card Issuer to see if your credit card qualifies for this benefit.

fields you find on the majority of websites. Examples include name, current address, e-mail address and date of birth. After filling out the proper forms, all you have to do is create a unique user ID and password and agree to the terms and conditions of each

> **Million $ Tip**
>
> When setting up your PayPal Account, use a credit card and not a bank account. This will add an extra layer of protection to all of your PayPal transactions.

website. Once this is completed, you are now officially registered with both eBay and PayPal.

Searching the Website

Searching for those buried treasures is a simple and easy process on eBay. All you have to do is to enter what you're searching for in the search criteria dialog box, click on the search button to the right of the search criteria dialog box and then the results of your search are listed on your computer screen. The best way to get more usable hits when you search for items on eBay is to be as detailed as possible. If you use a set of more generic search terms, your search may not yield as many usable results as you would like.

After your basic search results are displayed and you want to further refine your search criteria, you can do so by finding the Refine search box on the left side of the page. In this area of the page, more categories and empty data fields will be listed if you need to use them to help you find your search goal. Another way to refine your search is to check the Search including Title and description box and then retype your original search terms. Hopefully, what will be displayed will be the exact item you're look- ing for. Information such as featured items (the actual auction item and description), price (the current high bid in the auction) and time left (time remaining in the auction) will be displayed next to a picture of the item for auction. Sometimes, Free Shipping or a label of Top Rated Seller (for those sellers who meet certain suc- cessful sales criteria) will be listed for each sales entry to try to entice you to further investigate a particular auction.

All the pertinent auction information will be displayed for you on this page. Now it's up to you to either investigate a particular auction further or to keep on searching for the exact item you're interested in.

Before You Bid: Understanding the Auction Page

After finding an item you'd like to bid on, you'll need to click on the picture or description to select the item. The auction page you see displayed will have everything you need to make a proper decision whether or not to bid. It's on this page where your decision to either bid on an item or to look for other items will be made.

The auction page is split into two sections. The top half of the page gives bidders exact data about the current auction as well as the seller; the bottom half of the page gives more detailed information about the auction item and details regarding the auction process.

The top half of the eBay auction page displays for the bidder:

Item Condition—Is the item you are interested in new, used, never opened, refurbished or mint-in-box? You'll find that information here.

Time Left—The time remaining in the auction. If the auction is getting close to ending, the time left will countdown second-by-second directly on your screen.

Bid History—Shows how many bids have been made in this particular auction.

Current Bid—Shows the current price or what the high bid is so far in this auction.

Max Bid Field—If the auction is still open, you can place your bid here.

Sale Info—Shipping, payment and return information will be located under this heading.

Seller Info—Seller ID, link to feedback profile, feedback percentage and links to ask the seller a question are listed in this section of the auction page.

Miscellaneous—Item number, location and where the seller ships to are listed here.

The bottom half of the eBay auction page contains more information including:

Description—More specific details of the auction item are listed in this section.

Shipping and Payment Info—This section lists the terms and conditions of the sale such as shipping costs, estimated delivery time and any return policies.

Related Items—Many times a seller will have multiple auctions on eBay. This section gives you specific hyperlinks to access the auctions of those items.

You might see another option where the current bid price of the auction is listed known as Buy It Now. When this option is available, any bidder can pay the Buy It Now price and immediately win the auction item without having to go through the sometimes lengthy auction process. The Buy It Now option, when it's offered, is always available if no one has yet placed a bid on an auction. Once the first bid is made, the Buy It Now option disappears.

> **Million $ Tip**
>
> Not all auctions have a Buy It Now option. It is up to the seller to list this option on an auction item. You can still contact the buyer to see if they would take your offer on the item they are selling to end the auction early.

You need to be extra cautious when you are deciding on which items to place bids. Because you are not personally familiar with the seller, care must be taken to make sure the item you want to bid on is exactly what you are interested in buying. Never bid early on an item. The best time to bid on an item is the final two minutes of any auction. The best and most efficient way to do this is to use sniperware. I will discuss sniperware in much more detail later in the chapter.

Getting to Know the Seller

There are some great tidbits of information that will clue the bidder into whether or not the seller can be trusted and if he or she is legitimate. The Seller Info section is one of those areas you need to

> **Million $ Tip**
>
> When an item is first offered on eBay, always see if the seller will take less than the asking price. You will have a better chance to get a great deal if this item is from a person who maintains an eBay store and not one individual selling one individual item.

examine carefully and study before you bid on any item. This information is located on the right side of every eBay auction page. The seller info section details valuable information regarding the legitimacy of the seller, including:

The Seller's Name—This is the eBay user ID for the seller.

The eBay Seller's Star Rating—This rating denotes positive feedback for the seller participating in this auction. Obviously, the higher the star rating, the more you will trust and will want to do business with this person.

Positive Feedback Percentage—This section shows positive feedback from all bidders listed as a percentage. There is also a hyperlink included which will direct you to the seller's detailed Feedback Profile.

Ask A Question—Click this hyperlink if you need to ask the seller anything about the auction.

Save This Seller—You can add this seller to the list of your Favorite Sellers and Stores on your personal eBay homepage for quick reference.

See Other Items or Visit Store—If this seller has other items up for auction on eBay, those auctions will be linked to from here.

Other Item Info—Included here is the item number, the originating location where the item was shipped from and the destination location to where the item will be shipped.

Protecting Yourself as a Bidder

Properly evaluating the legitimacy of a seller is one of the foremost ways you can protect yourself as a bidder on eBay. There are a few things you can look for when examining the authenticity of a seller:

> **Million $ Tip**
>
> If the price seems too good to be true, be *very* careful.

Study the Seller's Feedback Score and Feedback Percentage. The higher the number score and percentage, the better the chance any transaction from this seller will be legitimate. You can view this data by clicking on the seller's name directly under the seller info header.

Go to the Ask A Question link to ask the seller a question about the item or to request more information about the item up for auction. Pay careful attention to how quickly the seller answers your questions and note the completeness of the answers. See if the seller offers extra useful information about an item.

View all the detailed pictures of the item if they are listed on the auction page. Every seller is different and may list this feature in different areas of their eBay auction website. If you don't see a picture listed on the seller's page or the pictures posted to the auction website are not to your liking, e-mail the seller and ask to see additional photos or more evidence to show the item is legitimate and to your liking before you make a bid.

In the *Latest Feedback section,* click on the See All hyperlink to the far right to see what other users think of this seller's business dealings and practices. A better breakdown of the seller's score will be listed here as well. This area of the eBay website is located with the seller's feedback score and feedback percentage as outlined above.

Million $ Tip

Be wary of spoof e-mails from seemingly legitimate sources such as eBay and PayPal asking for your financial information. The act of spoofing involves an e-mail that is sent to trick the recipient into thinking the e-mail is coming from a legitimate e-mail address. Instead, it comes from a criminal source in an attempt to trick the recipient into unknowingly releasing sensitive personal information, opening up the recipient to identity theft.

Million $ Tip

Never hesitate to ask for more photos and information if you are unsure about the quality, authenticity or legitimacy of the item you are considering. It is better to know all the facts up-front before bidding on something. The last thing you want to do is to pay for something that is not exactly as advertised.

Million $ Tip

Read the item description very carefully on any eBay auction. If you have questions about any part of that description or any part of the seller's auction, always e-mail the seller for clarification. If they don't answer your e-mail to your liking, do not bid on the item.

> **Million $ Tip**
>
> You are limited in the number of negative reviews before you get your eBay bidding rights suspended.

The higher the numbers for a seller in both total number of positive responses and percentage, the better. It's much easier to trust someone with a high number tally of 3,500 positive responses than it is if someone had only a score of 12. The same is true of feedback in percentage form. If a seller rates 99.0% to 100.0% in positive feedback, all potential buyers can be assured that the seller is trustworthy. Also, by clicking on the actual score the seller has received, you get a twelve-month breakdown in one-month, six-month and twelve-month increments of all sales activity rated as positive, negative or neutral. This hyperlink will be listed (the seller's score and a star icon) directly to the right of the eBay user's ID. Personal feedback from auction winners is another major plus in verifying how reliable the seller is. Of course, anyone on eBay can claim what they're selling is the most beautiful item of its kind in the world, but a seller's less-than-stellar reputation will make you think twice about bidding on that person's item.

eBay's Buyer Protection Programs

After the auction is concluded and you've sent your money to the seller, if you don't get what you paid for, there are certain avenues you can take with the assistance of eBay to help get some, if not all of your money back. eBay's buyer protection programs help you with what eBay calls transactional problems with a seller. eBay prefers you do most of the work yourself before you file a claim if you feel you've been cheated by a seller. eBay wants you to be proactive and try to solve your auction disputes on your own. If eBay handled every claim from millions of users around the world, website and company costs would rise exponentially.

A few of the steps you can take before contacting eBay about any problem include e-mailing the seller with questions about the situation, contacting the seller directly by telephone to try to solve a dispute (if the telephone number was given after the auction ends), filing a grievance with PayPal and contacting your credit card company. Only after the proper steps are followed can you file any protection claim with eBay and access their buyer protection programs. Any claim of this type may take up to 60 days or more after an auction ends before there is a decision made about your dispute. Detailed information on this topic can be found on eBay's Help Pages (http://pages.ebay.com/help).

You'll need to keep detailed documentation of your efforts if there's a dispute because eBay will require documentation proving what you've already done before filing a claim with them. It's not instant gratification, but by following the rules you will eventually get some help. The eBay buyer protection programs range from assistance in facilitating a communication process between the buyer and seller, to getting reimbursed up to $20,000 with a buyer co-payment of $500 when a vehicle is involved.

> **Million $ Tip**
>
> If you buy more than one item from a seller, ask them to combine shipments to save on the shipping costs.

Bidding on eBay

Bidding for items on eBay follows many of the practices and procedures found at a traditional auction house. The usual acts of bidding and re-bidding are the same and they are essential parts of the online auction process.

I do have one major word of caution about bidding for any item on eBay and I cannot stress this strongly enough: *every bid on eBay is a legally binding contract between the buyer and seller which cannot be retracted.* You must be very sure you want to bid on something before finally clicking that enter button.

The only exception to the legally binding bid rule is when a bidder mistakenly adds a zero or multiple zeroes to the end of a bid. For example, a bidder incorrectly makes a bid of $2,000 or $20,000 instead of a proper bid of $200. (eBay will allow you to make a few retractions per annum without consequence.) If you do renege on a bid, your user rating will be affected in a negative way. User ratings are similar to popularity contests. When you have a higher user rating as a buyer or seller, more people want to do business with you and, in turn, you become much more popular. As a bidder, being more popular means more sellers will sell to you with fewer or no restrictions.

As a seller, being more popular on eBay means more bidders will be attracted to your auctions because you're considered a legitimate and trustworthy vendor. The complete opposite occurs when your user rating is low. As a seller, not many people will take your auctions seriously. They will view your business dealings as untrustworthy because of your low rating. As a bidder, many sellers won't vend with you because you have proven yourself to be unreliable.

Being Outbid AKA Let the Bidding Wars Begin!

After you've placed your bid on an item, you might be outbid. That is usually the rule and not the exception. When you're outbid, eBay issues an automated e-mail reminder stating that, in fact, you've been outbid. In the e-mail, eBay provides a link back to the exact auction item website page so you may place another bid to outbid the higher bidder or, as I like to say, your competition. If you're like me, you really hate to be outbid in any auction.

Losing an auction you know you could have won and turned that item around and sold it for a handsome profit is a very bitter pill to swallow!

> **Million $ Tip**
>
> Sign up to have eBay text your mobile telephone on the auction status of every auction in which you are involved. Texts will advise of activity on the item and are helpful if you do not check your e-mail on a regular basis.

Being outbid is not really a problem in the early stages of an auction because of auto-generated outbid notices. The only time being outbid becomes a serious problem is if you don't check your e-mail often enough. If you can't check your e-mail frequently, you may come to the realization you're reading an outbid notice for the first time after the auction you're interested in has really ended. Not good. When this happens, the sting you feel knowing that an eventual profit was lost, lasts for a little while.

> **Million $ Tip**
>
> If you did not win an item at an auction, make an offer on the item anyway. This is sometimes a great way to get an amazing deal.

After bids have been placed and you're lucky

enough to be the high bidder when an auction ends, it's now time to pay for the item.

Payment on an Item

After you've won an item, eBay will contact you by e-mail to let you know you were the high bidder. The e-mail will contain a link to click on to go directly to the payment page for that auction. If you consistently monitor the page where the auction is being held, you can pay for the item from a direct link on the auction page.

The way you pay for an item depends on how the seller originally set up payment instructions for the auction. Even though PayPal is the usual method of payment on eBay, there are other electronic transfer options which I will discuss later in the chapter when I talk about avoiding fraud. For now, I will focus on paying for auction wins through PayPal.

Once you click on the PayPal link either from the e-mail sent to you by eBay or directly from the auction website, you will be redirected to the seller's PayPal website for the opportunity to transfer funds from either your credit card or bank account. Once you've put your data entry skills to work by filling out all the pertinent payment information, all you have left to do is to wait until you receive the item.

When you finally receive the item you've won on eBay, make sure you open and inspect it thoroughly within 48 hours so you can report any problems. After a certain amount of time has transpired, the seller will not feel liable for any problems and you will be stuck with something defective and non-returnable.

> **Million $ Tip**
>
> Always remember it is much safer to use your credit card for PayPal transactions than using your bank account.

> **Million $ Tip**
>
> Always give your feedback after you receive the auction item. The higher the feedback score you get as a great buyer, as well as the positive feedback score you give the seller after they deliver the item to you as promised, helps improve the status you hold in future dealings on eBay.

Sniping and Sniperware: Never Get Outbid on eBay Again

This brings me to snipers and sniperware and the bidding process. These terms might seem somewhat scary or mysterious, but they describe how individuals with little or no effort can swoop in at the very last moment of an online auction and steal the deal you thought you had won. This is even more painful when you realize the item you just lost out on would have made you a substantial profit upon resale.

So, what then is sniping? With just moments left to go in an auction or in many cases, with just one second remaining, someone enters the auction with just barely enough of a bid to outbid you and becomes the winning bidder. Because of the precise timing of that single strategically placed bid, so close to the end of the auction, you have no opportunity to counter and save your bid. You are stuck and you have just lost the auction. You have now been relegated to dreaming of what could have been.

Congratulations, or rather, my condolences . . . you have just been sniped by someone using sniperware.

The term sniping can also be used for someone manually outbidding you at the last moment without the use of a computer program. The term more commonly refers to electronic sniping using software, though.

In more civilized times, it used to be that the person sniping you to win an auction would do it manually. This was accomplished by physically waiting until the last moment to outbid you. This drawn-out process usually meant staying awake until midnight or later to try to win the auction by waiting until the last possible moment to (hopefully) enter and make a winning bid. As a result, you'd become sleep deprived despite the fact of knowing you had to wake up early the next morning to go to work. However, you waited patiently until the last conceivable moment in your attempt to try and win the auction item. Today, these snipers use technology in the form of computer-aided programs called sniperware to do all their dirty bidding work to out maneuver the non-sniperware-using public.

Sniperware can be found and downloaded from the Internet as shareware. Shareware programs are software programs that cost the user a fee after a short trial period. Just perform a Google search and you'll eventually find capable sniperware programs to incorporate into your bidding activities.

To better understand just how easily snipers using sniperware on eBay can really ruin your day, please continue reading.

How Co-Author Jeffrey Received an Assiduous Snipe He Won't Soon Forget ...

Jeffrey and his wife Mary absolutely love movie replicas, movie collectibles and almost anything else regarding the movies that looks like a really cool-to-own collectible. This time, the item in question that Jeffrey was aching for was a 1:1 scale movie replica of the Samaritan Gun from the first Hellboy movie. The main character Hellboy actually uses this gun throughout the film to get the bad guys. This collectible was much more valuable since it was no longer being manufactured and it was becoming increasingly rare as the weeks and months passed by. A 1:1 movie scale replica, for those not familiar with these sorts of things, is a replica produced in the exact measurements and specifications as those that were actually used and seen on-screen. Jeffrey described it to me as, "An awesomely wicked cool piece that had to be mine!"

To see someone actually selling this item from their movie memorabilia collection was a very rare occurrence indeed. To top it all off, the item was unopened. This meant the collectible was in perfect or mint condition.

Jeffrey was high bidder on the eBay auction for over a week. He really wanted this piece to add to his collection. He was also building a brand new custom home theater where this collectible would be prominently housed and displayed along with items from his prized movie and television memorabilia collection. Jeffrey had amassed a very substantial collection over the last ten years of collecting and this gun would become one of the crown jewels in his overall collection. It goes without saying the Samaritan Gun was going to have a very special place in the lobby area of his custom home theater.

The auction, like many eBay auctions, ended at midnight. On the night the auction concluded, Jeffrey was tired and exhausted and knew he had to get up early to go to work the next morning. As you may have already guessed, despite the situation, Jeffrey remained intensely focused and determined to win this item.

11:00 PM rolled by and Jeffrey was still the high bidder. Then it was 11:15 PM, 11:25 PM and 11:30 PM passed with no change. Jeffrey was still high bidder! About 11:40 PM, someone got into a minor bidding war with him and the price went up a bit, so Jeffrey matched his competitor each time and eventually rose to the position of high bidder once more. By 11:45 PM there was no more bidding activity. He thought he was in the clear and was surely going to win.

He continued reloading his web browser every few seconds to verify no one was slipping in any last second bids as the time quickly approached midnight. Depending on your Internet connection, it takes six to seven seconds from the time you are outbid to the time you get your next bid in to eBay to have it registered as a valid bid.

No more bids. 11:55 PM, 11:56 PM, 11:57 PM, tick, tick, tick; Jeffrey was golden for the Hellboy gun. He could smell the sweet smell of victory as it drew closer with the passing of every second. The clock continued to tick away, rapidly approaching the stroke of midnight and the end of the auction.

Then, with just two seconds remaining, someone stepped in with just barely enough of a bid to win, okay, steal the auction. Yes, Jeffrey is still bitter about his loss after all these years. By the time Jeffrey had reloaded his web browser, frantically putting in a counter bid, the auction had officially ended. Unfortunately his last bid didn't register in time and all was lost. What a SNIPE! That evening there was no thrill of victory, but certainly the bitter agony of defeat loomed in the midnight air.

Don't feel too badly for Jeffrey though. His fellow collectors all enjoy swapping similar war stories from time to time.

Luckily, a few months later, Jeffrey was finally able to purchase his Samaritan Gun from a respected movie and television memorabilia collectibles dealer. It did cost him a bit more than the eBay auction would have, but he finally had his treasured collectible.

As I mentioned earlier in the chapter, there are two avenues you can navigate when using eBay. We have talked about buying, and now we will discuss selling.

Creating a Seller's Account and Understanding How to Sell Your Items for a Profit on eBay

Creating Your Account

The first step you must take to become an eBay seller is to create a Seller's Account. You do this, of course, by filling out yet another online form. Although there are differences in registering as a seller compared to a buyer, these differences are minor. Some of the additional information you'll need to provide when registering as a seller includes a credit or debit card number. The rest of what needs to be filled out is the usual name and address information. Now that you have registered as a seller on eBay, you can begin the process of listing your items on the website.

Understanding the Different Types of Auctions on eBay and What These Levels Mean to Your Costs and Eventual Profits

Before you get ready to list your items for sale on eBay or even begin considering how you're going to describe your items to get the best response, you must first understand the different types of auctions eBay offers. There are two different types of auctions on eBay: fixed auctions and current auctions (see table below). Each different category offers distinct positives and negatives to the seller depending on which one the seller chooses.

The first classification of eBay auction is the fixed auction. With a fixed auction, you will be paying higher listing fees and more of a commission to eBay than someone selling in a store auction. The major benefit in comparison to store auctions is that you will get better placement on search results that potential bidders for your auction items will have access to. This translates into better opportunity to make more substantial profits. By choosing to sell your items in a fixed auction, you also get to use the Make An Offer option to enhance your selling chances. As previously discussed in this chapter, the Make An Offer option gives

Auction	Costs	Positives	Negatives
Fixed	• Not as much as the Current Auction fees	• Able to use the Buy It Now and Make An Offer options • Auto restart of auction after 30 days	
Current (1, 3, 5, 7 or 10 days)	• Most expensive option • Highest commissions • Highest listing fees		• Highest cost of the two options • Have to wait for the item until the auction is over

buyers a chance to approach the seller with a direct offer to buy an auction item.

The current auction is the other type of auction on eBay. The two major drawbacks of a current auction are that you will be paying the highest commission to eBay on every sale as well as paying the highest level of listing fees. The main benefits of a current auction are access to the Buy It Now option, which gives bidders the chance to pay for an item outright, the ability to have your auction roll over after 30 days if no one makes a bid on your auction and the best placement from search results eBay has to offer. The best benefit to listing your items under the current auction format is that you can set starting bids of $100 on every auction you hold.

Other Need-to-Know Criteria Before You Start Thinking About Selling Items on eBay

In speaking with representatives from eBay while researching this book, there was some essential information that all sellers need to know. Some of this information may seem strict or inflexible, but these caveats are put in place to help make eBay run like the well-oiled machine it is.

Before eBay puts an end to their scrutiny of you and your selling activities, you will need to obtain a score of 100. To score 100, you must have 100 sales on the website with positive feedback. Before reaching a score of 100, eBay will hold back all proceeds from every sale until the buyer receives the item they have purchased from you. eBay does this in order to make sure you have acted properly and ethically in all your financial dealings.

Another important piece of information concerns name brand items. Until you reach a score of 50, which signifies 50 positive feedback sales, you cannot sell any name brand items. You are absolutely forbidden to sell items from name brand companies such as Sony, Nike, Rolex and Samsung until you

> ### Million $ Tip
>
> When selling an item, make sure your auction ends at a proper time during the day. The optimal time to end an auction is between 10:00 AM and 7:00 PM Monday through Friday. This will insure more bidders can bid on your items.

reach that 50 mark. If you do list something with a name brand item before reaching that mark, eBay will immediately pull the item from the website. In the past, some unscrupulous individuals have signed up for selling accounts and immediately tried to move what was thought to be authentic name brand merchandise, only to take the money and run without shipping anything to their customers. eBay concludes from these sorts of negative experiences, if you try to sell these things before a certain experience level is reached, then you are a potentially fraudulent dealer with intentions of scamming people.

I have said it before in this chapter and I need to stress again, your feedback score is *very* important to your success and livelihood on eBay. Because eBay cannot work personally with every seller due to the overwhelming number of sellers participating on the website, they rely heavily on feedback information to make judgments on how well eBay vendors are conducting business.

Whenever you sell something on eBay, the buyer will usually fill out a feedback form with five topics on it to report how the sales experience went. Even though all five items are important, there are two main ratings you need to get right to do well consistently as a seller. First, communication is the key to a good transaction. The way to guarantee no problems occur during the selling process means you have to be very professional and open in all your communications with your customers. You need to answer all e-mails quickly, monitor your auctions closely in case people have questions for you, send buyers the tracking numbers when you ship items and make sure they always feel taken care of until they are satisfied with the item they purchased from you. When sending an invoice, put your e-mail address on the invoice as well as a telephone number if you want to take customer service to the highest level. Second, give free shipping. Buyers love free shipping and

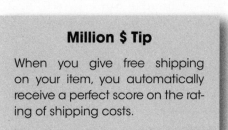

Million $ Tip

When you give free shipping on your item, you automatically receive a perfect score on the rating of shipping costs.

offering this relatively low cost option goes a long way towards ensuring your customers remain happy customers.

If these two factors are properly taken care of, there is a great chance you will get a perfect score on buyer feedback. Making sure the customer comes first and taking care of your customers from the start of any auction will eventually help you to secure lower fees on your future auctions.

Researching eBay for Better Profits

For the knowledgeable and successful Garage Sale Millionaire, doing proper research on marketing and selling your items on eBay means the difference between incremental profits and substantial profits. Along with spending quality time on eBay looking at what kind of items are being listed, how they are being listed, who may be buying items and for what amounts, take a few moments to look at and study the **eBay University Learning Center (http://pages .ebay.com/education/index.html)**. This section of the website offers invaluable tips and strategies on how to properly use eBay to your ultimate advantage. The topics at the eBay University Learning Center, listed in detailed tutorial form include:

New to eBay—How eBay works, how to register and how to buy with confidence are just some of the topics discussed.

How to Buy—Buying items on eBay, searching for auction items and paying for items are discussed in this section.

How to Sell—This section details everything you need to know about selling items on eBay.

Increase Your Sales—Tips about growing your business, opening an eBay Store, growth strategies and seller best practices are available in this section.

The Benefits of Becoming an eBay PowerSeller

There are sellers on eBay and then there are Powersellers on eBay. As the name would seem to imply, a Powerseller is a much better designation.

According to eBay, Powersellers rank among the most successful sellers on eBay for sales and customer satisfaction. The Powerseller's icon is placed next to each Powerseller's member ID which means the seller meets the criteria for being a Powerseller.

The criteria include consistent sales volume, a rating of 98% or above for total positive feedback, eBay marketplace policy compliance, an account in good financial standing and a detailed seller rating (DSR) of 4.5 or higher in all four DSRs. You will also need to sell a minimum of 100 items with feedback in order to apply. If a seller no longer complies with any one of the above requirements, they are removed from the program.

When a bidder sees the Powerseller icon in any auction, the bidder can be assured they will be dealing with someone who has earned a stellar reputation on the website. From eBay's website, the Powerseller program benefits include:

Prioritized Customer Service—Depending on a seller's level of sales, Powersellers receive prioritized support by e-mail or telephone.

Powerseller Fee Discounts—As a reward for excellent customer service, Powersellers with high DSRs over the past 30 days will receive discounts on final value fees for their prior month's sales.

Unpaid Item Protection—Powersellers receive a credit for any feature fees when a buyer doesn't pay for an item and the seller closes an unpaid item dispute. This program covers auction-style listings (excluding dutch and live auctions) and single-item fixed-price listings on eBay.com, eBay.ca and eBay Motors.

Expanded Seller Protection from PayPal—Items sold by Powersellers on eBay and paid for with PayPal accounts, will be covered against claims, chargebacks, reversals for unauthorized payments and merchandise not received. Transactions must meet the terms of coverage. This protection is free to Powersellers and eliminates the need for confirmed addresses.

Increased Visibility in Best Match Searches—To reward excellent customer service, eBay gives an advantage in the listings to those sellers rated in the upper half for buyer satisfaction. This advantage also applies to sellers outside of the Powerseller program.

UPS Rate Discounts—Powersellers can receive up to a 23% discount on UPS Ground daily rates.

Exclusive Networking—Powersellers share selling strategies on an exclusive discussion board open only to PowerSeller members.

Special Offers—eBay works with many companies that offer products, services and discounts available only to Powersellers.

Powerseller Business Templates—Access to eBay-approved templates to use in better marketing your business.

Powerful Giving Program—The eBay Foundation regularly donates to charities supported by Powersellers.

Understanding and Determining the Value of an Item—The eBay Way

Monetary Cost Versus Emotional Value

There are two ways to view any transaction for items being sold on eBay: monetary cost and emotional value. Many times emotional value or the emotional currency someone places on an item far outweighs the actual cost of an item or the monetary cost. In these instances, the idea of getting the best value or price for an item falls somewhat by the wayside. In an emotional value purchase, the buyer must have that item no matter what—*no ifs ands or buts!*

For example, when co-author Jeffrey bought his 1:1 scale, #288 of 500, life-size Star Wars' Darth Vader action figure, he spent approximately $6,100 for it (give or take a few cents). In referencing *The 4th Edition of the Star Wars Super Collectors Wish Book* by Geoffrey T. Carlton, Collectors Books (a Division of Schroeder Publishing Co., Inc.), to verify the piece's value and ascertain that this was a wise investment,

> **Million $ Tip**
>
> You certainly can use the emotional value of an item to your advantage as a seller on eBay. You could earn larger profits knowing the item you have up for auction on eBay will elicit an emotional response from your bidders. Many times bidders will easily pay above market value if that item means something personal to them. Also, if you have an item that would provoke this reaction amongst your bidders, you can set the starting price of your auction much higher.

he discovered the estimated value of the piece to be only $4,500. The difference in the cost of the item versus the estimated value of the collectible was $1,600. This difference was a substantial amount of money. Was that a bad investment? When considering the numbers . . . maybe. As it turns out, it was a great investment on several different levels.

The first question Jeffrey had to ask is, will the piece rise in value over time? The answer is, it probably will. Why? The value of the piece will probably increase due to the lower issue number. This piece is also a limited edition item with high overall quality and the fact that the company that made this collectible is not making the Darth Vader 1:1 scale replicas anymore influenced Jeffrey's decision to purchase this rare, hard-to-find item. What also had to be taken into consideration was this particular item was something Jeffrey had been feverishly trying to get his hands on for over a decade.

The emotional value compared to the monetary cost was very high and the thought of getting the piece solely for any monetary gain became secondary. Emotion completely won out over saving some money. Would Jeffrey have spent any more money than he eventually paid to acquire this collectible? The answer is probably yes. He happily accepted the offer and gladly paid the $6,100 because of the important emotional currency associated in the act of acquiring this item.

Estimating Value on eBay

So, how does one go about estimating the monetary value of an item on eBay? There are a several methods to use.

One proven method on eBay is to search for duplicate items or items very similar to your items of interest. By understanding how much others are bidding for similar items, you can see the real market value or at least the eBay market value that others are willing to pay. You can also do an advanced search

Million $ Tip

As a buyer or seller on eBay, it is extremely important to find out how to judge the value of an item so you have the best chance to either get a bargain (as a bidder) or make more money on an item (as a seller). If you're planning on using eBay a lot, you might want to consider joining Terapeak (www .terapeak.com). There is a membership fee, but once you're a member, you'll have access to a comprehensive database of buying and selling prices from eBay's history.

Million $ Tip

One key aspect of your research needs to include finding similar items already listed on eBay. By studying how others price and describe similar items, you can price and describe your items accordingly for profitable auctions.

Million $ Tip

Find the Completed Listings hyperlink on the Advanced Search page to view what items previously sold for and what the last sale was, to help you price your item more accurately.

on closed auction items and see how much these items may have sold for in previous auctions.

If the article in which you are interested is a one-of-a-kind piece or an item where you can't compare what similar items sold for on eBay, then you need to use other resources on the Internet to your advantage. Also search at bookstores for a collectibles price guide listing the item you're interested in. This is especially important for a buyer if the bidding or sales price on the item is escalating rapidly. You need to do as much research as possible on the value of the specific item you want to buy not only if you want to save money on the item, but also so you will make as much money as possible when you sell the item.

The time you spend making sure you're not getting ripped off and not paying the price on an item you think is too high is time well spent. Hopefully, you will come across the auction in its infancy so you have adequate time to do your research and make the proper decision.

Would I go to great lengths to research something in detail that is being sold or auctioned for a couple of dollars? Probably not. However, as the monetary stakes rise in a high-priced auction, the more informed you are, the better so you don't pay too much for an item. From the selling side, the opposite is true. As a true Garage Sale Millionaire, you can always hope eventually your inexpensive items advance to increased amounts of value as an uninformed public continues to line your pockets with higher bids.

In the end, you are the ultimate judge as to what may be too high a monetary cost for you with regard to acquiring an item or what you may find to be a financial steal. Once again, it's the monetary cost versus the emotional currency value argument I discussed earlier. Even when you weigh monetary cost against emotional value, in the end a dollar is still a dollar. If you've found the true value of an item that piques your interest and you've done the proper research to determine proper value, you're still the one who has to make the final decision.

Avoiding Fraud as a Seller

One of the more unfortunate facts about eBay is that the website will never be 100% free of individuals looking to make a quick buck by taking your money in an auction where the item is invalid, misrepresented or never even exists. With so many individuals making up a global Internet community, it's inevitable to have some evildoers lurking about within the system. eBay does an admirable job in policing their website to rid it of unsavory online predators seeking to defraud users via bogus auctions and fraudulent dealings. However, as diligent as eBay is, they cannot stop everyone from trying to take unfair advantage of honest, unsuspecting bidders.

As a seller, the only real type of fraud you need to be aware of is that which involves incoming sources of funds to pay for the items you've auctioned on the website. As long as you remember to use PayPal, which involves the use of credit card funds or a direct debit from a bidder's bank account, you're better protected. Other electronic options you can use to accept funds authorized by eBay are services from **ProPay (https://epay.propay.com), Moneybookers (www.moneybookers.com)** and **Paymate (www.paymate.com)**. You can also directly accept a credit or debit card which will be processed through your Internet merchant account. Although I will not go into detail about these additional services, you can readily find more information about these optional payment services on the Internet.

Sellers may also offer to accept payment upon pickup when they list payment terms for their auctions. Payment upon pickup means that alternative payment methods could be offered if the buyer picks up the item in person after winning an auction. Other means of payment such as cashier's checks, money orders or cash can only be accepted if the bidder picks up an auction win in this fashion. I highly recommend against this practice because of the potential fraud issues associated with accepting non-guaranteed funds.

Million $ Tip

The number one time of year to sell any item on eBay is 30 days prior to Christmas.

What is the second best time of year to sell on eBay? Right in front of any major holiday such as Mother's Day, Father's Day, Valentine's Day, etc. January is *the* worst time of year to sell anything on eBay.

Although stop payments are strictly regulated on cashier's checks or money orders, some banks will still place stop payments on these types of transactions. According to John Burnett of BankersOnline.com, "A bank may refuse payment of its cashier's check under certain circumstances such as alteration, forged endorsement or a claim against the payee/presenter. But it should be sure of its position before doing so, because the penalties for wrongfully refusing payment are stiff. Particularly when a holder in due course is involved, the bank that refuses payment of its own cashier's check is walking in a minefield. Another situation when a bank may refuse payment of a cashier's check is in the special circumstance of a lost, stolen or destroyed check."

Instead of having to deal with this type of potential fraud and financial headache, I believe it is really best to use electronic payment services for your business transactions. Just remember, when you list payment terms in your auction, you must make sure to detail what is considered acceptable payment and what the specific terms are. That way, you're protected from any misunderstandings that might occur when payment is due to you.

Preparing Your Item for Sale

Before you even consider listing an item on eBay, you will have to do research first. Why must you go through this seemingly dull process? It is a given you'll want to make the most money you can from the items you sell, but you must also give yourself every opportunity to distinguish your item from the extensive multitudes of listings found throughout the eBay website.

The Listing of Your Items on eBay

Considering all the detailed research you've conducted, you now know with certainty how to best describe your sale items and at what price you're going to start your auction for those items. It's time to fill in the proper listing information and get your item exposed so the eBay world can see your offering and, of course, bid handsomely on it. Here are areas you have to decide on regarding listing your item:

Proper category and subcategory—Under what categories will you list your sale items to best describe what you want to sell?

Listing your item in a second or third category—By listing your items in different categories, you will attract more bidders.

Starting bid price—What will the starting price be on your sale items? This is very important because you don't want to undervalue your sale items.

Minimum bid you will accept for the item—When you set up your auction, this is the bid you place as the minimum starting bid. This option can only be used if you are signed up for a current level type of auction on eBay. The minimum bid is also called the reserve price.

Specific item details—Color, size, speed and whatever makes the item you want to sell unique. Be very accurate when describing your sale items.

What pictures to upload—eBay bidders absolutely love to see detailed pictures of how your sale item looks. If you want to move your sale merchandise quickly, upload some great pictures of what you're trying to sell!

> ### Million $ Tip
>
> Offer free shipping for all your eBay auctions. Customers love free shipping. As a result, your satisfied customers will be much more likely to leave positive feedback regarding their business dealings with you. As a result of the positive feedback, eBay will give you a price break on their commission.

The duration of the auction—I recommend an auction length of seven days. By setting up an auction to last seven days, you have the best possible opportunity to receive the most traffic and highest number of webpage hits for your auction on eBay.

Terms of the sale—What types of payments will you accept for the sale of your auction items and what are the sale details of the auction? The acceptable methods of payment (e.g., PayPal), any additional shipping costs, listing a return policy and how long the winning bidder has to pay before he defaults on the auction must be listed in this section. The more clear you are when listing your auction details means less potential problems later down the road.

There are additional options from which you can choose to include with the listing of your sale items. These options are not free, but these will, in the long run, help your auction stand out that much more. Some of these options include extra pictures of your item, a border around your listing and having your item spotlighted in the Featured Area of the search and listings page.

Also, eBay doesn't like it when you use the adjective *like* in your auction descriptions. For example: Fontana Watch, just *like* a Rolex. Your item will be removed from the website if the term *like* is ever used. Instead try the terms *comparable to, matching* or perhaps *equivalent*.

Managing Your eBay Listing and Completing the Sale

From your personal My eBay page, you can constantly track multiple auctions and see the status of all those auctions in which you are involved. Your My eBay page is an essential element in becoming a successful seller, especially if you're buying and selling multiple items at the same time. This eBay control center helps you organize and refine your efforts and also see what's selling, what's not selling and if you are the big winner on items you've been bidding on. The My eBay page also has an abundance of other eBay options such as saving a list of your favorite sellers, monitoring feedback on your eBay activities, viewing messages sent to you by other bidders and sellers or by messages generated by eBay and viewing specific eBay announcements as well.

The Last Major Step in the Selling Process on eBay is to Complete the Sale

When one of your auctions is completed, eBay will auto-generate an e-mail to you stating who the high bidder was, their shipping address and the winning bid amount. Because you clearly stipulated payment terms when you originally set up your auction, you may not hear from the high bidder until funds are received from the auction. You might also get an e-mail from the buyer asking some additional questions about the payment process. This is a normal part of the eBay auction process even if you have one of the best, most detailed sales pages. Reply with the appropriate answers immediately.

Because you took great care and paid great attention to detail when posting your auction to the website, all you have to do now is wait for payment from the customer and ship the item. If, for some reason, the buyer delays sending in funds for several days, you can follow up with a friendly reminder e-mail about payment.

Always be a great communicator on eBay and your customers will love you! More importantly, they will love the way you do business. eBay is glutted with sellers who are terrible communicators, treat their customers terribly and make doing business with them a nightmare. A competent, successful sales- and businessperson stands out as being exceptional. After receiving repetitive positive feedback on your customer feedback page, people will more easily respect you and will want to continue to do business with you. By conducting business in a responsible manner, you will obtain repeat customers in no time and your business will consistently grow.

Logging Off eBay

As you explore eBay on your own, you will discover a treasure trove of valuable information at your fingertips just waiting to be discovered. eBay is a relatively simple website to get to know and one that is easy to navigate through and browse for hours at a time. With the information provided herein, as well as the knowledge you'll gain by cruising around the site and becoming an active day-to-day user on eBay, you will be a Garage Sale Millionaire in no time at all.

CHAPTER

7

How to Assign a Value to Your New Treasures

Properly valuing your new found treasures is one of the most important aspects of becoming a successful Garage Sale Millionaire. If what you find during your treasure hunting endeavors is not valued correctly, when you decide to sell your items, you could be short-changing yourself and losing out on a lot of money.

If you price an item too low, you'll lose out on the money you could have potentially made on the sale. If you price an item too high you may never be able to make the sale at all. The actual practice of putting a price tag on any item is never an easy one. Even the most knowledgeable experts can sometimes find it difficult to determine what the best price is for certain items.

There are two different options available for properly and accurately valuing your treasures. You can complete a self-valuation or you can pay a professional to do the job for you. No matter which direction you choose, you'll have to value your items as accurately as you can in order to make as much money as possible.

Self-Valuation

The main benefit to valuing items without any outside assistance is that you maintain lower overhead costs. The only cost associated with

> **Million $ Tip**
>
> Use more than one source to value your treasures.

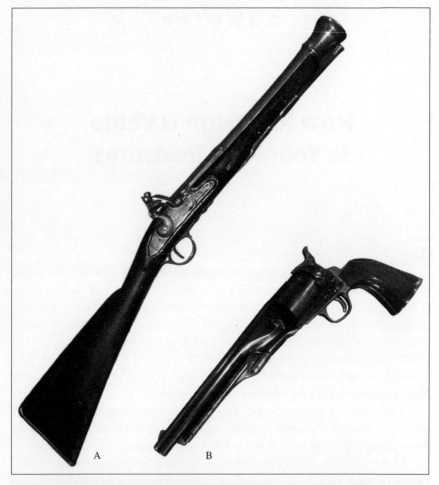

A. This is a 1700s-era Boatgun (although it does look like a Blunderbuss).
This is my favorite weapon. Its value is $4,500 to $7,000.
B. This is a collectible, replica western sidearm. I found it at a gun
auction for only $195!

self-valuing items is your personal time spent valuing items and perhaps buying a book or two to assist you with the self-valuation process. Used books are available at truly extraordinary prices at **Alibris** (**www.alibris.com**). Of course, if you do opt to hire a professional to value items for you, there are fees and expenses involved. There's nothing wrong with wanting to save some money valuing items yourself, but on certain occasions when you aren't confident you're capable of making an accurate evaluation or appraisal on your own, using an expert could very well be the best course of action you could take. I will elaborate about using a professional to value your items a little later on in the chapter.

Self-Valuation—The Traditional Way

The simplest, most inexpensive way to research and assign a proper value to your collectibles is to visit your local bookstores and libraries. There's an amazing selection of books available to help you find exact dollar values for items you've collected and are trying to sell. If you go to bookstores like **Barnes & Noble Booksellers** (**www.barnesandnoble.com**) and visit the collectibles section, there are dozens of books covering price guides of collectible items ranging from Matchbox cars, Barbie dolls, coins, stamps, antiques and G.I. Joes, to Star Wars and Star Trek memorabilia. The list is endless. When conducting a search for price guides in books on **Amazon.com** (**www.amazon.com**), over 15,200 books on this subject are listed. It goes without saying then that every Garage Sale Millionaire has an amazing amount of resource material on hand to properly self-value their items.

> **Million $ Tip**
>
> Make sure when you compare your item to others that you do your due diligence because many collectibles look alike but vary widely in value.

If you plan to specialize in certain collectibles, you should be willing to invest in a few books covering these items. Owning price guides that cover the items you want to specialize in provides a timesaving resource. By personally owning these price guides, you can establish proper values for your items quickly and as the saying goes, time is money. Whether you're searching online for items or trying to find them at a garage sale, you may only have a few moments to spare for verifying information before your competition swoops in to buy that highly valuable item right out from under you. Having your resource materials on hand for use at a moment's notice is a strong weapon in your Garage Sale Millionaire arsenal.

Look at as many price guides as possible before buying a single book. You'll quickly get an idea of which books work the best for your needs by understanding what subject matter is contained in each book, how detailed each book is and how experienced the authors are about the subjects they cover.

The best place to look for current price guides is your local bookstore. Libraries should be considered a secondary source because you'll only be able to check out books for a set period of time before having to return them. Having price guides on hand that cover consecutive years is another great way to understand how your item has been valued over the course of time. You'll be able to make better educated guesses as to which direction the value of your items will go based on collective historical data.

A key part in determining an item's physical condition and potential resale value is called grading. As we work our way through this chapter, I will discuss grading in more detail. I will also cover the top collectibles to buy and sell so you can increase your profits.

Self-Valuation Goes High Tech

Ah, the Internet! The glorious and wonderful Internet! How could society as we know it today possibly survive without e-mail, using our finely-tuned web browsers to explore infinitely informative and richly interactive websites, as well as texting, instant messaging and tweeting? The better question is, "How would we as collectors, treasure hunters and Garage Sale Millionaires be able to do business without the Internet?" Up until a few years ago, you could get away with using the Internet only as a supplemental way of doing business. Not any more. As traditional ways of business evolve and make way for an electronic future, so must all your Garage Sale Millionaire activities.

Now it's time to use the Internet to help establish more accurate values on your collectibles so you can turn around and make the best profit possible by reselling those items!

eBay

Although **eBay (www.ebay.com)** was covered extensively in the previous chapter, I feel it necessary to reinforce the importance of using this invaluable Internet community as an efficient and accurate resource for the purpose of determining the proper market value of items you're looking to buy and sell.

When buying and selling collectibles on eBay, the idea of market value plays a prominent role. Market value refers to the dollar amount people are willing to pay for an item. Every item listed on eBay, as well as every bid made on those items, continuously helps to set the current market value. For example, if an original 1984 edition of an Optimus Prime Transformers collectible toy is put up for auction on eBay at a price of $1,995, then that becomes the current market value for that type of item. The market value of an item is affected if people continue placing higher bids on that item. Based on the actual selling price, the new current market value gets established. Any subsequent listing of this collectible toy will similarly be priced at, or very close to, that final sales price.

In Chapter 6, I mentioned the fact that many individuals regard eBay as the world's largest garage sale. Now, I would like to take that concept a step further. I also believe that eBay must also be considered to be the world's largest pricing guide. I'd venture to bet not many people think of eBay along those lines. Although they're a fabulous resource to have, the obvious problem with price guides in book form is that once the word is printed on the page that price is finite. The stated market value of items is locked in when that book comes off the printing press for publication. eBay is the best price guide available because it evolves minute-by-minute. Every time an item is listed, bid on and sold, eBay becomes a newly updated price guide.

To verify what items have sold for at past auctions on eBay requires a little digging accomplished by performing an advanced search. On eBay's homepage, click the Advanced Search link directly to the right of the main item search box. You'll next be redirected and taken to a secondary search page. About a quarter of the way down the page you will find a Completed Listings box. Check the box and then re-submit the search criteria you originally entered on the previous page. After you've submitted your search criteria, all the completed auctions that contain the item you are looking for will be displayed on the screen in front of you.

Terapeak

Depending on how popular an item is, there could be hundreds of pages and thousands of search results to look through before you're able to find an item that interests you. Unfortunately, the advanced search function on eBay only stores historical data for the past few weeks. If you're attempting to find results from eBay auctions that were completed further back or you want to conduct more of a precise search on past auctions, try **Terapeak (www .terapeak.com)**. Terapeak tracks any item ever sold on eBay going back for at least a year. Basic searches on the website are free, but anything more will require a paid subscription.

Worthpoint

Another invaluable resource in valuing your treasures can be found at **WorthPoint (www.worthpoint.com)**. Experts contributing to the website are called Worthologists and bring decades of experience to the site. Worthpoint.com also houses one of the world's largest collecting databases. You can connect with other collectors interested in buying, selling or swapping stories and share your insight and knowledge through their forums.

After a free trial period, full access to the website is only available through a paid membership. Membership is offered on three levels: basic, professional and power. Some membership benefits include access to extensive valuation data, a collecting community of over 350,000 members and access to a wealth of information and data on the subject of collecting.

Google

Another avenue to navigate when valuing your collectibles is **Google (www.google.com)**. With any search on Google, especially when it involves collectibles, there is an upside and a downside as well. The good news is you will probably be able to find an extensive list of websites that deal in specific genres of collectibles. The bad news is it may take a substantial time investment to search through all those hundreds, thousands and sometimes even millions of search results to find specific areas of importance in which you were interested.

For example, try conducting a basic Google search for Barbie dolls. I entered this basic search string recently, and approximately 1,060,000 search results came back including pretty much everything under the sun and then some regarding Barbie dolls. Listed will be the official company's website that makes the dolls, some websites that cover the detailed history of Barbie dolls, a multitude of Barbie doll enthusiast websites that discuss methods for collecting the dolls, numerous enthusiast websites that just show pictures of doll collections, various listings for dolls like Bratz which are similar to Barbie dolls and retail toy websites that just sell the dolls. This is a lot of information to sift through. When you enter more detailed search criteria as in "Barbie Dolls + 1965 + Redhead," only 9,160 results are retrieved. This is more pertinent information which, as a result, will help you find more accurate valuation data.

> ## Million $ Tip
>
> For collectibles that are not so common, you will need to put in a little more effort to find the value. When you find a website that sells your item, make sure you compare size, color and any markings that are on the collectible. Give the owner of the website a call and compare your item to what they have. There is a good chance they may have an interest in your treasure and you will have a fantastic sales opportunity! If an offer is made, I recommend comparing the potential value of your item with a few other vendors before you accept. You might also check to see if the same item is being sold for more somewhere else on the Internet.

By making your Google search criteria more detailed, you will have the best success in finding specific data that best suits your needs.

Blogs, News Sites and Community Forums

After you've identified websites that have the information you need to value your items for eventual sale, delve a little bit deeper into each website. Many of them will also have blogs, news sites or community forums available for you to read and gather more information about the items in which you have an interest. There may also be hyperlinks to other websites with additional blogs, forums or news sites available for you to investigate. Blogs, news sites and forums contain quintessential reading material that could give you more insight on your items and the best opportunities to make valuable sales. Everything you learn from these resources will help shape your ideas and opinions on how to properly value your items.

Using Professionals: Appraisers and Professional Grading Services

Appraisers

Hiring an experienced appraiser is one of the most accurate ways to find current and future market value for your collectibles. Depending upon an appraiser's level of experience, if that appraiser is involved in the collectibles industry or perhaps if they own an art gallery, you could gain tremendous insight from their experience and knowledge of current and future selling trends. This information can certainly be used to your advantage when either selling an item or negotiating price with a customer.

> **Million $ Tip**
>
> Check with art gallery owners in your area. They will have expert knowledge and years of experience in the appraisal of items.

Appraisers can be found in almost every city. How good they are in their ability to properly and accurately appraise items is another question altogether. Checking credentials for a quality appraisal service can be as easy as making a few telephone calls. It's incumbent upon you to verify the experience a person or company has. You can do this via telephone, in person and over the Internet to see if the appraisal company you are interested in is certified with a national or international appraisal agency. **The American Society of Appraisers (www.appraisers.org)** is one of the better-known national certifying appraisal agencies and organizations. Also check to see if the appraiser is endorsed by the **Better Business Bureau (www.bbb .org)** and whether or not there are complaints filed against them. Another website that I have found useful is **Ripoff Report (www .ripoffreport.com)**. Founded in 1998 by Ed Magedson, the Ripoff Report is a website dedicated to informing consumers of potential marketplace ripoffs.

I have been appraising personal items; small, medium and large-sized personal collections and large family collections for years. Individuals worldwide have employed my services and they have trusted me time and time again as an expert appraiser. As a result of years of intensive study combined with expansive expertise and experience, I can look at collectibles and entire collections and know exactly what price the market will bear on such items. I represent the type of experienced appraiser you need to seek when hiring someone to make serious monetary judgments or decisions on what something is worth so you can sell it to make the best possible profit.

Professional Grading Services

Professional grading services are available to every collector, treasure hunter and Garage Sale Millionaire who wants to determine the actual physical quality and condition of a collectible. A grading service is usually dedicated to a certain type or category of collectible such as baseball cards, coins and comic books. Even though these grading services do not necessarily specify what the monetary value of an item is, by getting an item professionally graded, you give yourself the best opportunity to make more money upon resale.

Some of the benefits regarding hiring a professional to grade items include saving you a great deal of time from having to do the lengthy research needed to accurately grade items yourself and minimizing any evaluation mistakes you might make because you are not an expert in the respective field. Many times when a professional

> ### Million $ Tip
>
> If you feel the item you want to resell has the potential to make you a substantial profit, definitely use a professional valuation or grading service. By using these types of services, even if there is a fee involved, in many instances you will get a professional certification or expert appraisal value which can be used to drive up sale prices.

grading agency or company grades an item, the resale amount increases. At some point during the grading process, grading companies will usually seal your collectible in a protective casing and place certifying marks and labels that you can show to prospective buyers to prove the items in question have been professionally graded and certified by a respected organization or professional.

Of course, using someone else to grade your items will cost a fee depending on the items you want graded, the number of items to be graded and which certified professional or agency you take your items to. Costs can range from as little as just ten dollars to several hundred dollars.

Top Collectibles to Deal in for Substantial Profits and How to Accurately Value These Top Items Through Their Respective Grading Services

I regard coins, comic books, action figures, baseball cards, sports trading cards, non-sports trading cards and antique firearms to be some of the top collectibles in which to deal for substantial profits. The different types of collectibles listed in this section are graded by companies and agencies that specialize in that particular type of collectible. Additionally, each one of these collectibles has its own fervent, loyal and enthusiastic fan base—hungry collectors who will spend good money for the items and collectibles you are going to sell. If you're still in the mood to self-value your collectibles, you can use the following information in this chapter to better hone your self-valuing efforts.

Coins

There are many coin-grading services available to the treasure hunter trying to determine the quality and condition of their coins. Grading fees typically start at $10 for each coin and can increase from there. Once a

> **Million $ Tip**
>
> All dimes, quarters, half-dollars and dollar coins dated pre-1965 were made out of silver.

coin is graded, the professional coin-grading service that graded your item will enclose your graded coin in a certified and sealed coin holder that not only protects your newly graded coin, but also displays pertinent data about your coin and its respective grade. This data includes the year the coin was minted, denomination of the coin, actual grade of the coin and a bar code. The bar code is imprinted on the outside of the protective casing by the grading company in case they need to reference the coin at some future date.

The condition and grading of a coin plays a major role in determining its eventual resale value. According to the Professional Coin Grading Service website, the condition of a coin is defined as "the state of preservation of a particular numismatic issue," and grade is defined as "the numerical or adjectival condition of a coin." Professional coin-grading services use letter and numerical designations to show what they believe is a coin's most accurate grade. The numerical scale used by these grading companies is a 70-point scale that designates the incremental quality of each coin. The more pristine shape the coin is in, the higher the numerical grade will be. Letter designations are just as important as the numerical score. Each letter designation relates to the overall quality of the coin as well.

One of the best coin grading services available to the collector is the **Professional Coin Grading Service (PCGS) (www.pcgs.com)**. Much of the industry grades coins according to the PCGS grading system. Notice the following grading charts from the PCGS website. The first chart displays a particular coin grade and a description of what each grade means. The second chart explains what each letter grade in the first chart stands for.

Grade	Description
PO-1	Identifiable date and type.
FR-2	Mostly worn, though some detail is visible.
AG-3	Worn rims but most lettering is readable though worn.
G-4	Slightly worn rims, flat detail, peripheral lettering nearly full.
G-6	Rims complete with flat detail, peripheral lettering full.
VG-8	Design worn with slight detail.
VG-10	Design worn with slight detail, slightly clearer.
F-12	Some deeply recessed areas with detail, all lettering sharp.
F-15	Slightly more detail in the recessed areas, all lettering sharp.
VF-20	Some definition of detail, all lettering full and sharp.
VF-25	Slightly more definition in the detail and lettering.
VF-30	Almost complete detail with flat areas.
VF-35	Detail is complete but worn with high points flat.
EF-40	Detail is complete with most high points slightly flat.
EF-45	Detail is complete with some high points flat.
AU-50	Full detail with friction over most of the surface, slight flatness on high points.
AU-53	Full detail with friction over 1/2 or more of the surface, very slight flatness on high points.
AU-55	Full detail with friction on less than 1/2 the surface, mainly on high points.
AU-58	Full detail with only slight friction on the high points.
MS/PR-60	No wear. May have many heavy marks/hairlines, strike may not be full.
MS/PR-61	No wear. Multiple heavy marks/hairlines, strike may not be full.
MS/PR-62	No wear. Slightly less marks/hairlines, strike may not be full.
MS/PR-63	Moderate number/size marks/hairlines, strike may not be full.
MS/PR-64	Few marks/hairlines or a couple of severe ones, strike should be average or above.
MS/PR-65	Minor marks/hairlines though none in focal areas, above average strike.
MS/PR-66	Few minor marks/hairlines not in focal areas, good strike.
MS/PR-67	Virtually as struck with minor imperfections, very well struck.
MS/PR-68	Virtually as struck with slight imperfections, slightest weakness of strike allowed.
MS/PR-69	Virtually as struck with minuscule imperfections, near full strike necessary.
MS/PR-70	As struck, with full strike.

Grade	Condition
PO	Poor
FR	Fair
AG	About Good
G	Good
VG	Very Good
F	Fine
VF	Very Fine
EF	Extremely Fine
AU	About Uncirculated
MS	Mint State
PR	Proof

The condition and subsequent grade of a coin and how these qualities equate to market and potential resale value can be explained in the following example.

Let's say you owned two 1893-CC Morgan Dollars. Both coins look the same although one is a bit more worn than the other, have the same design, have the same mintmark and have the date of 1893. After getting the coin graded, you realize that one of your 1893 Morgan Dollars was graded as an EF-40 and the other was graded as an MS/PR-67. The difference in grade seems minor at first. Is the difference between an EF-40 (extra fine condition) grade compared to an MS/PR-67 (mint strike/proof condition) grade that important? Yes! According to the PCGS Price Guide (www.pcgs .com/prices), as of October 2010, an EF-40 graded 1893-S Morgan Dollar was valued at $8,750 whereas an MS/PR-67 1893-S Morgan Dollar was valued at $1,000,000.

The detailed differences and nuances in the quality and condition of coins and their subsequent values based on particular sets of grading criteria can affect the value of every coin. By using a professional coin grading service, the potential of inaccurately grading valuable coins will be avoided.

Comic Books

The **Certified Guaranty Corporation Comics (CGC Comics) (www .cgccomics.com)** is the only professional grading company available for comics and comic books. Fees start in the $10 range for the grading of one comic and can escalate to hundreds of dollars if multiple comics or comic books are submitted. The success of CGC Comics comes from their attention to detail and thoroughness throughout all facets of the comic book grading process. Their four-step process in the valuing of comic books involves receiving (getting the comic book shipped from the customer), grading (judging the physical condition of the comic book and assigning a grade), encapsulation (placing the comic in a protective sleeve or casing) and shipping (sending the comic book back to the customer). The industry standard for grading comic books is based on the 0.5–10.0 CGC Corporation Scale. A grade of 0.5 is the lowest score a comic can receive and it is an example of a comic in poor quality. A grade of 10.0 is the best grade score a comic can possibly achieve and denotes this collectible is in the best possible condition or gem mint condition.

The CGC Scale is as follows:

Grade	Condition
0.5	Poor
1.0	Fair
1.5	Fair/Good
1.8	Good –
2.0	Good
2.5	Good +
3.0	Good/Very Good
3.5	Very Good –
4.0	Very Good
4.5	Very Good +
5.0	Very Good/Fine
5.5	Fine –
6.0	Fine
6.5	Fine +
7.0	Fine/Very Fine
7.5	Very Fine –
8.0	Very Fine
8.5	Very Fine +
9.0	Very Fine/Near Mint
9.2	Near Mint –
9.4	Near Mint
9.6	Near Mint +
9.8	Near Mint/Mint
9.9	Mint
10.0	Gem Mint

Top comic books, when properly graded by a professional grading company, can be valued at more than \$1 million. You can view a current listing of the 100 most valuable comic books at **Nostomania (www.nostomania.com/servlets/com.nostomania.CatPage?name= Top100ComicsMain)**. Comic book values, like the values from any type of collectible, are always in a state of flux. The chart showing the values of the top 100 comic books is just a snapshot of a particular comic book's value on a particular day.

Action Figures

Action Figure Authority (AFA) (www.toygrader.com) is the only professional grading service available for action figures. AFA uses three very detailed grading scales to accurately grade action figures: the C-Scale (Condition Scale), the AFA 3-Tier Grading Scale (for items produced from 1995 to present) and the AFAM (M for "modern") 3-Tier Grading Scale (for items produced from 1995 to present).

As with all grading scales in the collectibles market, a higher score given to any collectible equates to a higher assigned value. A higher value means that higher potential profits can be made. The three AFA grading scales (courtesy of Action Figure Authority) are:

C-Scale

Grade	Condition
C1–C4	Very poor, badly damaged, basically only useful for spare parts.
C5	Poor condition with heavy wear, broken parts will impair function.
C6	Fair, significant wear, may have some broken parts.
C7	Good, noticeable wear but no broken parts, items may be missing accessories.
C8	Very good, some minor wear, no broken or missing parts.
C9	Near mint condition, very minor imperfections apparent.
C10	Mint condition, unused.

AFA 3-Tier Grading Scale (for items produced from 1995 to present)

Level	Grade
AFA Gold	Gem Mint (100), Mint (95) and Near Mint/Mint (90)

AFA Description/Condition

The AFA Gold level consists of the grades 100, 95 and 90. The select few figures receiving these grades are among the highest quality in existence. A very small percentage of figures submitted to AFA receive a Gold grade. The flaws are very minor, very subtle and are sometimes very hard to identify with the naked eye. The collector who is extremely condition sensitive will be satisfied with the condition of a Gold-level figure.

Level	Grade
AFA Silver	Near Mint Plus (85), Near Mint (80) and Excellent Plus/Near Mint (75)

AFA Description/Condition

The AFA Silver level consists of the grades 85, 80 and 75. The figures that receive these grades are in excellent condition. A figure graded an 85 will often be referred to as case fresh and should be very close to gold level condition. The term case fresh is certainly justifiable as the average figure pulled from a sealed case will grade an 85 due to small flaws that occur when the figures are packaged or shipped in the case. The average figure pulled from a store shelf is usually an 80, which represents a nice specimen with minor flaws apparent upon close inspection. The final Silver-level grade, a 75, represents an item with more minor flaws than the average Silver-level piece. An item grading 75 does have significant wear but does not have major flaws that would draw the eye to them at first glance. For most high grade collectors, an 85 is satisfactory. For most discriminating collectors, an 80 is satisfactory. A 75 will be satisfactory to those who are not overly concerned with light stresses, small bubble imperfections and other flaws that do not jump out at first glance. Therefore, the Silver-level grades do represent a much larger range than the gold level grades.

Level	Grade
AFA Bronze	Excellent Plus (70), Excellent (60), Very Good (50), Good (40), Fair (30), Poor (20) and Very Poor (10)

AFA Description/Condition

The AFA Bronze level consists of the grades 70, 60 and below. The figures that receive these grades typically have damage ranging from simply noticeable upon first glance to extremely significant. The card may have creases on the front and the blister may be crushed or cracked. The Bronze level covers a large range of figure conditions and the scope of the flaws range considerably. Condition for Bronze level figures is determined by how many major flaws are present on the card and how severe each flaw is. Bronze-level figures may have major flaws such as a torn off POP or other large paper tears. Bronze level figures may not be satisfactory to condition sensitive collectors.

AFAM 3-Tier Grading Scale (for items produced from 1995 to present)

Level	Grade
AFAM Gold	9.0, 9.25, 9.5, 9.75 and 10.0

AFAM Description/Condition

The AFAM Gold level consists of the grades 10.0, 9.75, 9.5, 9.25 and 9.0. The figures that receive these grades are among the highest quality in existence. The flaws are very minor, very subtle and are sometimes very hard to identify with the naked eye. A collector who is extremely condition sensitive should be satisfied with the condition of a Gold-level figure.

Level	Grade
AFAM Silver	7.5, 8.0 and 8.5

AFAM Description/Condition

The AFAM Silver level consists of the grades 8.5, 8.0 and 7.5. The figures that receive these grades are in decent condition. A collector would be able to spot a few small flaws on an 8.5 and would see several moderate flaws on a 7.5.

Level	Grade
AFAM Bronze	1.0–7.0

AFAM Description/Condition

The AFAM Bronze level consists of the grades 7.0 and below. The figures that receive these grades typically have damage ranging from simply noticeable upon first glance to extremely significant.

Since modern items are typically in good condition, very few items will be low enough to receive these grades.

As a Garage Sale Millionaire, leaving grading judgments to the professionals regarding action figures is one of the best decisions you can make. Because there are so many variables that can determine the condition of your action figure, it's really best to leave grading decisions to the experts. When the discussion moves to potential future profits, having the proper grade on an action figure collectible is key in making the most money possible from every sale.

Baseball Cards, Sports Trading Cards and Non-Sports Trading Cards

Consider the following: there are 30 professional Major League Baseball teams playing every year, every team's roster is made up of 40 players, many players get called up from the minor leagues every year to the big leagues, the sport has been played professionally since 1871 and hundreds of baseball cards are made for each player in the big leagues every single year. You can only imagine how much profit potential there is to be made from buying and selling baseball cards.

And that's just baseball!

The baseball card, sports trading card and non-sports trading card market is a treasure trove ready to be discovered and exploited by Garage Sale Millionaires everywhere. The baseball card and sports trading card market includes every sports trading card manufactured. Non-sports trading cards consist of television and movie trading cards, entertainment trading cards, pro-wrestling trading cards and various stiffeners from cigarette packs from the late-1800s through the early-1900s. Although football, basketball and hockey are all viable sports trading card markets and non-sports cards are still a novelty in comparison to sports trading cards, the baseball card market continues to be the most lucrative.

Some of the top grading companies in this field are **Professional Sports Authenticator (PSA)** (www.psacard.com), **Beckett Grading Service (BGS)** (www.beckett.com), **GMA Grading** (www.gmagrading .com), **Sportscard Guarantee (SGC)** (www.sgccard.com) and **International Grading Service (IGS)** (www.igsgrading.com). By choosing to get your cards professionally graded, you'll get increased value from your card. Also, your card will be protected in a sturdy and durable card holder and you will get your card expertly authenticated.

Baseball cards are unique in the world of collectibles. Only baseball cards are graded based on three unique criteria:

The physical condition of the card—Is the card in good condition or mint condition?

The star quality of the player—A rookie card of Babe Ruth is much more valuable than a rookie card of John Kruk.

The era a player played the game—Older cards of superstar players will be more valuable overall than the superstars who have played the game of baseball within the last few years.

Besides grading a baseball card on the star quality of a player and what era that player played the game, baseball grading companies use four criteria to grade the physical quality of a card. According to **Baseball Cards Buyers.com (www.baseballcardsbuyers .com)**, the basic criteria for grading baseball cards are:

Centering—This refers to the evenness of the white space or border (if any) around the baseball card's main image. Centering is measured left to right and top to bottom and is defined in percentages. For example, if a card is slightly off-center (to the right) and way off-center (to the bottom), grading might be 55–45 and 65–35. That means that to the naked eye the baseball card's left border is just noticeably wider than the right border, but the top border is almost twice as wide as the bottom border.

Corners—This refers to the sharpness of the corners and any creases in the corner. Dinged corners will drop the value of a baseball card almost more quickly than any other factor. To the naked eye, if the corners are a very sharp point, that's a good thing. Experts at professional card-grading companies check corners under magnification for complete accuracy. Some unscrupulous sellers will re-cut a card, which gives it sharp, new corners. This trick is easily detected with a metal template that is cut to the exact size at which that particular card was originally manufactured.

Edges—While not as important a factor in grading baseball cards as the previous two items, chipped edges will reduce a card's value. The two causes of imperfect edges are poor card cutting at the time the card was originally manufactured and edge damage due to extensive or improper handling of the card. Of course, there's nothing you can do about how well the card was made, but you can reduce handling damage by keeping valuable baseball cards in protective sleeves.

Surface—This refers to coating on the image of the baseball card as well as, but to a lesser degree, the printing on the back of the card. Other than unacceptable problems such as pin holes, tape, staples or writing, the biggest de-valuation factor is creases in the card that are typically visible to the naked eye. The very rarest of baseball cards are not subject to the same stringent surface criteria due to their age and uniqueness. Less obvious, but nearly as important, are scratches in the surface of the baseball card. These scratches can be observed by the naked eye without magnification when held closely under a normal light bulb. You should also rotate the card so that the light hits it at different angles. A third flaw can be printing dots that are a different color than the area around it.

Antique Firearms

If you're not familiar with how valuable the collectible and antique firearms market is, take one look at the auction listings on **GunBroker.com (www.gunbroker.com)**. The amounts are staggering and are a real eye-opener. Many firearms sales start in the hundreds of dollars and the price ranges increase until they hit six figures. Antique firearms are a hot market because of their steady popularity over the decades and sales don't appear to be letting up anytime soon. Antique firearms and their associated values are based on the physical qualities of the firearm and its provenance.

Provenance relates to the place of origin or earliest known history of an item. **Gun-Appraisals.com (www.gun-appraisals.com)** states that, "One thing we have noted throughout the years of doing appraisals is that if a gun can be tied to a historic person or event, the value of that firearm will escalate tremendously. This is no easy task however. Irrefutable proof must be provided and not just a letter from Grandpa saying that he got this from a friend as payment for a debt and the friend was related to Geronimo and the friend swore it was a present from Geronimo to him. What you will need to provide is a myriad of supporting documentation. If you are able to prove that your weapon is tied to someone important or an important event and this proof is accepted by the top dealers and collectors, then you have a great chance of getting a nice premium at one of the top auction houses. Of course the more historic and important the person or event is, the better your chances of a big score!"

Gun-Appraisals.com will value your collectible and antique firearm. Besides information concerning provenance, Gun-Appraisals.com uses a certain set of criteria to determine if a firearm has value:

Desirability/Aesthetics—People collect weapons that personally appeal to them and ones that have a desirable aesthetic quality. This is not to say that an ugly, yet unique firearm will not be sought after. It's more of a general statement regarding what the majority of collectors look for.

Condition—Condition definitely makes or breaks the value of any collectible. Now, thanks to the **National Rifle Association (www.nra.org)**, a gun collector has at their disposal a very sophisticated system of grading. Since grading remains a subjective art, there will always be differences in opinion as to the actual grade of an individual weapon. (Please see the charts later in this section for the National Rifle Association Standards for modern and antique guns, and visit www.armchairgunshow.com).

Price—Most firearms have been catalogued and priced in various guides. A search on the Internet can give you a good idea of the going rate for any particular weapon.

Maker/Manufacturer—Many collectors specialize according to manufacturer. The appeal and recognition of large name makers is usually much broader than the smaller and usually defunct companies. Firearms bearing the trademarks of a reputable firm will usually have a larger collector base than a lesser-known maker.

Rarity—*Not every old gun is rare and not every rare gun is old.* If your gun is indeed rare, it will be of interest to someone, somewhere. The trouble is that often locating that special someone is just as difficult as finding the gun itself! Don't mistake rarity for desirability. Rarity is but one factor to take into account when determining the value of a gun. Some collectors will only collect weapons that are MIB (Mint in Box) condition and are not so interested in the rarity. Other collectors would do anything to have a rare gun in their collection no matter what the condition . . . believe it or not! The original condition of an old gun is usually what is rare and not necessarily the gun itself.

Special Order Features—Firearms fall into a special category when it comes to special features. Almost every gun manufacturer has numerous options available to the buyer. From engraving, wood carving, checkering, special finishes, sights and everything in-between, there are literally hundreds of special features in the firearm world. To top it all off, not all of these special features were completed at the factory. Many were custom, after-market options. All of these features must be taken into consideration when determining the collectible value of your weapon. What is desirable to one collector may not necessarily intrigue another.

Market/Economic Factors—In North America, we usually talk about values of firearms in relation to the U.S. marketplace; however, even within the United States the values of a particular gun will be quite different, varying from region to region. This is particularly true when attending gun shows. Dealers notice higher demands for certain types of weapons in different states. The ability to post your gun for sale on the Internet has rapidly removed the distance barriers typical of gun shows. For the person who has the disposable income available, this is the best time to buy. It's supply and demand in its purest form.

The NRA Modern Gun Condition Standards

Grade	Condition
Fair	In safe working condition, but well worn, perhaps requiring replacement of minor parts or adjustments that should be indicated in advertisement; no rust, but may have corrosion pits that do render the gun unsafe or inoperable.
Good	In safe working condition; minor wear on working surfaces; no broken parts; no corrosion or pitting that will interfere with proper functioning.

Grade	Condition
Very Good	In perfect working condition; no appreciable wear on working surfaces; no corrosion or pitting; only minor surface dents or scratches.
Excellent	New condition; used very little; no noticeable marring of wood or metal; bluing perfect (except at muzzle or sharp edges).
Perfect	In new condition in every respect.
New	Not previously sold at retail; in same condition as current factory production.

NRA Antique Firearm Condition Standards

Grade	Condition
Poor	Major and minor parts replaced; major replacement parts required and extensive restoration needed; metal deeply pitted; principal lettering, numerals and design obliterated; wood badly scratched, bruised, cracked or broken; mechanically inoperative; generally undesirable as a collectors firearm.
Fair	Some major parts replaced; minor replacement parts may be required; metal rusted, may be lightly pitted all over, vigorously cleaned or re-blued; rounded edges of metal and wood; principal lettering, numerals and design on metal partly obliterated; wood scratched, bruised, cracked or repaired where broken; in fair working order or can be easily repaired and placed in working order.
Good	Some minor replacement parts; metal smoothly rusted or lightly pitted in places, cleaned or re-blued; principal letters, numerals and design on metal legible; wood refinished, scratched, bruised or minor cracks repaired; in good working order.
Very Good	All original parts; none to 30% original finish; original metal surfaces smooth with all edges sharp; clear lettering, numerals and design on metal; wood slightly scratched or bruised; bore disregarded for collectors' firearms.
Fine	All original parts; over 30% original finish; sharp lettering, numerals and design on metal and wood; minor marks in wood; good bore.
Excellent	All original parts; over 80% original finish; sharp lettering, numerals and design on metal and wood; unmarred wood; fine bore.
Factory New	All original parts; 100% original finish; in perfect condition in every respect, inside and out.

Now You Know the Rest of the Story

The best decision you can make to guarantee that you receive proper value for your collectible items at resale is to have your items graded. There are two directions you can take to have your collectible items graded: self-grading or hiring a professional. When you are ready to sell your valuable treasures, be it in person or online, all of your potential customers will want to know everything there is about what you are trying to sell. All this is accomplished through the process of grading. By providing your customers with as much detail as possible about your items, you will have a better chance to complete every sale and also make the most money.

Million $ Tip

If your treasure is a baseball card, comic book, limited edition collectible or coin, you will have no problem finding a value.

Million $ Tip

The condition of your item will greatly change the value.

Million $ Tip

Retail value and what you can get selling it to a retailer are going to be different. Stores that are known for collectibles have a following and can receive top dollar for an item. If a store is selling something for $100, they probably paid about $50 for the item.

Million $ Tip

If a dealer offers you money for your item and the amount is not enough, you can negotiate the price with them. I recommend you always ask for more during your negotiations. Dealers' first offers are usually low.

CHAPTER 8

Putting on the World's Greatest Garage Sale

My lifelong fascination with garage sales began at a very young age. I was only seven years old when I held my first sale with my mom. I didn't really know why I even wanted to hold a garage sale. I saw other families in my neighborhood having garage sales but I just didn't quite get it. What was the big deal, anyway? When you're seven years old, it seemed as though people were going though a lot of trouble and effort for nothing. Since garage sales were usually held on a Saturday and Sunday, like *all day* Saturday and Sunday, that meant the sale took away a chunk of some very serious play time. Why would I ever want to sacrifice having lots of fun? What a totally boring way to waste the weekend!

It couldn't have been about the money. The concept of free market economics in buying and selling physical goods for money and hopefully turning a profit was just barely starting to sink in at such a young age.

I did notice one characteristic all the families who did hold garage sales had in common. Every single one of our neighbors seemed to be having serious amounts of fun when they did this sort of thing. Of course, being seven years old, I wanted to have fun too! After a lengthy discussion with my mom, I convinced her we needed to have some fun like the neighbors, so we should have a

My favorite place in my home is the Presidents Room.

garage sale of our own. My mom agreed and my first garage sale was a go.

After my first sale ever was over, I finally understood why everyone seemed to have such a great time holding garage sales. I also learned my first worldly lesson. In the end, it is really all about the money! People actually came up and gave you handfuls of cash for a bunch of old stuff that you didn't want anyway. I can't remember how much my mother and I made at our first sale together, but I do remember seeing more cash than I had ever seen before in my life. Safe to say, I was immediately hooked on the idea of holding garage sales. I had been bitten by the garage sale bug and bitten badly. A new world seemed to open up for me. After all these years, I still can't wait for the arrival of summer so I can have yet another sale!

The Need-To-Know List: Essential Information for Holding The World's Greatest Garage Sale

There are certain things you need to know in order to hold a successful, moneymaking garage sale. In this section, I will discuss some of the key elements necessary for making your garage sale the best it can be.

When to Hold the Sale

One of the crucial elements in conducting a successful garage sale is to know when the right time is to have one. Picking the right days of the week to conduct your sale is absolutely crucial.

You really need to hold your garage sale when as many people as possible can attend. The more foot traffic you can generate at your sale, the better chance you have for success and of course turning substantial profits. Well, that

Million $ Tip

If you want to have a garage sale and have just one day for such an event, make sure you hold your sale on a Saturday. As a second option, try to choose a Friday. Between Friday and Saturday, you'll get the most traffic possible. People tend to not attend garage sales between Sunday and Thursday like they do on Fridays and Saturdays. On these other week days you will just be spinning your wheels and wasting your own time, hard work and effort.

and having some seriously cool things to sell, but I will talk about these points later in the chapter.

The best day to hold a garage sale is on Saturday. Sunday through Thursday are generally not good days at all to have a sale. You will waste plenty of time and effort on any of these days. While some people may show up if your sale is between Sunday and Thursday, most people have other obligations that will take priority, especially on a Sunday. On Sunday the priority will be attending church and family events. During the week, the obvious priority will be work. This doesn't mean you won't have some success on other days of the week, but usually the most sales will be made on Saturdays.

If you insist on having a sale on a weekday, pick Friday. Friday is an excellent secondary day to hold a garage sale. Some people might take Friday off as part of a three-day weekend and some good sales may be made, providing you publicize your sale with street signs and in the local paper. Even if individuals don't take the whole day off, by Friday afternoon they may leave work early and be ready to get a jump on finding some great sales in their area. If you want to do a two-day garage sale, definitely plan for a Friday and Saturday.

If you live where you have four distinctive seasons, it's best to schedule your sales for the warmer weather months. That means anytime during the late spring, throughout summer or into the early fall. Scheduling your garage sale for a potentially non-rainy day is also a key to success.

You can usually rely on the accuracy of advanced local weather predictions up to a week in advance. Many people just don't attend garage sales when the weather is bad. If you live in a part of the country that has great weather all year long, then every weekend offers you the potential to bring garage sale success and profitability.

Getting People to Your Garage Sale—and Managing Them Once They've Arrived

Getting as many people as possible to attend your garage sale is a key component for achieving financial garage sale success. Additionally, how you inform your customers is another key to making your garage sale more profitable.

Many individuals plan their entire weekend solely based on going to garage sales. When they see a sign or advertisement for your garage sale, they may arrive at least ninety minutes early. If you think I'm kidding, just wait until you have your first sale. For as long as I've been involved in the business and too many times to count, I've seen people actually camp out on the seller's front yard before the sun even rises so they can be the first one there. Even if your sign states that the sale doesn't start until 9:00 AM, people will still get there while you're setting up everything. Even when you're pulling items out of your garage to place on the sale tables, they will be walking with you trying to carry on a conversation and may ask if they can help you set up. Experienced garage sale shoppers do this sort of thing to try to not only get a look at what you have to sell, but this also places them in the best possible position so they can have a first go at all of your great sale items.

It is important how you handle garage sale early birds because these early arrivals could make or break your garage sale. Don't shoo them away like my mother always wanted to and did, on many occasions. I suppose she just didn't understand the business as well as I did even at my young age. As a child, I wanted to let all my early bird customers into our house and have them start picking up our furniture and taking it home with them. *For a price, of course!* Enjoy your customers, even if they prove to be difficult to handle. People like to shop in a jovial environment. Definitely make sure you hold a garage sale that has an element of fun attached to it. In many cases,

> ### Million $ Tip
>
> Half the fun of going to any garage sale is doing the buying. But people also want to be entertained! No, you do not have to do cartwheels, juggle or put on a magic show. All you have to do is be kind, chatty and make the process for the buyer an enjoyable experience. I guarantee if you are a great garage sale host, people will buy more of your wares and will come back when they know you are having another sale.

a garage sale mixed with a relaxed shopping and sales environment equals bigger profits! I will discuss some of the ways to spice up a garage sale later in the chapter.

Preparation and Setup

How do you prepare for and set everything up for the world's greatest garage sale? You need to arrange the details for your sale a few weeks in advance, not just days in advance. If you want to make the most profit possible from your garage sale, you need to make sure everything regarding the upcoming sale is in order and ready to go before the sale begins. This, of course, takes a little bit of planning.

Having a garage sale is a great opportunity for you to go room to room, closet to closet and drawer to drawer throughout your home to identify all the items for which you have no need or use any longer. This includes unwanted gifts . . . things you may never have liked or needed at all. Have you used, worn or even looked at something you have tucked away collecting dust in the past year? If not, then you more than likely need to get rid of it. You can choose to sell it, give it to charity or just throw it out if it isn't in good condition. Why have something lying around if you do not use that item?

I truly believe if you can find all the stuff in your house that you don't use, you can make very good money from it. If, for some reason, you sell something and decide you need it again, go to the store and buy it new again. Or go to another garage sale and buy it!

I usually begin preparing for my garage sales about a month before the actual date of the sale so I can be thorough in my preparations. I want to make sure I've gone through my house from top to bottom so I don't overlook something of value I can sell. The worst thing that can happen is that you discover things that you could have sold, after your garage sale is history. After I've exhausted the search throughout my own home for salable items, I move on to my office and look for even more items to sell.

> **Million $ Tip**
>
> You will want to try to inform the customers at your garage sale about the history behind the items you are trying to sell. The amount of information you do or do not provide could make or break any sale! Customers at garage sales absolutely love hearing value-added information and background stories about the items they are getting ready to buy.

Parents, family members, neighbors and friends are fantastic sources for finding more valuable items to sell at any garage sale. Over time, miscellaneous items always seem to get stuck in people's basements and as a result, all those long-forgotten items just end up gathering dust and cobwebs. Always ask people you know if there's anything of theirs you can put in your garage sale. You can always arrange to split the money you make on their items with them. It really is a win-win situation for all involved. They give you their old stuff; you do all the work. They make a percentage on the sales! Many times family and friends want to help you out and will even work at your garage sale because these types of events are so much fun.

> **Million $ Tip**
>
> Use TagSellIt.com to advertise your garage sale. You can also use it to find all the great garage sales in your area. It is a excellent resource for all garage sale fanatics.

Throughout the years, I've developed a proven timeline that has helped me stay organized and get ready for any garage sale. By always adhering to my timeline, I can 99.99% guarantee myself that I make sure that everything I want to sell will be at my garage sale.

Let's look at the timeline and then I will discuss some key points in more detail.

Time Before Sale	Things to Do
1 Month	✓ Start looking for and gathering up items around your house and office that you do not use.
	✓ Ask your family members if they have any items for you to sell.
	✓ Try to get as many items as possible for your sale. Size matters!
	✓ Overdo it if you have to. More items are better.
	✓ The more items people see at your garage sale, the more motivation they will have for stopping and shopping.
	✓ Clean and fix your sale items (if necessary).
	✓ Look for original packaging on the items you have, especially if you have collectibles to sell.
2 Weeks to 2 Days	✓ Create your signs and flyers for your sale (extra credit points are awarded for very colorful and eye-catching signs and flyers).
	✓ Get a change purse together so you are prepared to make correct change when your garage sale starts.

(continued)

(*continued*)

Time Before Sale	Things to Do
2 Weeks to 2 Days	✓ Place your advertisements in your local newspapers or in any free newspapers in your area to announce your sale. ✓ Use social networking Internet websites such as Twitter, Craigslist and Facebook to get the word out on the location and date of your garage sale. ✓ Start methodically pricing your sale items. ✓ Make sure you have enough tables for all of your sale items.
The Night Before	✓ Put your signs and flyers out in the busiest traffic areas and around your neighborhood where you believe the most people will see the announcement of your garage sale. ✓ Look over and meticulously double-check everything you want to sell at least one more time to guarantee accuracy in the pricing of your sale items.
The Morning of Your Garage Sale	✓ Two hours before your sale, start physically setting up your garage sale.
Your Garage Sale Begins	✓ **Smile and watch the money pour in!**

Key Elements from My Tried-and-True Garage Sale Timeline

I cannot tell you how many garage sales I've seen where people will slow down, stick their heads out the car window, take a look around and keep on driving. This is definitely not what you want to have happen at your sale.

Size Matters

Implement this *key element* one month before the date of your garage sale

To make sure your garage sale is an even bigger eye-catcher, you'll want to have as many items as possible in view to sell and have them spread out on as many tables as possible. By having enough tables to display all your merchandise, your garage sale will look nice and big. When you have people driving by to see if your sale is worth the time and energy to get out of their cars to shop, bigger is most definitely better. Also, when you have a larger sale, people will take more time to browse and eventually to shop. In my decades of garage sale experience the more time people spend at a garage sale, the more money they seem to spend.

By including as many other people's stuff that you can get your hands on, the better opportunity you'll have to make a bigger profit.

> **Million $ Tip**
>
> The more treasures, trinkets and goodies you have in your garage sale, the bigger it will look. By having a fully stocked sale, your chances for garage sale success and making as much money from your sale as possible will increase exponentially. When people drive by and see a lot of great items at a garage sale, they will almost always stop, get out of their cars and walk quickly into your sale.

Clean and Fix Everything

Implement this *key element* one month before the date of your garage sale

After you've gone to family and friends to look for salable items for your enterprise, next look through your house inside, out and upside down identifying the items people might be interested in buying. Then, take time to scour your office for finds you didn't even know you had lying around. Make sure everything is clean and in working order. If something needs to be fixed, you need to fix it before the sale so you avoid having customers bargain you way down on the price. There's nothing worse than going to a garage sale and finding something you really want to buy that is in absolutely awful shape. I have seen it all in my experience with garage sales. If you're selling stuffed animals,

This Iron Man #1 in very good to fine condition was bought at one of the first garage sales that I attended for roughly fifty cents. It is now worth between $175 and $250, depending on where you look. Not a bad investment when you're only nine years old.

furniture with cushions or even pillows, give them a good spritz of Febreze®! Dirty, malfunctioning and broken items don't bring in very much revenue! Following is a list of things that are deal-breakers for me:

- I've found so many items that look dusty, unclean and noticeably in a state of ill-repair that I've passed on buying these items even if there was an inkling I could have sold them for a profit later on.
- Items that physically fell apart in my hands when I picked them up get a pass from me every time.
- Discovering when I went to plug an electrical item into the outlet, the item for sale started smoking . . . no thanks.
- I've found items that smelled so horribly awful that they were a complete turn off . . . a definite NO!
- I've found rusted-out items that lost all their value many years ago. Sometimes it seems decades ago. It doesn't take a very keen eye to pick up on this.

Million $ Tip

By inviting more people to help you at your garage sale, you increase your chances for garage sale success and you will more than likely have a great turnout.

Million $ Tip

Have an extension cord available for your customers to use if you are selling any electrical items. Your customers may want to test them out before they buy.

My list could have been longer, but you get the idea. Always make sure the items you have are in decent working order. People will ask you to plug in an item to see if it really works and they will pick up items to see if they completely fall apart. The opportunity to test your items is in the days leading up to your garage sale. The opportunity to get the most money for every item lies in whether or not it's in proper working order and how good it looks when it's sitting on the sales table. If you have something to sell and it's missing a part, believe me, your garage sale visitors are going to ask if you have that missing part. It's an inevitable garage sale truth

. . . they will always ask! If you happen to have the part, it will usually guarantee the sale. If not, then good luck.

Customers will ask you questions you never thought they would come up with in a million years. Be ready for anything and always be honest with your reply. If you are dishonest at any time during your sale, buyers will be upset. If you ever have another garage sale, they will not stop by again. More importantly, they could warn many others to stay away from any garage sale you hold in the future.

Million $ Tip

When someone is trying to buy one of your treasures, they are going to ask questions. Sometimes, many questions! Try to give as many answers as you can and do not ever rush them. This kind of interaction is considered great entertainment for the garage sale enthusiast! This is what garage sale customers look forward to every weekend. If you are short with them, treat them unkindly and show disinterest, I can guarantee they will not buy anything and they will never come back to another one of your garage sales.

Original Packaging Greatly Adds Value to Your Items

**Implement this *key element* one month from
the date of your garage sale**

It's very important, especially if you're selling collectibles, to include the original box or packaging that came with the item. Why? Items with the original packaging, along with the instructions (if there were any), will sell for much more money than items being sold without their original sales packaging. *A lot more money!* In my experience, an item with its original packaging will sell for at least 20% to 40% more than an item sold by itself. If it's a collectible and you have the box and certificate, this will raise the value about 50%. If your collectible came with a wind-up key, it's essential to find that key to keep the item fully intact. Anything you can find to help add value is crucial to include with the item at your garage sale.

It's worth your while and will result in bigger profits, to take the extra time needed to make certain that everything is in perfect order for your big day. Do everything in your power to present the world's greatest garage sale. Run your event like a well-oiled machine and your pocketbook, as well as your bank account, will be happy that you did.

Pricing Your Items

Implement this *key element* one week from the date of your garage sale

Pricing is another crucial element to any garage sale. *To place prices on items or put them out without pricing . . . that is the question.* You would think prices should be placed on everything at a garage sale. This is not always the case. I've gone to a multitude of garage sales where items for sale fall into two categories . . . items with pricing and items without any price attached.

Why would someone not put a price on something at a garage sale? By not placing a price on an item, the person holding the garage sale forces the potential buyer to personally inquire about the price or to make an offer. This gives the seller a potential amount of leeway in determining the price of the item. This non-pricing of items occurs most often on items of very little value. With less expensive items selling for as little as a dollar or less, it will take you hours to price out everything. On these types of items, try omitting the price altogether and bargaining with your customers. You're not going to make much from these items anyway. You know people are going to probably spend the minimum so why waste your valuable time marking a price on insignificant smaller items?

When pricing items, don't be greedy. If you're too greedy with your pricing, people will walk away from your sale with nothing in hand. Place a fair price on your items, but always leave yourself some room to bargain. If you have an item that cost $100 when it was new, your sale price should not exceed $45. Also, be ready to accept $30. If you're not prepared to take an offer of $30 for the item, then slightly raise your sales price to $47, $48 or even $50. Remember, the goal at any garage sale is to have nothing left over at the end of the day. Try to sell everything on hand so you can begin building a fresh new inventory for your next sale.

> **Million $ Tip**
>
> Always leave room to "horse-trade" when pricing an item. Make sure you price your sale items 15% to 20% higher than the minimum price you would accept so you can negotiate the price when someone makes you an offer.

If you're unsure of something when it comes to pricing your sale items, search out eBay (see Chapter 6 for an extensive discussion of eBay). eBay will give you an up-to-the-minute idea of what an item is worth. If an item is worth only a few dollars, price it to sell. It's better to put it on your table and have someone make you an offer than to hold onto it for another ten years! If you really don't know how to value an item, price it at what you believe to be fair and be very observant of your customers during your sale. If someone wants to buy an item you marked at a certain price and it looks like they are ready to walk away from the sale, go over and ask, "Would you like to make me an offer?" If they come up with a number that's below the price you had listed for the item, counteroffer. You can always suggest meeting in the middle between your final price and your customer's offer. If they offer $2 and you make a final counteroffer of $3, then $2.50 will be the final sales price. That's the normal flow of the garage sale.

There are so many opportunities for people to buy new merchandise at great prices. New means items are in perfect or near-perfect condition. New may also mean this year's model. I can guarantee you that almost every item sold at a garage sale is not going to be this year's latest model. If an item is in perfect condition, you can't expect to make all your money back or even consider charging retail value. Don't forget! You are conducting a garage sale where full price is almost never paid. That's just the way it works. You're doing extremely well if you get between 25% and 35%, or sometimes even 45% of what you originally paid for an item.

When you're thinking about what's valuable and what could be worth good money at your garage sale, don't consider used books. If you charge more than a few dollars per book, people will quickly walk away. No sale, my friends! Used books don't hold much value.

Computers, old appliances and tube televisions (not flat screens) don't sell for much, either. Of course, you can always try to sell these items, but don't expect much in return for them. This doesn't mean you shouldn't sell everything and anything you want, just be cognizant of what you might or more than likely might not get for older items way past their prime.

One of the reasons you should try to sell everything you can has to do with trash removal. Whatever you have left after your sale that needs to be disposed of will cost you money to haul away. Trash companies won't even take the majority of larger items that you were unable to sell and you'll be forced to hire a private junk hauler to get rid of your items for you. Trash companies also don't like taking obsolete computer monitors and printers or anything that could be considered hazardous to a dump site. Secondhand stores are also not taking everything as readily as they once did. In the end, you'll be stuck spending your hard-earned garage sale profits on hiring a hauler to move anything that was unsold. It's sometimes better to take an offer of less money for your sale items so you don't have to dispose of them yourself if they are left over after the sale.

Advertising

**Implement this *key element* beginning two weeks and
up until two days before the date of your garage sale**

Your sale items have all been exhaustively acquired, painstakingly organized for your garage sale and are all ready to go. They are priced, cleaned up and looking good . . . as though they are ready to literally leap from the table into your customers' hands. Now, all you have to do is figure out a way to get people to your sale.

From my experience, most people believe that the advertising aspect of any garage sale is an extremely complicated process. Nothing could be further from the truth. Advertising for your garage sale is the easiest component within the sales process. Publicizing your garage sale does take some attention to complete, but it's a very straightforward exercise.

Two weeks to go before your sale is when you need to start taking advantage of many of the free advertising resources at your disposal. Your advertising must all be in place a couple of days before your target day. Not only are most of these resources free of charge, but they are also very effective and proven methods for making your forthcoming event known.

These free resources include:

- **Advertising on the Internet.** There are many garage sale websites that will let you post your garage sale information for free.

- **Various Internet Social Networking Websites. Facebook** (www.facebook.com), **Twitter** (www.twitter.com) and **Craigslist** (www.craigslist.org).
- **Advertisements in Flyer Form at Local Libraries, Coffee Shops and Your Neighborhood Recreation Centers.** Always be sure to get permission to place your garage sale advertisements so your hard work will not be torn down and thrown in the trash before your sale.

The week before your sale is when you need to start posting information about your sale on Twitter. You must have your sale posted to Craigslist three days before your sale. On Facebook, you need to have everything in place within a few days of your sale. Although the use of free advertising options are excellent cost-effective ways to get the word out, don't overestimate the power of spending a little money by placing an ad in your local newspaper's classifieds section. One of the main benefits of advertising in your local paper is for whatever the small expense might be, you will be reaching many more potential customers than with free advertising alone. Serious garage sale aficionados, who are often big spenders at every sale they attend, scour the classifieds sections of the paper every week to map out a plan and decide which sales they will attend. Of course, every newspaper's fee structure is different, so contact your local classifieds section advertising sales rep to get an idea of what the actual fees are. Because of today's very tough economic climate, you may get a great deal to advertise your garage sale in your local newspaper. Why? For some time now, free online advertising websites such as Craigslist have been taking bigger and bigger bites out of the newspaper industry's advertising profits. Because of this trend in advertising, you may get a great deal on the ad rates. I can't guarantee anything, but you can always try.

You will need to begin creating all the signs for your sale a week prior to the sale. These signs will be placed around your immediate area and neighborhoods. They need to be placed in designated, high-traffic locations within twelve hours of your garage sale. The higher and faster the traffic area, the bigger your signs should be. I recommend obtaining white posterboard from an art or office supply store. You can even try going to frame stores that have tons of leftover scrap board you might be able to get for free. Once they use part of the mat board or cardboard, they throw away the other part. Trust me. I own an art gallery and I go through a lot of it myself: it really is a huge waste. My art gallery is just starting to recycle the mat board we don't use. So, going to a frame shop is one great way to get colorful mat board for your low-budget sale. You also need to make your sign extremely visible. Choose signs or boards that are either red or white. For lettering, use thick-tipped magic markers. On white signs or white boards, always use a red magic marker. If you're using red signs or red boards, always use a black magic marker. Green or brown colors get lost in the background of trees and yards.

If you're placing signs in speedy traffic areas, you'll want to use big mat boards. *When I say big, I mean BIG!* I am talking boards at least 3' high X 3' wide. If you're in an area where people are using pedestrian walkways and are leisurely walking with their children or dogs or going out for their daily jog, then you can use smaller signs to advertise your sale.

I recommend making about 20 signs and placing them on busy streets within three to five miles of your home. Be sure to take a staple gun with you as well as some duct tape. Never put your signs on traffic markers; that is against the law. Take the signs to as many busy streets as close to your home as possible. By placing the majority of your signs near stop signs or stop lights, people will have ample time to read them. If libraries, grocery stores or shopping malls are within three to five miles of your home, then these are also great places to put up signs. Be sure to place these signs near the parking lot exits as well.

Don't place signs in locations where traffic is moving very fast and streaking past. When you place a sign along a busy street and the cars are going about 45+ mph, what are the chances anyone is going to see that garage sale sign? The answer is little to none.

What should be written on your signs to achieve the best financial success at your sale? The address is the very first piece of information that needs to be listed. The day and time of your sale goes directly under the address. Also, with bullet points, include some key items you will have at the sale. Be focused. Only list the five most-sought-after main selling items. Anything more and your sign gets too crowded. People often make the big mistake of trying to squeeze too much information on a sign. Here are the top items people sell and what people look for most at garage sales—when these items are listed on a garage sale sign, people take notice and will make it a point to stop by and spend their money:

- **Antiques**
- **Tools**
- **Electronics**
- **Baby anything (i.e. clothes, cribs, toys)**
- **Bikes**
- **Collectibles**
- **Furniture**

Extras to Have at Your Sale that Will Help It Achieve World's-Greatest-Garage-Sale Status

A Refreshment Stand

When people come to a garage sale, especially in the hot summer months, they're going to get thirsty. The larger your sale, the longer people will pause and spend time looking at as many items as they can. As a result, they will want something to drink. *A refreshment stand at your sale will help make the shopping experience for your guests a much better one. It may also add some extra money in your pocket because people will stay longer if they are not hungry or thirsty.* If you have children of your own or know of some neighbor kids between the ages of five to sixteen years old, see if they want to have a lemonade or refreshment stand right next to your garage sale. Having kids selling soft drinks (that's pop or soda), iced tea, lemonade and/or bottled water will save you from having to run into your house for a cup of water when someone inevitably asks for a drink. Also, consider selling food items at your refreshment stand. These items could include cookies, candy, chips, popcorn or a variety of homemade baked goods. Shoppers will invariably be more relaxed and will have a more enjoyable time at your sale if they can quench their thirst and enjoy a snack! Always remember that if your customers are enjoying themselves, there's a good chance that they will spend more time and spend more money at your sale.

If you want to do the refreshment stand on a larger scale, contact your church or a local charity to see if they would like to host one at your garage sale. Good refreshment stands at garage sales easily net between $50 and $200. I've seen some refreshment stands take in almost as much as the actual garage sale itself.

More Tables Equal Better Profits

Earlier, I mentioned the necessity of having an adequate number of tables. When you hold your garage sale, you're going to need as many tables as possible to sufficiently display your items. *The more tables you have, the better a garage sale becomes . . . it never fails.* If you put all of your items in boxes, potential customers will have to make an exerted effort to rummage through everything. Sometimes people like that, but more often they don't. One of the most universal garage sale rules is *all items need to be laid out in plain sight.* If you're asking good money for something, you don't want to display your valued objects in a crowded pile or hidden in a box. If items are hidden in a box, there's a very real chance someone might not even see what you're trying to sell. Having all your treasures nicely laid out is a monumental plus. This means you're going to need those tables I mentioned earlier to show off your wares.

When you put the tables out, people might ask if you're going to sell the tables as well as what's on each table. When I say everything must go at a garage sale, I was not joking! You will need to determine ahead of time if you want to sell the tables and at what price you will want to sell them. Of course, only sell them if they're yours and aren't borrowed. If you have really ugly-looking tables, always cover them with attractive tablecloths. If you have items lying on top of an ugly, old and weathered table without a proper covering, the items for sale will appear to be ugly too.

Volunteers

When your garage sale is quite large, one or two people working the sale just won't do. There's no chance to be able to cover everything and help every customer with just a few people. This is especially true if you have multiple families selling their treasures at your garage sale. This is where having multiple volunteers comes in handy. If there are several families selling items at your garage sale, then each family really needs to have several helpers present. There are a few positive reasons for this:

> *People usually come to garage sales in groups.* There won't be anyone at your sale for a while and then all of a sudden, you'll find yourself inundated with 5 to 15 people all at once. One or two people staffing your sale won't be able to

provide the level of customer service your potential customers require. As a result of being understaffed, you'll end up losing money.

Shoppers need ample time to look at everything. Not only that, but they are going to want to chitchat with you and negotiate the price on almost everything. If you rush them, they'll become dissatisfied with your sale and walk away without buying anything. At a large garage sale, it is good to have at least three to five volunteers standing by, ready to help, answer questions and assist with getting items into shopper's cars.

There is a really good chance if you sell something large it's going to take a little time to settle on a price and help load it into a customer's car or truck. Having a volunteer who can just hang out and talk with the other customers, process any sales or just supervise the sale with help as needed (while you're busy helping others) will be a huge asset.

What Not to Do at Your Garage Sale

Do Not Let Strangers in Your Home ... EVER!

The major point I want you all to know and never forget, is to *NEVER LET ANYONE INTO YOUR HOME UNDER ANY CIRCUMSTANCE.* There are a few essential reasons why this is a good strategy:

People have been known to get into your house and case it. These strangers look over the contents within your home, see what they can find of value and check how your home is laid out for easy access and a quick exit. This is commonly referred to as casing the joint. Experienced thieves take everything they see into consideration so they can return later and rob you. Not good!

People have also been known to come into your house and take items while you're distracted or when you're not paying attention. Again, not good!

The shoppers and customers who come into your home to use the bathroom facilities might not be up to your level of cleanliness. The last thing you want to do is to clean up after a stranger who improperly uses your bathroom. This goes way beyond not good!

As you can see by the previous examples, nothing good can result by letting strangers into your house. In advance of your garage sale, make up some plausible excuses you're comfortable with using to avoid these types of situations. For example, you have a baby asleep inside, you have a sick parent or you own a dog that doesn't really get along with strangers. Whatever the reason is, always be prepared to convey it at a moment's notice.

Never Take Checks

It gets very difficult to turn down any sale especially in this economy and most especially when you are talking hundreds of dollars. People will try to convince you the only form of payment they have at the moment is a personal check. Some customers will go to great lengths to reassure you their check is legitimate. If you accept a check from someone you don't know and it turns out to be no good as is often the case, then you have only yourself to blame for your predicament. Not only will you have to pay your bank any NSF (Non-Sufficient Funds) fees for accepting a bad check, but you also get to keep the worthless check as a truly wonderful souvenir from your sale. Avoid these problems by never accepting a personal check.

> **Million $ Tip**
>
> Even if you post a sign stating "NO CHECKS WILL BE ACCEPTED" at your sale, people will still offer them as a viable payment option. Be firm. Sticking to your guns will save you a substantial amount of money.

You just can't afford to accept checks from people frequenting garage sales. Unfortunately, it's very likely that they don't have the money in their account to cover the amount written. A possible sale-saving solution for those experiencing financially rougher times is to ask them for a small cash deposit instead of a check. Tell them you'll hold the item they want for 48 hours so they can get the money when their bank opens or when they get paid. If they don't return at a certain time, advise them that their deposit is non-refundable. To prevent them disputing the deposit situation after the 48 hours time period has passed, or if you feel they might demand their money back, write a very informal agreement and have them date and sign it. That way you're completely covered from a legal standpoint. Under no circumstances would I ever accept a check from someone I don't know personally.

The Cash Back Artist

One of the biggest ripoffs at garage sales is one I call the Cash Back Artist.

Many garage sales get very busy and the owner of the garage sale is somewhat overwhelmed and usually distracted. Customers are constantly asking you for details about this item and that, negotiating prices on what they want to buy and confusion reigns supreme. Occasionally, you'll have a customer who may ask you to take a check, but then ask to write the check for more than the sales price of the item. The customer will then request the amount over the cost of the item to be handed back to them in cash.

For example, a seemingly decent looking, well-groomed shopper at your sale wants to buy a couch. You've priced the couch at $200. Then, the shopper says very convincingly, "Oh, man, I don't have enough cash on me. I'm so sorry. When I left the house this morning, I thought I put enough cash in my wallet. I must have gotten busy and I only have about $60 or $80 on me. The customer lets you see the actual cash in their wallet to suggest subliminally that you're dealing with what appears to be an honest person. "Can I write this check for $250 and could you give me the difference in cash?" The unknowing garage sale owner takes the check for the couch and feels good about the sale, but seven days later the check bounces.

Congratulations. Thanks to the Cash Back Artist you don't have your sofa, you are out an extra $50 in cash (that you handed out to the customer when you accepted his/her check) and you now owe your bank money to cover the NSF fees you accrued when the check bounced.

Additionally, Cash Back Artists may also use fake certified checks. This kind of activity happens often when you're dealing with transactions through Craigslist.

Do Not Give Out Your Telephone Number!

I never put my telephone number on any of my garage sale signs or in any of the advertisements I place. If you list your telephone number, you'll have people calling you at all hours of the day and night.

Incoming calls about your sale will sometimes last for weeks after the sale is over. You really need to think seriously about whether or not you want to divulge your number to the general public and exactly what the repercussions may be if you choose to do so. The only exception to this rule is if you give someone your telephone number because they are interested in buying an item from you after your garage sale ends.

Another reason not to display your number is that people don't value your time the same as you do. With your best intentions, you give the customer your telephone number so they are able to call back regarding an item if they have any questions or to arrange payment. The customer then decides to call you when you're in the middle of dinner, after you've gone to bed for the night or at any other extremely inconvenient time of day.

So remember, when you do give out your telephone number, you must consider what could happen in a worst-case scenario. If you must advertise your telephone number, use only a cellular telephone number that you can control.

Do Not Sell Anything Illegal

You may read this and think it's the most ridiculous thing I could say. You might also say, "Of course, who would be dumb enough to sell illegal items?" It's not as stupid a statement as you might think. I've been to many garage sales where honest people have unknowingly sold illegal items. Besides the obvious illegality of selling drugs, drug paraphernalia and fireworks, I need to clue you in on some very popular legal items that might be misconstrued as illegal if the circumstances were right.

Firearms and ammunitions are one of the biggest categories sold at garage sales. However, if not sold properly, the sale can constitute an illegal act. People don't usually set out to sell entire arsenals of illegal firearms, but if they sell their firearms and ammunitions improperly, they could end up serving jail time. If you want to sell firearms or ammunitions, you need to let a licensed gun store clear them for you first. Licensed gun stores will make all the proper background checks to ensure that people who are not allowed to purchase these items will not wind up getting them. Better yet, by going through licensed gun stores, you can almost assure yourself that you won't get into any legal trouble selling firearms.

The worst-case scenario you could encounter is if you were to sell a firearm improperly at your event and then, that firearm was used in the act of committing crime. In the event that this did happen, the authorities will come directly back to you and you will be entangled in a web of legal problems.

Fireworks are another item with tricky legal issues to sell at garage sales. Time and time again, I have seen people selling fireworks that are not legally allowed in their city or county. The worst-case scenario associated with selling fireworks is if someone becomes injured or has an accident with the fireworks you have sold. Profits from fireworks, whether illegal or not, would never be worth the risk of selling if they might potentially cause someone bodily harm. If a person gets hurt after they buy something from you, the most likely outcome will be that they will come back and aggressively sue you. We live in a very litigious society (if you haven't noticed already) and people are always looking for an easy way to make quick money from lawsuits. Be very mindful to ensure that anything you sell cannot harm anyone in any way.

Recalled items must never be sold at any garage sale. If you have something that has been recalled and you know it has been recalled, please don't ever try and sell it. The best thing you can do with any recalled item is throw it away or send it back to the manufacturer if there is a recall notice. Obviously, you don't want to sell an item such as baby furniture or children's toys that pose a potential health risk to anyone's family. So please, if you know something could be harmful, especially if it's been officially recalled, don't sell that item.

What Do You Do if You Can't Sell All of Your Items?

Here are some other possible options for disposing of things you couldn't sell at your garage sale. I mentioned using a private trash-hauling company to come to your home and remove any remaining items and I even talked about taking your items to secondhand stores to see if they could resell any of your unsold items, giving you a portion of the proceeds. What I didn't mention was using charities to take those leftover items. The benefit of donating your unsold items to a charitable organization comes in the form of potential tax write-offs. Of course, please consult with your personal tax professional to get an exact idea of what you can or cannot deduct from any charitable donation. By donating items to charity, not only will you be helping others in need, you will be helping yourself as well.

Now You Can Have The World's Greatest Garage Sale

I have to say that buying and selling items at estate auctions, garage sales and everything in-between is a highly enjoyable activity to engage in not to mention a highly profitable endeavor! Personally, I've had so much fun holding garage sales that I have hosted nearly 50 of them in my life and I don't plan on stopping any time soon. I absolutely know you're going to have a tremendous time holding your own garage sales as well.

By actively participating in estate auctions, buying and selling items online and using other means to buy and sell collectibles as outlined in this book—in addition to holding garage sales—you'll be making yourself some serious money.

My Last Million $ Tip for The Garage Sale Millionaire

The information I've presented in this book has helped me buy and sell tens of millions of dollars worth of collectibles over the course of 30+ years—not only as a fine art and collectibles gallery owner, but also as a Garage Sale Millionaire. If you adhere to the principles detailed in this book, you too can become a Garage Sale Millionaire.

Fortunately, all the profitable fun doesn't stop where this book ends. Please visit my website at www.thegaragesalemillionaire.com for more insider tips and need-to-know money-making information so I can continue to guide you in your quest in becoming the best Garage Sale Millionaire you can be! Also, if you have any questions for me about the book, the buying and selling process or if you want to share your successes with me (which I could possibly highlight in my next *The Garage Sale Millionaire* book), I'd love to hear from you at thegaragesalemillionaire@gmail.com.

I hear remarkable success stories all the time from other Garage Sale Millionaires. You now have the essential tools to successfully navigate your own course to become a Garage Sale Millionaire too! Those hidden gems and buried treasures are always out there just waiting for you to discover them. ***Get out there and claim your fortune!***

Conclusion

I wrote this book with the understanding that a lot of people have gotten into financial trouble and despair with the way the economy has been going. Many people over the last several years have lost their jobs and their home and don't know how to make ends meet. I, too, felt the crunch of the bad economy in my business as an art gallery owner. Since buying art is not on the top of the necessities list for people during financial hardships, my business suffered.

I had a lot of friends tell me I should teach others how I made my money both growing up and again in saving my business. This book is meant to be a resource for other people to have and learn from. I truly believe that if you follow the steps in this book, chapter by chapter, and start doing your research on becoming an expert in your own fields of items to buy and sell, you should be able to go to any garage sale, estate sale, storage unit auction or second hand store and feel comfortable looking at any of the items they have and be able to convert them into cold hard cash when you buy and flip them.

Please, after you've read all of the chapters, and when you feel like it's time for you to go out on your own and start your new venture of becoming a Garage Sale Millionaire, don't get caught up in the excitement of an auction or a sale and feel you have to buy things right away. Always do your research. Have fun. And good luck on your new journey to become a Garage Sale Millionaire.

Happy hunting!

Aaron

Glossary of Terms

#

3-D Card   A sports trading card that appears to be three-dimensional (3-D) when it is moved or tilted.

9-Up Sheets   Uncut sh eets imprinted with nine cards, usually used as promos. A term commonly used with sports and trading cards.

A

About Good   Refers to a coin with a grade of AG-3.

About Uncirculated   (1) Coins with grades of AU-50, AU-53, AU-55 and AU-58 on the Professional Coin Grading Service (PCGS) Grades and Grading Terms scale. (2) A coin that, at first glance, appears uncirculated, but upon closer inspection has slight friction or rub.

Abraded Corner   The grinding of a corner area on a comic book caused by improper handling or storage.

Absentee Bid   When this type of bid is allowed at an auction, a person can bid on any item without actually attending the event. The buyer submits in advance a written or oral bid that is the top price he/she will pay for a given auction item. Only the auctioneer knows this amount and the bid amount is kept private. The auctioneer bids on behalf of the absentee bidder until the buyer either wins the auction item or when the absentee buyer's maximum bid is exceeded.

Absolute Auction   An auction where property is sold to the highest qualified bidder with no limiting conditions.

Accessory Pack   A set of accessories, typically intended for a specific line of action figures and/or toys, which come packaged by themselves instead of with an individual action figure and/or toy.

Acid Cutting   A process used for decorating glass where objects were coated with an acid-resistant substance.

Action Figure   A doll-like plastic figure, that can be made to pose in different configurations. Action figures have come a long way over the years and many are now collected for the quality of manufacturing and for their resale potential. Action figures are usually licensed by comic book or entertainment companies.

Action Figure Authority (AFA)   Professional grading agency that verifies, authenticates and certifies items such as action figures, toys, die cast items and dolls. www.toygrader.com

Action Figure Authority (AFA) C-Scale Grading Scale:

C1–C4—Very poor, badly damaged, basically only useful for spare parts.

C5—Poor condition with heavy wear, broken parts will impair function.

C6—Fair, significant wear, may have some broken parts.

C7—Good, noticeable wear but no broken parts, items may be missing accessories.

C8—Very good, some minor wear, no broken or missing parts.

C9—Near mint condition, very minor imperfections apparent.

C10—Mint condition, unused.

Action Figure Authority (AFA) 3-Tier Grading Scale (for items produced from 1995 to present):

AFA Gold   Graded as Gem Mint (100), Mint (95) and Near Mint/ Mint (90). The AFA Gold level consists of the grades 100, 95 and 90. The select few figures that receive these grades are among the highest quality in existence. A very small percentage of figures submitted to the AFA receive a Gold grade. The flaws are very minor, very subtle and are sometimes very hard to identify with the naked eye. The collector who is extremely condition sensitive will only be satisfied with the condition of a Gold-level figure.

AFA Silver   Graded as Near Mint Plus (85), Near Mint (80) and Excellent Plus/Near Mint (75). The AFA Silver level consists of the grades 85, 80 and 75. The figures that receive these grades are in excellent condition. A figure graded as an 85 will often be referred to as case fresh and should be very close to Gold-level condition. The term case fresh is certainly justifiable, as the average figure pulled from a sealed case will grade an 85 due to small flaws that occur when the figures are packaged or shipped in the case. The average figure pulled from a store shelf is usually an 80, which represents a nice specimen with minor flaws apparent upon close inspection. The final Silver-level grade, a 75, represents an item with more minor flaws than the average Silver-level piece. An item grading 75 does have significant wear but does not have major flaws which would draw the eye to them at first glance. For most high-grade collectors, an 85 is satisfactory. For most discriminating collectors, an 80 is satisfactory. A 75 will be satisfactory to those who are not overly concerned with light stresses, small bubble imperfections and other flaws which do not jump out at first glance. Therefore, the Silver-level grades do represent a much larger range than the Gold-level grades.

AFA Bronze   Graded as Excellent Plus (70), Excellent (60), Very Good (50), Good (40), Fair (30), Poor (20) and Very Poor (10). The AFA Bronze level consists of the grades 70, 60 and below. The figures that receive these grades typically have damage ranging from simply noticeable upon first glance to extremely significant. The card may have creases on the front and the blister may be crushed or cracked. The Bronze level covers a large range of figure conditions and the scope of the flaws range considerably. Condition for Bronze-level figures is determined by how many major flaws are present on the card and how severe each flaw is. Bronze-level figures may have major flaws such as a torn off POP or other large paper tears.

Advance One Sheet   A 27- X 41-inch poster usually issued several months prior to the release of the movie.

After-Market   The market in which an item is sold after its initial retail availability.

Airbrushing   The art of touching up a photo prior to a sports trading card being printed to remove imperfections or to update the player's jersey or cap logo.

All Bisque   A doll, usually under eight inches in length, made entirely of bisque parts.

American Numismatic Association (ANA)   A non-profit numismatic organization founded in 1888. www.money.org

American Numismatic Association Certification Service (ANACS)   A third-party coin grading service. www.anacs.com

American Numismatic Society (ANS)   An organization dedicated to the study of coins, currency, medals, tokens and related objects from all cultures. www.numismatics.org

Animation Production Cel   A transparent sheet on which objects are drawn to create an animated cartoon. Animation production cels are currently hand-painted from behind onto celluloid acetate. In the early years of animation, these cels were made out of a thin plastic or nitrate with paint on the back or front of a cel. Each cel also represents one frame of a character's movement on film. Also known as a cel.

Annual   (1) A comic or comic book that is published yearly. (2) Some square-bound comics.

Annual Edition   A new collectible piece created each year.

Antiquarian Book   Originally this referred to an old and rare book, preferably at least 100 years old, similar to an antique, but the term has come to mean also any book that is out-of-print, old, rare, scarce, common, used or remaindered. Virtually any book that is not a new or in-print book.

Antique   Any work of art, piece of furniture, decorative object, created or produced in a former period or, according to United States Customs laws, 100 years before date of purchase.

Antiquities International   A retailer of one-of-a-kind collectibles, nostalgia and memorabilia from the worlds of history, entertainment and sports. Antiquities International coined the term *autographistry* to describe its technique of turning a piece of history into a work of art. The company was founded in 1984 and is headquartered in Las Vegas, Nevada. www.antiquitieslv.com

Anvil Die   The lower die used to stamp a coin, usually the reverse.

A/O   An abbreviation for All Original. An A/O action figure or toy comes complete with everything it came with, new and in its original packaging.

Appraisal   The process of evaluating the quality, condition, rarity, provenance and source of a particular item in order to establish its value.

Archival Mount   The way to have your art properly framed using acid-free materials that affix your art inside the frame.

Archival Quality   The conservation materials and techniques accepted by libraries for the preservation and permanent housing of their old and rare materials.

Armoire   A French term for a large freestanding closet for hanging clothes.

Artificial Toning   The coloring added to the surface of a coin by chemicals and/or heat.

Ask   The selling quotation of a coin either on a trading network, pricing newsletter or other medium.

Assay   To analyze and determine the purity of a metallic alloy.

Association Issue   A paper or magazine that can be verified and authenticated to have been owned by a person of historical importance.

Atom Age   The period recognized by the comic book industry between 1946 and 1956.

Attic Mint   A term used to refer to a collectible found in an attic or area of a building that has been left untouched for many years. This item may be dirty but in perfect condition.

Attributes   The elements that make up a coin's grade.

AU-50   Refers to the grade or quality of a particular coin based on the Professional Coin Grading Service (PCGS) Grades and Grading

Terms scale. This designation is for About Uncirculated (the grade) and 50 (the numerical designation of the grade). Also called Almost Uncirculated 50. This is the lowest of the four AU grades, with the others being AU-53, AU-55 and AU-58. Between 50% and 100% of the surfaces will exhibit luster disturbances and perhaps the only luster still in evidence will be in the protected areas. The high points of the coin will have wear that is easily visible to the naked eye.

AU-53   Refers to the grade or quality of a particular coin based on the Professional Coin Grading Service (PCGS) Grades and Grading Terms scale. This designation is for About Uncirculated (the grade) and 53 (the numerical designation of the grade). Also called Almost Uncirculated 53. There is obvious wear on the high points with light friction covering 50–75% of the fields. There are noticeable luster breaks, with most of the luster still intact in the protected areas.

AU-55   Refers to the grade or quality of a particular coin based on the Professional Coin Grading Service (PCGS) Grades and Grading Terms scale. This designation is for About Uncirculated (the grade) and 55 (the numerical designation of the grade). Also called Almost Uncirculated 55. There is slight wear on the high points with minor friction in the fields. Luster can range from almost nonexistent to virtually full, but it will be missing from the high points. The grade of Choice AU equates to AU-55.

AU-58   Refers to the grade or quality of a particular coin based on the Professional Coin Grading Service (PCGS) Grades and Grading Terms scale. This designation is for About Uncirculated (the grade) and 58 (the numerical designation of the grade). Also called Almost Uncirculated 58. There is the slightest wear on the high points, even though it may be necessary to tilt the coin towards the light source to see the friction. In many cases the reverse of an AU-58 coin will be fully Mint State. Less than 10% of the surface area will show luster breaks. The grade of Borderline Unc equates to AU-58.

Auction   The process of selling items through open, competitive bidding.

Auction Block   The specific area, usually on a podium or platform, where the auctioneer stands while conducting an auction.

Authentication   The process of determining the authentic qualities of a collectible item.

Authorized Issue   An issue or set of sports trading cards that are produced and distributed with the permission or written consent of the given league or player's association.

Autographed Card   A sports card that has been autographed, almost always by the player depicted on the card.

B

B&W   The abbreviation for black and white.

Backstamp   A legal mark or logo put on the bottom of a figurine or the back of a plate as proof of authenticity.

Bag Mark   The mark on a coin, made from another coin, while placed in a coin bag.

Bag Toning   The coloring on a coin acquired from the bag in which a coin was stored.

Bank Wrapped Rolls   The rolls of coins wrapped at a Federal Reserve Bank of the United States from original mint bags.

Barber Coinage   An alternate name used to describe the Charles Barber–designed Liberty Head dimes, quarters and half dollars struck between 1892 and 1916.

Barn Find   A car found in long-term storage, in highly original, although not necessarily orderly or complete condition. This term applies to cars and motorcycles.

Base Sets   A complete set of base cards for a particular trading card series.

Baseball Card   A sports trading card that features a professional baseball player or team.

Baseball Hall of Fame (HOF)   Located in Cooperstown, New York, the Baseball Hall of Fame features thousands of artifacts from the game of baseball including many game-used pieces of memorabilia. Any memorabilia associated with a player who is enshrined as a member of the Baseball Hall of Fame will carry more resale and collectible value. www.baseballhalloffame.org

Basining   The process of polishing a die to impart a mirrored surface or to remove clash marks or other injuries from the die.

Bazooka   A bubble gum–making subsidiary of Topps which made baseball cards between 1959 and 1971 and, once again, between 1988 and 1991. www.topps.com/candy/brands/Bazooka

Beckett   A well-known publisher of sports and specialty market collectible publications. Founded in 1984. www.beckett.com

Bibliophile   Someone who collects books.

Bid   (1) A prospective buyer's indication or offer of a price he or she will pay to purchase property at auction. (2) The buying quotation of a coin either on a trading network, pricing newsletter or other medium.

Bid Increments   The amount that a bid must be raised in an auction to be considered as acceptable. The proper bid increment amount depends on what the current bid is and the individual auction house's rules.

Bidder   A participant in an auction.

Bidder Number   The unique numbers assigned by auction houses to the various participants in their auction.

Bindery Defect   The defects associated with the binding process.

Bisque   Unglazed porcelain that is molded into a particular shape, then baked in high temperatures in a kiln to form doll heads and doll body parts.

Bisque Pottery   Unglazed porcelain or china that has had only one firing in the kiln.

Blacklist   A list that actively blocks certain bidders from participating in an auction. On eBay, a blacklist is the Blocked Bidder list.

Blank   The flat disk of metal before it is struck by the dies and made into a coin. Also known as coin blank.

Blank Back   A trading card that has nothing imprinted on the reverse side of the card.

Blind Box   A style of packaging that does not allow the purchaser to see the enclosed action figure inside its packaging.

Blister   The clear plastic shell attached to a card that encases an action figure or toy.

Blister Packs   A means of packaging action figures or toys within a clear plastic bubble glued to a cardboard backing. Many times blister packs are fitted with J-cards for better product placement in retail stores. Also known as a blister card.

Bobble Heads   A series of dolls that have heads that bobble and wobble. Bobble heads are manufactured in both limited and mass quantities.

Bowman   A well-known sports trading card manufacturer, established in 1948. Topps purchased the company in 1956.

Branch Mint (BM)   Any United States mint other than the mint located in Philadelphia, Pennsylvania.

Brass   A metal alloy comprised of approximately 50% copper and 50% zinc.

Breweriana   A category of beer-related antiques and collectibles such as advertisements, coasters, openers, labels, signs, steins, mugs, odd-sized cans, bottles and trays. www.americanbreweriana.org

Brilliant   A coin with full luster, unimpeded by toning or impeded only by extremely light toning.

Brilliant Uncirculated   Any coin that has never been in circulation.

British Issue   Comic books printed for distribution in Great Britain.

Brittleness   A severe condition of paper deterioration where paper loses its flexibility and easily chips, flakes and tears.

Brockage   A mint error that includes an early capped die impression where a sharp image has been left on the next coin fed into the coining chamber.

Bronze   A metal alloy comprised of approximately 83% copper, 13% tin, 3% zinc and 1% lead.

Bronze Age (B.A.)   (1) The Age of comic books after the Silver Age (S.A.). (2) A non-specific term that denotes comics published between 1970–1980.

Brown   A copper coin that no longer has the red color of copper.

Browning   (1) The aging of paper characterized by the ever-increasing level of oxidation characterized by darkening. (2) The level of paper deterioration one step more severe than tanning and one step before brittleness.

Buckled Die   A coin die that has warped in some way, possibly from excess clashing. A buckled die produces coins that are slightly bent.

Buffet   A French term for a small dining room sideboard used for dish storage, with drawers, cupboards and a flat surface for serving. The term is often used interchangeably with sideboard.

Buffalo Nickel   An Indian Head nickel struck between 1913 and 1938.

Bullion   A slang term used to describe coins, ingots or private issue numismatist items that trade below, at or slightly above their intrinsic metal value.

Burl   An abnormal growth on a tree such as found in the roots and crotches that produces a beautiful strongly grained wood prized in veneers.

Burnished   Refers to specially prepared planchets used for specimen coins or other special coins.

Burnishing   A process by which the surfaces of a planchet or a coin are made to shine. Acheived through rubbing or polishing.

Burnishing Lines   Lines resulting from burnishing, seen mainly on open collar proofs and almost never found on close collar proofs. This term is commonly used with coins.

Burnt   A slang term used to describe a coin that has been over-dipped to the point where the surfaces are dull and lackluster.

Burr   A type of veneer.

Bust Dollar   A particular type of silver dollar that was struck and minted between 1795 and 1803.

Buyer's Premium   The additional fee paid to the auction house by the buyer or winning bidder at an auction.

C

C Mint   The term applied to gold coins struck and minted at the Charlotte, North Carolina branch mint. This mint uses the C mintmark.

C Scale   A common grading system used to convey the condition of a toy being sold or traded among collectors. See *Action Figure Authority (AFA) C-Scale Grading Scale.*

Cabriole   A style of leg on a chair or table that has an S shape.

Cameist   A person who collects glass or stone cameos.

Cameo   The brief appearance of one character in the comic strip of another.

Cameo Glass   A technique used on glass or stone to create a decorative effect of contrasting colors.

Canadian   Coins and other numismatic items from Canada.

Canadian Silver   Describes silver coins struck and minted from Canada.

Carbon Spot   A spot seen mainly on copper and gold coins, though also occasionally found on U.S. nickel coins and silver coins.

Carded   Denotes an unopened action figure. A carded action figure is understood to be in mint condition.

Cartwheel   The visual effect seen on some coins when they are rotated in good light. The luster of the coin then rotates around the coin like spokes of a wagon wheel.

Case Fresh   A toy or action figure that has come directly out of the factory case or box.

Cases   A factory-sealed crate filled with card boxes. A case usually includes 6 to 12 card boxes per case with 24 packs of cards per box.

Cast Counterfeit   A replication of a genuine coin usually created by making molds of the obverse and reverse then casting base metal in the molds.

Caveat Emptor   A Latin term meaning let the buyer beware. A buyer takes the risk regarding quality or condition of the property purchased, unless that item is protected by a warranty.

CC Mint   The term applied to coins struck and minted at the Carson City, Nevada branch mint. This mint uses the CC mintmark.

CCA Seal   Emblem that was placed on the cover of all Comics Code Authority-Approved (CAA-Approved) comics beginning in April and May of 1955.

Cel   See *Animation Production Cel.*

Cello   A type of trading card pack whose wrapper is plastic and see-through. Those packs that haven't been opened, with a major star's card showing, have a premium value.

Celluloid   (1) The earliest plastic used to make dolls. (2) The full name used for an Animation Production Cel.

Cent   A coin with a denomination valued at one-hundredth (1/100) of a dollar.

Centerfold   (1) The two folded pages in the center of a comic book at the terminal end of the staples. Also known as center spread. (2) Usually a portrait such as a pin-up or nude inserted in the middle of the publication. Commonly found in adult magazines.

Centering   Refers to the evenness of the white space or border (if any) around a baseball card's main image. Centering is measured left-to-right and top-to-bottom and is defined in percentages.

Ceramic   A product of baked clay, porcelain, pottery, tile or earthenware.

Certificate of Authenticity (COA)   (1) A document issued by a seller that guarantees that the item is authentic. (2) A document that accompanies a piece denoting the name of the manufacturer, artist, date, size of the edition, etc.

Certification   The professional evaluation of the grade and condition of a collectible (e.g., comic books, movie memorabilia, signatures and autographs, etc.), including examination for restoration and other characteristics of an item's integrity.

Certified Coin Exchange (CCE)   The largest online dealer-to-dealer numismatic network in the world dealing in rare coins. You must be a professional numismatist with extensive experience and excellent trading references from current dealers to be a member of CCE. www.certifiedcoinexchange.com

Certified Guaranty Company (CGC)   The first independent third-party grading service specializing in comic books and photographs. www.cgccomics.com

Certified Guaranty Company (CGC) Grading Scale

    0.5—Poor

    1.0—Fair

    1.5—Fair/Good

    1.8—Good−

    2.0—Good

    2.5—Good+

    3.0—Good/Very Good

    3.5—Very Good

Chasing   (1) A method used by forgers to create a false mintmark on a coin. (2) Process of engraving or embossing to decorate a toy or bank. (3) In antique furniture, a method of decorating silver and other metals by creating a raised pattern using a hammer or punch.

Chip Cut   A missing piece of a comic or comic book that is smaller than one square millimeter.

Chippendale   A neoclassical style of furniture developed in the mid-18th century by English designer and furniture maker, Thomas Chippendale.

Circa   Applied before each approximate date, while dates without a circa immediately preceding them are generally assumed to be known with certainty.

Circulation   A term applied to describe coins that have been used in everyday commerce.

Clamshell   Action figure and toy packaging designed to be resistant to dents and bending. Clamshell packaging is also extremely difficult to open.

Clash Marks   The images of the dies seen on coins struck from clashed dies.

Clashed Dies   Coin dies that have been damaged by striking each other without a planchet between them.

Classic Car   (1) Any car that is 25 years old or older. (2) A range of vehicles built mostly from 1925 to 1948. (3) Made to describe a new vehicle, one that is immediately sought after such as a Ferrari, Lamborghini or Aston Martin, from the moment the vehicle leaves the manufacturing plant.

Classic Cover   A comic book cover considered by collectors to be highly desirable because of its historical importance, subject matter and artwork.

Classic Era   The period between 1792 and 1964 when silver and gold coins of the United States were issued.

Cleaned   A coin whose original surface has been removed.

Clip   A coin struck from a clipped planchet.

Clipped   A coinage term for an irregularly cut planchet.

Clogged Die   A die of a coin that has grease or some other contaminant lodged in the recessed areas.

Close Collar   The edge device, sometimes called a collar die, that surrounds the lower die of a coin.

Closing   The time that the last bid at an auction will be accepted.

Club Piece   A piece, usually considered a collector's item, that is included in the annual membership dues of a collector's club.

CNP   An abbreviation for Complete No Package.

Coach's Card   A sports trading card that features a coach or group of coaches.

Coat-Tail   A political item or pin where local political candidates take advantage of the popularity and/or awareness of the national candidate to enhance their own chance for being elected. A coat-tail pin would have a local candidate's picture displayed alongside a national candidate's name or picture.

Coin Blank   The flat disk of metal before it is struck by the dies and made into a coin. Also known as a blank.

Coin Silver   The proportion of silver used in American coins.

Coin Universe Daily Price Guide   A price guide which lists approximate selling prices for Professional Coin Grading Service (PCGS) graded coins. www.pcgs.com/prices

Coinage   The issuance of metallic money from a particular country.

Cold-cast   A type of resin that is set by a chemical process as opposed to the application of heat.

Cold Paint   The finish of a pottery and/or ceramic item.

Collar   A metal piece that either positions a planchet beneath the die and/or restrains the expanding metal of a coin during striking.

Collectible   An item or items people like to acquire and collect. Some individuals obtain items to add to their specific collections while other individuals acquire items to resell for profit.

Collectible Doll Authority (CDA)   Professional grading agency that verifies, authenticates and certifies all packaged dolls and related items. www.dollgrader.com

Color Flake/Color Fleck   This happens when the color layer has been lost on a comic, making the white paper substrata (the underlying layer) visible.

Colorist   The artist who applies color to black and white (B&W) pen and ink art.

Color Touch   A comic book restoration process by which colored ink is used to hide color flecks, color flakes and larger areas of missing color.

Comic Book Restoration   Any attempt, whether professional or amateur, to enhance the appearance of a comic book.

Comics Code Authority (CCA)   Also known as the Comics Magazine Association of America, which was founded in 1954.

Commemorative   Specific coins issued to honor a person, place or event. Commemoratives are also issued to raise funds for activities related to a particular theme.

Commercial Strike A synonym for a coin's regular strike or business strike.

Complete An action figure or toy that comes with all its accessories included.

Complete Run All comic book issues from a specific title grouping.

Con A convention or public gathering of fans. The annual San Diego Comic-Con International, held in San Diego, California, draws over 100,000 attendees during its four-day event. www.comic-con .org/cci/

Condition The state of preservation of a particular collectible item.

Condition Census A listing of the finest known examples of a particular issue.

Conditions of Sale The legal terms that govern the conduct of an auction. Conditions of sale include acceptable methods of payment, buyer's premiums, seller's premiums, terms and any other important rules of an auction.

Consensus Grading The process of determining the condition of a coin by using multiple graders.

Contact Marks Marks on a coin that are incurred through contact with another coin or a foreign object.

Contemporary Counterfeit A coin, usually base metal, struck from crudely engraved dies and made to pass for face value at the time of its creation.

Continental Dollars Dollar coins struck in 1776.

Copper Spot A spot or stain commonly seen on gold coinage.

Copper Nickel This alloy, composed of approximately 12% nickel and 88% copper, was used for small cents between 1856 and 1864.

Copper Nickel Cent A copper nickel alloy used in cents struck between 1859 and 1864.

Corrosion The damage that results when reactive chemicals act upon a metal.

Counterfeit A coin that is not genuine or authentic. Many times the term counterfeit is used when discussing paper currency. This term has the same meaning for both coinage and currency.

Counterstamp An impression or stamp placed on a coin after it has left the originating mint.

Counting Machine Mark Refers to a dense patch of lines caused by the rubber wheel of a counting machine. This defect occurs when the rubber wheel of a counting machine was set with insufficient spacing for the selected coin at the time in which the coin was struck and minted.

Coupon Cut/Clipped   A comic book with a missing coupon. Also known as coupon missing.

Cover Gloss   The reflective quality of the cover ink.

Cover Loose   (1) Cover has become completely detached from the staples. (2) Cover moves around on the staples but is not completely detached from the staples.

Cover Off   Refers to when a comic book cover is completely detached from the staples.

Cover Reattached   Refers to when a comic book cover has been repaired/restored to hold staples and reattached to comic interior.

Cover Trimmed   Refers to a comic book cover when it has been reduced in size by neatly cutting away rough or damaged edges.

Crazing   (1) A close network of very fine cracks on the top surface as in the glaze of ceramics. (2) Aging lines that run through the paint on vintage toys and banks.

Crease   (1) A fold in a comic, periodical, book, or magazine that causes ink removal usually resulting in a white line. (2) A paper wrinkle defect caused by bending a trading card.

Crossover   (1) A coin that was graded the same at two different grading services. (2) A comic book story where one character appears prominently in the story of another character. Also called X-Over.

Crystal   A type of fine quality glass created in 17th-century England that is highly transparent and contains a larger proportion of lead oxide. The percentage of lead oxide required to be defined as crystal varies according to the country. In the United States an item is considered being authentic crystal with only 1% lead oxide content, while in Europe a 10% lead oxide content is required.

Cud   An area of a coin struck by a die that has a complete break across part of its surface.

Cull   A coin that is basically non-collectible due to its extremely bad condition.

Custom   An action figure not released in stores, but made by a collector usually by using parts from existing action figures.

Cut Signature   A signature that was cut away from a document, book or photo and, as a result, the signature stands alone.

CVR   An abbreviation for comic book cover.

D

D Mint   (1) Coins struck and minted at the Dahlonega, Georgia mint between 1838 and 1861. (2) Coins struck and minted at the Denver, Colorado branch mint starting in 1906. These mints use the D mintmark.

Date Stamp   The arrival date or other date printed in ink somewhere in or on a comic by use of a stamp and stamp pad.

De-Acidification   The process of neutralizing harmful acids from the paper in a comic book, by applying a special solution of calcium carbonate.

Dealer   (1) Someone whose occupation involves the buying, selling and trading of numismatic materials. (2) An individual who sells toys, action figures and collectibles on the after-market.

Debut   The first time a character ever appears in a comic. Debut may also refer to the first issue of a comic book.

Deep Cameo   A proof and proof-like coin, that has deeply frosted devices and lettering that contrast with the fields. Also known as a black and white cameo.

Deep Mirror Proof–Like   Any coin that has deeply reflective mirror-like fields.

Defect   Any fault, flaw or negative characteristic in the quality of a comic book that detracts from its perfection.

Denomination   The value assigned to a specific coin by a government. For example, the denomination of a U.S. nickel is five cents.

Dent   An indentation usually on the cover of a comic, that does not penetrate the paper nor remove any material or gloss.

Denticles   Small, toothlike design elements all the way around the perimeter of some coins, especially of the 18th and 19th centuries.

Depression Glass   Glassware manufactured around the time of the Great Depression between the late 1920s and the early 1940s.

Designer   An individual whom is responsible for a particular design used in a numismatic series.

Device Punch   A steel rod with a raised device on the end used to punch the element into a working coin die.

Die   A steel rod that is engraved, punched and/or hubbed with devices, lettering and the date for use in the minting of a coin.

Die Alignment   Indicates the relative positioning of the obverse and reverse dies used on a coin.

Die Break   A defective area of a coin that is the result of a broken die.

Die-Cast   An action figure or toy that is manufactured out of metal.

Die-Cast Authority (DCA)   Professional grading agency that verifies, authenticates and certifies die-cast and various other related items. www.diecastgrader.com

Die Crack   A raised and irregular line on a coin.

Die-Cut Cover   When areas of a comic book cover are precut by a printer to a special shape or to create a desired effect.

Die Line   Raised lines on a coin that result from the polish lines on the die.

Die Rust   Rust that has accumulated on a coin die that was not properly stored.

Die Stage   Refers to the specific status of a certain coin's die state.

Die State   A readily identified point in the life of a coin die.

Die Striations   Raised lines on coins which were struck with polished dies.

Die Trial   A test striking of a particular die of a coin in a different metal.

Die Variety   A coin that can be linked to a given set of dies due to the characteristics possessed by those dies and imparted to the coin at the time it was struck.

Die Wear   Deterioration in a die caused by excessive use.

Dipped   A coin that has been placed in a commercial dip solution. This solution consists of a mild acid wash that results in the removal of the toning from most coins.

Direct Metal Mastering (DMM)   During the vinyl record production process the master disc is cut on a copper-coated disc which produces a high-quality audio record. The use of the DMM process also seemed to improve the lifetime of the vinyl discs.

Disme   The original spelling of the U.S. dime.

Distressed   An object that has been artificially aged.

Distributor Stripes   Color brushed or sprayed on the edges of comic book stacks by the distributor/wholesaler to code them for expedient exchange at the sales racks. Also referred to as DISTRO Ink.

Doctored   A numismatic item that has been enhanced by chemical or other means.

Double Cover   A bindery defect where two covers are stapled to the comic book interior instead of the usual one.

Double Eagle   Refers to a twenty dollar United States gold coin which was issued between 1850 and 1932.

Doubled Die (DD)   A die that has been struck more than once by a hub in misaligned positions, resulting in doubling of design elements. The most famous Doubled Die coin in United States numismatics is the 1955 Doubled Die Lincoln cent.

Double Struck (DS)   A condition that results when a coin is not ejected from the dies and is struck a second time.

Dovetail   An antique furniture-making term used to describe a joint that fits two pieces of wood tightly together. The wedge-shape resembles a dove's tail and is used to join corners of case pieces and drawers.

Draped Bust   A coin design that features Miss Liberty with a drape across her bust.

Dribbler   The nickname for solid brass, steam-powered toy locomotives manufactured in Britain from the 1840s to the early 1900s.

Drift Mark   The area on a coin that has a discolored or streaky look.

Dry Press   The machine used to flatten out comics with rolled spine and folds.

Due Diligence   The process of gathering information about the condition and legal status of assets to be sold.

Duotone   Comics printed with black ink and one other color of ink.

Dust Jacket   A paper cover used to protect the binding of a book from dust and wear.

Dust Shadow   A darker, usually linear area at the edge of some comics stored in stacks.

Dutch Auction   This occurs when a seller has several, sometimes many, identical items for sale at an auction. Every winning bidder pays the exact same price for each auction item no matter the amount of their bid. The final sales price of each item will be the lowest bid that is successful on all of the same items up for that particular Dutch auction.

E

E-Unit   The mechanism that provides the reverse sequence on toy trains. There are two-position (forward-reverse) models and three-position (forward-neutral-reverse) models.

Eagle   A gold coin which has a face value of ten dollars U.S.

Ear   The area of a coin that is most important to the strike.

Early Strike   One of the first coins struck from a pair of dies.

eBay   The biggest worldwide online sales and marketing site. www.ebay .com.

Ebonized   A term used to describe antique furniture stained with a black color imitating the color of ebony.

Edge   The third side of a coin. Not the obverse or reverse of a coin, but the side or rim of a coin.

Edge Defects   Defects that occur to the edges of a comic or comic book.

Edge Device   A group of letters or emblems on the edge of a coin.

Electrotype   Refers to a duplicate coin created utilizing the electrolytic method.

Elements   The various components used for grading a coin.

Embossed   Refers to the raised, relief or dimensional design on paper or cardboard.

Embossed Cover   When a pattern is embossed onto the comic book cover that creates a raised area.

Emission Sequence   The order or sequence in which coin die states are struck.

Engraver   The individual who is responsible for the design and/or punches used for a particular numismatic item.

Envelope Toning   The toning or discoloration of a coin, which results from storage, mainly in a small 2 × 2-inch manila envelope.

Environmental Damage (ED)   The corrosion effects seen on a coin that has been exposed to the elements.

Eraser Mark   Damage that remains when pencil marks are removed from the cover or inside of a comic.

Eroded Die   Also known as a Worn Die.

Error Coin   A coin that accidentally varies from the norm.

Error Card   A sports trading card that contains some sort of mistake or error, such as a misspelling or a photo of someone other than the athlete named on the card.

Escrow   A transaction that involves a buyer, seller and an escrow company. The buyer pays the cost of the item directly to the escrow company and the escrow company holds the money from the sale until the buyer receives the item and is completely satisfied with his/her purchase. Once the buyer is completely satisfied the item is as advertised, the escrow company releases the held funds and pays the seller.

Essai   The term for trial, pattern or experimental strikings on a coin.

Estate Sale   The sale of property left by a person after his/her death.

Event Piece   An item or piece that is made specifically for a particular event. This item is available only to those who attend the particular event.

Ex-Libris A book that was once owned by someone whose ownership adds value, often from someone who is famous or notable. An ex-libris item is typically indicated by some ownership marking such as a stamp or seal, a signature or handwritten note.

Excellent Condition An item not in mint or perfect condition, but one that is found to have no major flaws.

Exclusive A specific type of action figure or toy, sold through only one store or a limited number of specific stores, often considered rare.

Exhibit Card A larger size of sports or non-sports trading card, usually the size of a postcard.

Extremely Fine Refers to the coin grades of EF-40 and EF-45 on the Professional Coin Grading Service (PCGS) Grades and Grading Terms scale. This grade has nearly full detail with only the high points worn, the fields rubbed often with luster still clinging in protected areas.

Extremely High Relief A feature on a coin where the mint engraver lowers the design on a coin.

Eye Appeal (1) The element of a coin's grade that makes a coin more appealing to a collector. (2) A term that refers to the overall look of a comic book when held at approximately arms length.

F

Face Value The stated value on a coin that can be spent or exchanged.

Facsimile Autograph A simulated, usually machine-printed autograph designed to duplicate a player's signature on a sports trading card. Not an authentic autograph.

Factory Sets Trading card sets, typically complete base sets, sorted and sold directly from the factory.

Fading Color fading that occurs on a comic exposed to sunlight or certain fluorescent lights that give off a moderate to high concentration of ultraviolet light.

Fake Also known as a copy, replica or faux. (1) A copy of a legitimate item that is created to deceive the buyer. (2) A slang term used to describe a counterfeit or altered coin.

Fanboy A fan, aficionado or supporter is someone who has an intense, occasionally overwhelming liking and enthusiasm for a sporting club, person (usually a celebrity), group of persons, company, product, activity, work of art, idea or trend. Fans of a particular thing or person constitute its fanbase or fandom. They often show their enthusiasm by starting a fan club, holding fan conventions, creating fanzines, writing fan mail or promoting the object of their interest and attention.

Fantasy Piece   (1) An item made to look like an authentic item that was never manufactured, produced or licensed by the company that holds intellectual rights property of that particular item. Many modelers and hobbyists on the Internet make items that replicate a specific collectible out of their love and fandom for a particular item. (2) A term applied to coins struck at the desire or whim of mint officials.

Fashion Doll   A French or German female doll made generally with a bisque head and dressed in fashions of the day.

Faux   Another term for a fake item. See *Fake*.

FAQ   The abbreviation for Frequently Asked Questions. FAQs are listed questions and answers, all pertaining to a particular topic. This is a commonly used term on the Internet.

FC   An abbreviation for front cover, the first page of a comic.

Feedback   On eBay, the positive or negative comments left by both buyer and seller for each other. Feedback helps establish the reputation of the buyer or seller. Receiving positive feedback is extremely important for any seller on eBay if that seller wants to run a successful business on the website.

Fiat Currency   Coins and paper money (for example a U.S. one-dollar bill) that do not have metal value.

Field   The area on a coin where there is no design.

File Copy   A high-grade comic book originally from the publisher's own files.

Fine   The term referring to the coin grades of F-12 and F-15 on the Professional Coin Grading Service (PCGS) Grades and Grading Terms scale. Most of a coin's detail is worn away although some detail is present in a coin's recessed areas.

Finest Known   The best known example of a particular coin.

Finger Oils   Finger oils cause a damaging effect when comics and comic books are handled with bare hands. The oil from an individual's hands and fingers degrade the comic or comic book over time.

First Appearance   See *Debut*.

First Shot   A slang term used to describe the opportunity to get the first opportunity to buy items from a particular numismatic deal or from a particular dealer.

Five Indian   Also known as an Indian Head Half Eagle coins, which were struck between 1908 and 1929.

Five Lib   Also known as Liberty Head Half Eagle coins, which were struck between 1839 and 1908.

Flange Neck   A flange neck or the cup and saucer joint as it is occasionally called, is when the bottom of the dolls head piece and the top of the doll's shoulder piece fit together on a flat surface. This is most commonly found on cloth-bodied dolls with a rim around the neck.

Flashback   When a previous story in a comic is recalled in a later story.

Flat Luster   A subdued type of luster that can be seen on coins struck from worn dies.

Flatware   Any flat or shallow tableware.

Flats   Two-dimensional lead soldiers with engraved decorations.

Flip   (1) The plastic sleeve in which coins are stored. (2) To quickly sell a recently purchased coin or any collectible for that matter, usually for a quick profit.

Flip Rub   The discoloration of the highest points of a coin resulting from contact with a flip.

Flirty Eyes   The eyes of a doll that can move from side to side.

Flop   To sell a new coin purchase for a quick profit.

Flow Lines   The lines on a coin that result from the metal flowing outward from the center of a planchet as it is being struck.

Flying Eagle   Another term used to describe a Flying Eagle cent.

Flying Eagle Cent   A small cent that replaced the large cent. Also known as a Flying Eagle.

Focal Area   The area of a coin to which a viewer's eye is drawn.

Foil Cover   A thin metal foil that is hot stamped onto the cover of a comic book during manufacturing.

Folding Error   A bindery defect in which a comic is folded off-center, resulting in part of the front cover appearing on the back cover or more seriously, part of the back cover appearing on the front cover.

Folds   Linear dents in comic book paper that do not result in the loss of ink. Not considered a crease.

Four Color Process   The name given to the process of comic book printing which includes three primary colors (red, yellow and blue) plus black.

Foxed A defect caused by mold growth that results in a spotting effect usually at the edges of a comic.

Franklin Half Dollar One of the United States' official fifty-cent coins minted from 1948 to 1963 which featured the image of Benjamin Franklin. This fifty-cent coin was replaced by the Kennedy half dollar in 1964. Like the Kennedy half dollar, this coin carries a value of fifty cents or fifty one-hundredths (50/100) of a dollar.

Fugio Cents Refers to one of the first coins authorized by the Continental Congress for minting in 1787.

Full Strike A coin that displays the full detail intended by the designer.

G

Gem The description applied to a Mint State and Proof 65 (MS/PR-65) coin.

Genre A category defining a comic book's subject matter—science fiction, super hero, romance, funny animal, teenage humor, crime, war, western, mystery and horror are all examples of specific genres.

Gift Pack A toy train set sold without a track or transformer.

Gilt Also known as gilding, it is a process by which an object is decorated with a thin layer of gold, gold leaf or gold foil. This technique is used on glass, ceramics, furniture and picture frames.

Glue (or) **Glued** A restoration method in which some form of glue was used to repair or reinforce a comic book defect.

Golden Age of Comics (G.A.) The Golden Age of comics occurred between June, 1938 (with the publication of Action Comics #1) and the end of World War II (approximately 1945).

Good The term that corresponds to the coin grades of G-4 and G-6 on the Professional Coin Grading Service (PCGS) Grades and Grading Terms scale. Coins in these grades usually have little detail but outlined major devices.

Googly Eyes A doll that has big, round and side-glancing eyes.

Goudey A very popular sports trading card manufacturer that produced cards between 1933 and 1941.

Grade The numerical condition of a coin.

Grader An individual who evaluates the condition of coins.

Grading The process of numerically quantifying the condition of a coin.

Grease Pencil A wax-based marker commonly used to write on cardboard.

Grease Pencil on Cover   Indicates that someone marked the cover of a comic with a grease pencil, usually with a resale price or an arrival date.

Grey Tone Cover   A comic book cover art style that uses an underlying pencil or charcoal under the normal line drawing to enhance the effects of light and shadow.

Gum Stain   A trading card that is marred by bubble gum that was once inserted in the pack. This term usually refers to sports trading cards.

H

Hairline(s)   (1) The term associated with pottery items when a small crack, with the approximate thickness of a strand of hair occurs. (2) A type of crack in bisque dolls that can often only be seen upon close examination with the help of direct lighting. (3) Fine cleaning lines found mainly in the fields of proof coins.

Half Cent   The lowest value coin denomination ever issued by the United States.

Half Eagle   A coin with a face value of half the value of an Eagle. The Eagle has a face value of ten silver dollars U.S.

Halftone   The process by which photographs are converted into printable images.

Hallmark   (1) The distinguishing mark used by silversmiths and goldsmiths to identify who made a particular piece. (2) A mark used to guarantee an item was made from metal of a high-quality. (3) The mark(s) stamped on silver or gold objects when passed at assay. See *Assay*.

Hammer Price   The price established by the last bidder. This final bid is acknowledged by the auctioneer before he officially drops the hammer or gavel.

Hard Plastic   A type of durable plastic used to make dolls from the 1940s and 1950s.

Heavy Creasing   A crease in a comic book that is longer than two inches.

Heavypack   An action figure included in a pack in excess quantities. There are more per case of this one item than the rest of its companions. The opposite of a shortpack.

Hickory   A hardwood tree that grows in the eastern half of the United States. It is a very tough, heavy wood used on furniture requiring both thinness and strength, such as veneers and woven seats.

High Number   The last or near the last series in a sports trading card set.

Highboy (1) A tall chest of drawers on a four-legged base. (2) A two-part case piece.

Hoard A group of coins, large or small, held by a coin collector for either numismatic or monetary reasons.

Hoarder (1) Someone who buys action figures and/or toys solely with the intent to resell. This person will buy as many of a single item as they can and stockpile them away, in the hope that the item's collectible and resale value will increase. (2) A coin collector who amasses a very large collection of coins.

Hobby Cards Items sold mainly to collectors through stores dealing exclusively in collectible cards.

Hobo Nickel An Indian Head or Buffalo nickel which has been engraved with a portrait of a hobo or character other than a buffalo or Indian head.

Hockey Card A sports trading card that features a professional hockey player or team.

Holder Toning Any toning on a coin's surface that appears as the result of its storage in a coin holder.

Hologram A three-dimensional image. Unlike regular images, which are usually two dimensional, a three-dimensional image, or hologram, appears to pop out of the media it is printed on or illuminated from. When collectible merchandise and memorabilia is professionally graded, the agency verifying an item's authenticity will affix a sticker that displays a one-of-a-kind image in the form of a hologram. This proves the item is deemed to be authentic.

Hologram Cover True 3-D holograms are prepared and affixed to comic book covers and trading cards for special effects.

Hot Stamping The process of pressing foiled prism paper and inks on comic book cover stock.

HTF An abbreviation for hard to find.

Hub A coin minting term for the steel device from which a die is produced.

Hutschenreuther The family name of the German company known for their fine porcelain plates, dinnerware and figurines which was established in 1814.

I

IBC The abbreviation for inside back cover.

Iconophile Someone who collects prints, engravings and is a connoisseur of icons or images.

IFC An abbreviation for inside front cover.

Imbrication   A decorative design carved into a piece of furniture that resembles overlapping fish scales.

Impaired Proof   A proof coin that grades less than an MS/PR-60. Also known as a circulated proof.

Incomplete   An action figure or toy that comes with some accessories.

Incomplete Strike   A coin that is missing design detail because of a problem during the striking process.

Incremental Bidding   Occurs when you bid enough to be high bidder, but not your maximum and then bidding again when someone tops your bid. In this instance, it's important to stay close to the computer in the last hours of bidding to continue bidding if you're outbid. This is also the time when sniping can come into play. If you're not willing to put your maximum bid up early, someone could come in and bid their maximum in the last few seconds not leaving you enough time to respond.

Note: Online auction houses will use an automatic incremental bidding system that allows you to secretly bid your maximum, but only comes into play when there are other bids.

Incuse Design   The intaglio design used on an Indian Head quarter, Eagle or Half Eagle.

Indian Cent   The common name used for an Indian Head cent.

Indian Head Cent   Refers to cents minted between 1859 and 1909 which have an Indian head on the front side of the coin.

Indian Head Eagle   The Saint Gaudens–designed ten dollar gold coin minted between 1907 and 1933.

Indian Penny   Also known as an Indian Head Cent.

Indicia   Publishing and title information usually located at the bottom of the first page or the bottom of the inside front cover of a comic book. In some pre-1938 comics, the indicia was sometimes located on an internal page.

Initials on Cover   Someone's initials in pencil, pen or grease pencil on the cover of a comic. Also known as Init. on CVR.

Ink Skip   A printing defect in which the printing roller momentarily receives no ink causing a streak or blank spot.

Ink Smudge   A printing defect in which ink is smeared, usually by handling or binding before the ink is completely dry.

Inker   The artist who lays the inks over the penciler's artwork.

Insert Cards   Non-rare to rare cards which are randomly inserted into packs in various ratios such as one per 24 packs. An insert card is often different from the main set and contains a different number on the back such as SS01 to SS10. Also known as chase cards.

Inset Eyes   A doll's eyes that are set into the doll's head and do not move.

Intaglio   An incised gemstone or any incised decoration on furniture.

Intaglio Eyes   A doll's eyes that are molded into the head. Intaglio eyes are meant to be painted.

Intaglio Print   An image that is printed from a recessed design incised or etched into the surface of a plate.

Intrinsic Value   The value of the metal(s) contained within a coin.

Investment Grade Copy   (1) A comic of sufficiently high grade and demand to be viewed by collectors as instantly liquid should the need to sell it arise. (2) A comic purchased primarily to achieve a profit.

Irvington Cars   Lionel's pre-war (#2623 and #2624) and post-war (#2625, #2627 and #2628) and 12-wheel semi-scale passenger cars. Made of compression-molded Bakelite. Irvington Cars were styled after 1920s-era Pullmans.

Issue Number   The actual edition number of a given comic or comic book title.

Issue Price   The manufacturer's suggested retail price (MSRP) of an action figure or toy when it is first introduced in the marketplace.

J

James Spence Authentication (JSA)   Internationally recognized memorabilia authentication experts based in Parsippany, New Jersey. www.spenceloa.com.

Jefferson Nickel   The official U.S. five-cent coin picturing President Thomas Jefferson. The Jefferson nickel was first minted in 1938 and carries a value of five cents or five one-hundredths (5/100) of a dollar. Also known as a nickel.

Jersey Cards   A sports trading card containing a piece of material taken from a jersey worn by a player or athlete.

Joined Pages   (1) A bindery defect in which pages of a comic book are trimmed long and are not separated at right-hand corners or along the right edge. (2) A rare printing defect where a new roll of paper is glued to the spent roll while still on the press.

Jugate   A political item, such as a button or pin, that includes two images. A jugate pin may have the presidential and vice-presidential candidates pictured. Jugate images are also found on various forms of political campaign items such as postcards, pennants and posters. Similar to a trigate item.

K

Kennedy Half Dollar One of the official U.S. fifty-cent coins picturing President John F. Kennedy. The Kennedy half dollar was first minted in 1964 and carries a value of fifty cents or fifty one-hundredths (50/100) of a dollar. The Kennedy half dollar replaced the Franklin half dollar which was minted from 1948 to 1963. Also known as a half dollar.

Key Coin The number one, most important coin of a particular series. Also known as king.

Key Issue A comic or comic book issue that contains a first appearance, origin or other historically or artistically important feature considered especially desirable by collectors. Also known as a key book.

L

Label Displays the title, issue number, publisher and grade of a comic book.

Lamination (1) A thin piece of metal that has nearly become detached from the surface of a coin. (2) A clear plastic cover with adhesive used by early collectors to protect comics.

Large Cent A large copper United States coin, which carries a value of one cent or one one hundredth (1/100) of a dollar.

Large Letters (LL) The size of the lettering of the date on a coin. The large letters designation refers to the large letters displayed in a coin's date.

Large Motto (LM) A common name for the particular variety of two-cent coins minted in 1864. The large motto designation refers to the large letters displayed in the coin's motto.

Large Scale Model and toy trains made since 1970 that use No. 1 gauge track. The model and toy trains are scaled to different ratios including 22.5:1.

Laserdisc A laser-read large optical disc playback device used for the reproduction of audio and video signals. The laserdisc was a precursor of the smaller DVD format, which was a precursor for the high-definition Blu-ray format.

LBC An abbreviation for the lower or left side or edge of back cover on a comic book.

Legend A specific phrase that appears on a coin. For example, E PLURIBUS UNUM.

Lenticular A piece of plastic that changes the image seen when the plastic piece is moved back and forth. Theatrical release movie posters are sometimes made from lenticular materials and are quite valuable. Also known as a flasher.

Lenticular Cover Images on a comic or comic book cover that move when viewed at different angles, specially prepared and affixed to the cover. Also known as a flicker cover.

Letter of Authenticity (LOA) May be provided by a seller to prove an item is verified as authentic. Similar to a Certificate of Authenticity (COA).

LFC An abbreviation for the lower, left side or edge of the front cover on a comic.

LFT An abbreviation for left.

Liberty The symbolic figure used in many U.S. coin designs.

Liberty Cap The head of Miss Liberty, with a cap on a pole by her head, used on certain U.S. half cents and large cents.

Liberty Head The design used on most United States gold coins from between 1838 and 1908.

Liberty Nickel Refers to the Liberty Head nickel or V nickel minted between 1883 and 1912.

Light Creasing A crease 2 inches long or less on a comic book.

Light Line The band of light seen on photographs of coins. A light line is especially visible on proof coins.

Limited Edition (1) This term is usually associated with art and fine art prints although limited edition items may be associated with various collectible items such as action figures, toys, coins, trading cards and Barbie dolls. (2) A manufacturing run restricted to a limited number of pieces or figures that are not produced in large quantities.

Limited Production A manufacturing run restricted to a limited time span.

Lincoln Head Cent The United States of America's official one-cent coin picturing President Abraham Lincoln. The Lincoln Head cent was first minted in 1909 and carries a value of one cent or one one-hundredths (1/100) of a dollar. Also known as a penny.

Line Drawn Cover A comic book cover published in the traditional way, whereby pencil sketches are overdrawn with India ink and then colored in. Also known as a grey tone cover, photo cover or painted cover.

Liner A coin classified in between two different grades.

Lint Mark A repeated depression on a coin caused by a thread that attached itself to the die during the manufacturing process.

Lionel Trains A toy train manufacturer established in 1900. www.lionel .com.

Lithograph A method for printing utilizing a lithographic limestone or a metal plate with a completely smooth surface.

Live A sports trading card product is referred to as live when it has been released by its manufacturer and is available for sale. The date when a product goes live is called its release date.

Live Auction An auction that takes place in real time. Live auctions also include those conducted online.

LLBC An abbreviation for the lower left corner of back cover on a comic.

Logo The title of a strip or comic book as it appears on the cover or title page.

Long Arm A firearm with a long barrel.

Loose An action figure or toy that is sold or purchased without its original packaging and having no accessories.

Loose Staples Refers to staples which can be easily moved and no longer hold comic pages tightly. Also known as a popped staple.

Lot (1) The unique number assigned by an auction house to an item that is to be sold in a particular sale. (2) A grouping of trading cards.

Loupe A loupe (pronounced loop) is a type of magnification device (usually set in an eyepiece) used by numismatists, jewelers and horologists to see things more closely.

LRBC An abbreviation for the lower right corner of a comic book's back cover.

LRFC An abbreviation for the lower right corner of a comic book's front cover.

LSH The acronym for the Legion of Super Heroes in comics.

Luster The result of light reflecting on the flow lines of a coin, whether it is visible or not. Alternate spelling is lustre.

Lustrous A term used to describe coins that still have their original mint bloom.

M

Mail Bid Sale An auction or sale where bidding is limited to bids by mail.

Major Variety A coin that is easily recognized as having a major difference from other coins of the same mint, date, design and type.

Manufacturing Fold A defect in which some pages of the comic are folded during the printing and/or the paper manufacturing process.

Mark(s) or Markings   (1) The imperfections found on a coin that are acquired after its striking. (2) The letters, numbers and symbols placed by the manufacturer of a doll on the doll's head or body. These markings are used as a means of identification. (3) The imperfections found on a coin acquired after its striking.

Market Grading   (1) A numerical grade that matches the grade at which a particular coin generally is traded in the marketplace. (2) The grading standard used by the Professional Coin Grading Service (PCGS).

Market Price   The economic price for which a good or service is offered in the marketplace.

Market Value   (1) The price at which an asset would trade in a competitive auction setting. (2) The price at which an asset is valued in the marketplace.

Married Item   A term in the antique trade used to describe furniture when it is composed of parts that were not originally made together.

Marvel Chipping   A bindery defect that causes a series of chips and tears at the top, bottom and right edge of the cover of a comic.

Master Die   The main coin die produced from the master hub.

Master Hub   The original hub created by the portrait lathe. This term is commonly used with coins.

Maverick Pages   Interior pages of a comic that are not the same size or shape as the majority of the rest of the pages. Most commonly known as a bindery defect. Also known as a maverick signature.

Maximum Bid   The upper bid limit set by the buyer when using proxy or automatic bidding.

McFarlane Toys   An action figure manufacturing company which produces many extremely sought after and highly collectible lines of action figures and toys from sports, comic books, the military, video games, horror, fantasy, sci-fi, music, television and movies. McFarlane Toys was established in 1994 and is currently the fifth largest action figure manufacturer in the United States of America. www.spawn.com.

Medium Date (MD)   Refers to the size of the digits of the date on a coin.

Medium Letters (ML)   Refers to the size of the lettering of the date on a coin.

Melt   A slang term used to describe the intrinsic value of a particular numismatic item.

Mercury Dime   The common name for the Winged Liberty Head dime which was issued between 1916 and 1945.

Metal Stress Lines   Radial lines, sometimes visible, which result when the metal flows outward from the center of the planchet during the minting process.

Mid-Spine   The section of the comic book's spine which is in between the staples.

Milling Mark   A mark which results when the reeded edge of one coin hits the surface of another coin.

Minimum Bid   The smallest amount a buyer can bid.

MINMB   An abbreviation for mint in near mint box.

MINMP   An abbreviation for mint in near mint package.

Minor League Card   A sports trading card featuring players and teams from the minor leagues.

Minor Variety   A coin that has a minor difference from other coins of the same design, type, date and mint.

Mint   An official coining facility of the U.S. Government.

Mint Bloom   The original luster still visible on a coin.

Mint Mark   A variation of the coinage term mintmark.

Mint Set   A set of uncirculated coins from a particular year comprising coins from each mint.

Mint Set Toning   The colors and patterns mint coins have acquired from years of storage in the cardboard holders.

Mint State   Coins with numerical grades of MS/PR-60 through MS/PR-70. Mint state coins also represent business strike coins that have never been in circulation.

Mintage   The number of coins of a particular date struck at a given mint during a particular year.

Mintmark   The tiny letter stamped into the die of a coin to denote the mint at which a particular coin was struck.

Miscut   A bindery defect where cover and/or pages are not cut square or are cut to the wrong size. Also known as mistrimmed.

Mis-Struck   Refers to error coins that have striking irregularities.

Mishandled Proof   A proof coin, which has been circulated and/or cleaned. If a proof is mishandled, the grade of a coin is reduced to below MS/PR-60.

Missing Edge Lettering   A coin which does not display any of the intended design on the edge of the coin.

Modern Era of Toy Trains   All model and toy trains manufactured since 1970.

Mohair   The hair of the Angora goat used in the wigs of antique dolls.

Moisture Damage   The wrinkling and/or stains on a comic caused by absorption of a liquid.

Moisture Ring   The circular wrinkling and/or stain caused on the paper of a comic by absorption of moisture from the bottom of a cup or glass.

Molded Ears   Doll ears which are molded right onto a doll's head. The opposite of molded ears are applied ears.

Morgan Dollar   The common name used for the Liberty Head silver dollar minted between 1878 and 1904. The Morgan Dollar was also minted in 1921.

Mother of Pearl   Refers to the iridescent lining of certain shells such as oyster or mussels used as a decorative inlay in furniture and other smaller decorative items.

Motto   An inscription or phrase on a numismatic item.

Mule Error   A rare mint error where the obverse die is of one coin and the reverse die is of another coin.

Muscle Car   American mid-size cars manufactured from 1964 to 1972 which were supplied with large, powerful V8 engines, superchargers and special exhaust systems. The first true muscle car was the 1964 Pontiac GTO.

Mutilated   A term used to describe a coin damaged to the point where it no longer can be graded.

Multiple Bindery Staples   A bindery defect in which the comic book is stapled additional times unnecessarily.

Multiple Reading Creases   Creases in the pages of a comic book. Also known as reading creases.

Multi-Seller Auction   Refers to an auction in which properties owned by many sellers, offered through a common promotional campaign, are auctioned in a single event.

Mylar™   An inert, very hard, space-age plastic used to make high-quality protective bags and sleeves used for comic book storage.

N

Name Stamp   Indicates an ink stamp with someone's name and sometimes someone's address that has been stamped in or on the comic or comic book.

National Rifle Association (NRA) Standards of Condition for Grading Antique Firearms:

Excellent—All original parts, over 80% original finish. Sharp lettering, numerals and design on metal and wood, unmarred wood, fine bore.

Factory New—All original parts, 100% original finish. Perfect condition in every aspect, inside and out.

Fair—Some major parts replaced, minor replacement parts may be required, metal rusted, may be lightly pitted all over. Vigorously cleaned or re-blued, rounded edges of metal and wood. Principal lettering, numerals and design on metal partly obliterated. Wood scratched, bruised, cracked or repaired where broken. In fair working order or can be easily repaired and placed in working order.

Poor—Major and minor parts replaced, major replacement parts required and extensive restoration needed. Metal deeply pitted, principal lettering, numerals and design obliterated. Wood badly scratched, bruised, cracked or broken. Mechanically inoperative, generally undesirable as a collector's firearm.

Fine—All original parts, over 30% original finish. Sharp lettering, numerals and design on metal and wood. Minor marks in wood, good bore.

Good—Some minor replacement parts, metal smoothly rusted or lightly pitted in places, cleaned or re-blued. Principal letters, numerals and design on metal legible. Wood refinished, scratched bruised or minor cracks repaired. In good working order.

Very Good—All original parts, none to 30% original finish. Original metal surfaces smooth with all edges sharp. Clear lettering, numerals and design on metal. Wood slightly scratched or bruised. Bore disregarded for collectors' firearms.

National Rifle Association (NRA) Standards of Condition for Grading Modern Firearms:

Excellent—New condition, used but little, no noticeable marring of wood or metal, bluing perfect (except at muzzle or sharp edges).

Fair—In safe working condition, but well worn, perhaps requiring replacement of minor parts or adjustments, which should be indicated in advertisement; no rust, but may have corrosion pits which do render the gun unsafe or inoperable.

Good—In safe working condition, minor wear on working surfaces, no broken parts, no corrosion or pitting which will interfere with proper functioning.

New—Not previously sold at retail, in same condition as current factory production.

Perfect—In new condition in every respect.

Very Good—In perfect working condition, no appreciable wear on working surfaces, no corrosion or pitting, only minor surface dents or scratches.

New   A term for a numismatic item that never has been in circulation.

Nickel   See *Jefferson Nickel.*

Nickel-Plating   The technique used for coating cast-iron or steel toys with molten nickel to prevent rusting and enhance appearance.

Nippon   A country of origin mark of Japan. The Nippon mark was used on exported porcelain items from Japan between 1891 and 1921.

NM   An abbreviation for near mint.

No Arrows   Coins without arrows by their dates during years when other coins had arrows by the date.

No Cents Nickel   Liberty Head or V nickels struck in 1883 without any sort of denomination engraved on the coin.

No Cover (NC)   A comic book with the cover missing. Also known as cover missing.

No Date (ND)   Refers to a comic book that has no date given on the cover or indicia page.

No Grade   The term applies to a coin returned from a grading service which was not encapsulated due to a variety of reasons.

No Motto   Coins struck without the motto, IN GOD WE TRUST.

No Number (NN)   Occurs when there is no number given on the cover or indicia page of a comic book.

Non-Paying Bidder   A bidder who does not pay for items they have won. Also known as a deadbeat bidder.

Non-Sport Card   A trading card that depicts something other than sports, such as movies, television, entertainers and celebrities.

Notching   Indentations along the edge of a sports or non-sports trading card, sometimes caused by a rubber band. Notching decreases a trading card's value.

Numbered   (1) Collectibles that are numbered, with lower serial numbers, within a specific edition are considered more desirable to a collector. (2) A sports trading card whose print run is limited to a specific quantity that is stamped or printed on the card itself. A trading card or collectible that is stamped 25/1000, is read as "25 out of 1,000."

Numbered Print   A print that is part of a limited edition and has been numbered by hand. Also see *Numbered.*

Numismatic Guaranty Corporation (NGC)   A third-party coin grading service based in Parsippany, New Jersey. www.ngccoin.com

Numismatic News   A weekly numismatic periodical which provides weekly reports on market trends and news concerning collectible

U.S. coins and paper money which was established in 1952. www
.numismaticnews.net

Numismatics   The science of money. Coins, paper money, tokens and all
related monetary items are included.

Numismatist   A person who collects coins, paper money (currency),
tokens and medals.

O

O Mint   Refers to coins struck and minted at the New Orleans, Louisiana
branch mint. This mint uses the O mintmark.

Oak   The more common name of several hundred trees and shrubs of
the genus Quercus. Its durability lends itself well to furniture making. The wood color varies from light tan to deep leathery brown with
black grain. Variations are due to differences in the soil and climate.

Obverse   (1) The front or heads side of a coin. (2) The front of a trading
card which displays the picture.

Off Center   A coin struck on a blank that was not properly centered over
the anvil or lower die.

Oil Stain   A defect in which oil has penetrated the cover and/or interior
pages of a comic or comic book causing them to become translucent
in the area of the stain.

Oleographs   Chromolithographs printed on a textured surface. See
Chromolithographs.

On-Site Auction   An auction conducted on the premises of the property
being sold.

One Sheet   A 27- × 41-inch poster usually printed on paper stock and
usually folded; the standard movie advertising poster size in the
United States.

Open Head   A doll's head with the crown cut out so its eyes can be
inserted.

Opening Bid   The first acceptable bid at an auction.

Orange Peel Surfaces   The dimple-textured fields seen on many proof
gold coins. The surfaces on these coins resemble the surface of an
orange.

Origin   When the story of a comic book character's creation is introduced.

Original   A term used to describe a coin which never has been dipped,
cleaned or struck from original dies in the same year as the date it
bears.

Original Art   A one-of-a-kind piece of art created by an artist.

Original Roll   Coins in fixed quantities which are wrapped in paper and stored at the time of their issuance.

Original Toning   The term used for the color acquired naturally by a coin that has never been cleaned or dipped.

Over Cover   A condition common in 1950s-era comic books where the cover extends approximately one-sixteenth (1/16) of an inch beyond its interior pages.

Over Mintmark   A coin struck with a die on which one mintmark is engraved over a different mintmark.

Over-Dipped   A coin which has become dull from too many baths in a dipping solution.

Overdate   A coin struck from a die with a date which has one year punched over a different year.

Oversized Cards   Any base, common, insert or other trading cards not of standard or wide-vision size.

P

P Mint   Refers to coins struck and minted at the main U.S. Mint located in Philadelphia, Pennsylvania. This mint uses the P mintmark.

Packs   The original wrapper with base and insert cards within, often called wax packs, typically containing two to eight trading cards per pack.

Pages Out of Order (POOO)   A rare bindery defect in which the pages are bound together in the wrong order, causing the pages of a comic book to be out of sequence.

Pages Trimmed   The top, bottom and right-hand edge of the comic book or possibly some interior pages, have been trimmed with a paper cutter, hand blade or pneumatic cutter to hide edge defects.

Painted Cover   (1) The cover taken from an actual painting instead of a line drawing. (2) An inaccurate name for a grey-toned cover. Also known as a line-drawn cover.

Pannapictagraphist   Someone who collects comic books.

Paper Abrasion   A rough patch or area where paper has been abraded on a rough surface, leaving a rough texture which is often faded.

Paper Cover   A comic book cover made from the same newsprint as the interior pages.

Partial Edge Lettering   A coin which has at least one complete letter or star missing.

Patina   (1) A greenish coating on the surface of bronze or copper that develops with age. (2) The mellowing of age on any object or material due to exposure, handling, repeated waxing or polishing. Also known as toning.

Pattern   A test striking of a coin produced to demonstrate a proposed design, size or composition.

Pave   Stones or jewels set closely together so no metal is seen between the settings.

PCGS   Abbreviation for the Professional Coin Grading Service.

Peace Dollar   The common name for silver dollars struck and minted between 1921 and 1935.

Pedigree (Coin)   A detailed and exhaustive listing of a coin's current owner plus all known previous owners of the same coin.

Pedigree or Pedigreed Collection   The status given to certain highly-publicized and usually high-grade comic book collections and finds.

Penciller   The artist who creates the original line drawings used in a comic book.

Perfect Binding   A process whereby pages are glued into the cover of a comic or comic book as opposed to being stapled to the cover. Also called square bound or square back.

Perforations   A small hole in the page margins of a comic which sometimes occurs as part of the manufacturing process.

Period   An item or piece made at the time its style first originated.

Peripheral Toning   Light, medium or dark coloring around the edge of a coin.

Pewter   An alloy of tin and lead that produces a metal with a dull gray appearance. Used for tableware and other small objects copying silver forms. It was replaced by chinaware.

Philadelphia Gum Co.   A major manufacturer of professional football trading cards in the 1960s.

Philatelist   A person who collects postage stamps.

Photo Cover   A comic book cover made from a photograph instead of a painting or line drawing. Also known as a line-drawn cover.

Photomechanical Prints   Prints made from photographically prepared printing surfaces.

Photo Reactive Inks   Certain inks used in the printing of comics which contain a higher proportion of metals, thus decreasing their stability and resistance to fading.

Pickle Smell A description of the odor of ascetic acid, which is often associated with browning and/or brittle paper on a comic.

Piedfort Refers to French coins which were once made with the double thickness of regularly minted coins to signify double value.

Pioneer Gold Privately issued gold coins struck and minted prior to 1861.

Plain Edge A flat, smooth edge seen mainly on a small denomination coinage.

Planchet The blank disk of metal before it is struck by a coining press transforming it into a coin.

Planchet Defects Any abnormality found on a coin blank.

Planchet Striations Fine lines found on some proof coins.

Plated A coin to which a thin layer of metal has been applied.

Platinum A precious metal sometimes used in the striking, manufacture and minting of coins.

Platinum Age The first age of comics beginning in 1897.

Playmates Toys A popular maker of toys and action figures established in 1966. Major properties include Teenage Mutant Ninja Turtles (TMNT), Terminator Salvation, Star Trek, Rainbow Brite, The Simpsons, Strawberry Shortcake and Nickelodeon's iCarly. www.playmatestoys.com.

Plugged A coin which has had a hole expertly filled which can only be detected and analyzed under magnification.

Pneumatic Cutter An industrial tool used to cut large amounts of paper.

PNG Certificate A certificate from the Professional Numismatists Guild (PNG) which guarantees the authenticity of a coin.

POC An abbreviation for pencil on cover regarding comics.

Polished Die A die which has been basined to remove clash marks or other die injury.

Polypropylene A type of plastic used in the manufacture of comic book bags.

Polyvinyl Chloride (PVC) A chemical used in coin flips to make them more pliable.

Pop Top A coin which scores the maximum number of points on the PCGS Set Registry.

Popped Staple A term used to describe a condition where the comic book cover has split at the staple and has become detached or popped loose.

Porcelain   A hard, translucent, white ceramic material. Porcelain created a sensation when it was first imported from the Far East to 17th-century Europe due in part to the mystery surrounding its creation. It started an intense competition among European factories searching for the formula.

Porous   A description indicating a rough or granular surface. A porous quality on a coin is typically seen on copper coins minted before 1816.

Post-Golden Age   Comic books published between 1945 and 1950.

Post-Silver Age   Comic books published after 1969.

Pottery   Refers to all ceramic wares with the exclusion of porcelain.

Pre-Golden Age   Comic books published prior to Action Comics #1 in June, 1938.

Premium Quality (PQ)   A term applied to coins that are the best examples within a particular grade.

Presentation Copy   A copy of a printed item inscribed and signed by the author or publisher and provided as a gift.

Presentation Striking   A coin, often a proof or an exceptionally sharp business strike, that is struck specially and given to an important person or dignitary.

Preview   The specified time frame available for individuals to view, examine and critique items offered at an auction.

Price Realized   The final selling price of a particular item at an auction.

Price Stickers   Adhesive-backed stickers applied to comic covers to alter the cover price.

Print Through   The printing on the inside of the front cover of a comic book which is visible to varying degrees if one were looking through the front of the cover. Also known as a transparent cover.

Pristine   A term applied to coins in original and unimpaired condition which are graded at MS/PR-67 or higher.

Private Auction   A seller may choose this option for his or her eBay auctions to hide the bidder's identification from the other bidders and visitors to that seller's eBay auction site.

Professional Numismatists Guild (PNG)   A dealer organization established in 1955. Membership in the Professional Numismatists Guild is restricted by financial and longevity requirements. www.pngdealers.com.

Progressive Rolled Spine   The spine roll of a comic book is more pronounced on one end than the other.

Promo Cards Trading cards that are distributed, typically in advance, by the manufacturer to enhance sales.

Prototype A type of action figure designed never to make it to final production or manufacture.

Proof (PR) A coin usually struck from a specially prepared coin die on a specially prepared planchet.

Proof Dies Specially prepared dies, often sandblasted or acid picked, used to strike proof coins.

Prooflike (PL) Term to designate a coin that has mirror-like surfaces. The term is especially applicable to Morgan dollars.

Proof-Of-Purchase (POP) The white area that displays the bar code for a retail item.

Proof Only Issue A coin struck only in proof.

Proof Set A coin set containing proof issues from a particular year.

Provenance (1) The documentation of the history of ownership of an item. If provenance can be verified during the authentication process of an antique, signed document or painting, then the value of the item will increase. (2) The place of origin or earliest known history of an item.

Proxy Bid The auctioneers who accept and perform the bidding on behalf of buyers who are unable to attend an auction. Buyers will inform the auction house personnel of the maximum amount they will bid for a particular item and the auctioneers will bid on behalf of the buyers incrementally, going up to, but not above the buyer's stated maximum bid.

PVC Damage A thin film left on a coin after its storage in flips containing polyvinyl chloride (PVC).

PVC Flip Any of the various soft coin flips which contain polyvinyl chloride (PVC).

Q

Qualified A label used by the Certified Guaranty Company (CGC) which designates those comic books with a significant defect that needs specific description.

Quarter Eagle A two-and-one-half dollar gold coin (with a face value of $2.50).

Questionable Toning The term used to describe the color on a coin which may not be its original color.

Quinone The substance in ink that promotes oxidation and discoloration and is associated with transfer stains.

R

Rain Check   A request form offered by a store for items carried by the store but not available in existing stock. Also known as a waiting list.

Rainbow Toning   The term used for the non-original color seen on silver dollars which are stored in bags.

Rare   (1) Indicates a coin within a series which is very difficult to find. (2) Denotes a comic with very limited numbers in existence; approximately 10–20 copies.

Rarity   (1) The number of specimens existing of any particular numismatic item. (2) The state or quality of being rare.

Rarity Scale   A term referring to a numerical rating system.

Raw   (1) A numismatic item, usually a coin, that has not been encased by a grading service. (2) A trading card that has not been graded or sealed in any type of permanent holder.

RBC   An abbreviation for the right side or edge of the back cover of a comic book.

Readers Crease   A defect in the spine of a comic book caused by someone folding back the pages.

Recessed Staples   These occur when the staple lateral bar penetrates below the plane of the cover of a comic without breaking through.

Red (RD)   A copper coin which still retains 95% or more of its original mint bloom or color.

Red Back   A trading card with a red back. Most common with trading cards of 1951 from Topps called the Topps Red Back Set.

Red Brown (RB)   A copper coin which has from 5 to 95% of its original minting color.

Redbook   An annual price guide sometimes referred to as the bible of printed numismatic retail price guides. This price guide was first issued in 1947.

Redemption Cards   Special trading cards which are mailed back to the card's manufacturer for a special card or some other gift.

Reeded Edge   Term for the grooved notches on the edge of some coins.

Reeding Mark(s)   A mark or marks, caused when the reeded edge of one coin comes in contact with the surface of another coin.

Regional Set   A sports trading card set issued only in a specific geographic area.

Reglossing   A comic book repair technique whereby silicone or other clear sprays or varnishes are applied to comic book covers in an attempt to restore cover ink reflectivity.

Regular Issue   Coins that are struck and minted for commerce.

Regular One Sheet   When a one sheet poster with credits follows the release of an advance one sheet or teaser one sheet.

Regular Strike   Denotes coins struck with normal coining methods on ordinarily prepared planchets. Also referred to as business strike.

Re-Issue   A manufacturing process of reproducing or recasting an action figure or toy from an existing mold and redistributing it to retailers.

Relief   The height of the devices of a particular coin design.

Re-Listing   The process of listing an item again if it did not sell initially.

Remainders   Comic books which remain unsold at the newsstand.

Repaint   A type of manufacturing process regarding the casting or repainting of an existing item in a different color plastic in order to create a new action figure or toy.

Replica   A copy or reproduction of a particular item. Also see *Fake.*

Reprint Comics   Comic books which contain newspaper strip reprints.

Reprint Poster   A poster which has been exactly duplicated in image, color, etc. though it may vary slightly in size from the original.

Reproduction Poster   When an old movie poster is reprinted. Also known as a reprint poster.

Repunched Date   When a date on a coin was punched into the die and then punched in again at a different position.

Reserve   The minimum price that a seller is willing to accept for an item to be sold at auction. Also known as the reserve price.

Reserve Auction   An auction where the seller reserves the right to establish and implement a reserve price. The seller at a reserve auction may opt to accept or decline any and/or all bids or to withdraw the item up for auction at any time prior to the announcement of the completion of the auction.

Reserve Price   The minimum price an item will sell for, which is set by seller and/or the auction house prior to the start of the auction. If auction bidding does not reach the seller's required minimum price, the item will not be sold.

Resin   A plastic material that allows for fine detailing in collectible sculptures.

Restoration   A treatment that returns a collectible to a known or assumed state through the addition of non-original material for aesthetic enhancement.

Restored Copy   A comic book that has had restoration work.

Restrike A coin struck later than indicated by its date, often with different dies.

Retail Cards Trading cards, packs, boxes and cases sold to the public, typically via large retail stores, such as K-Mart, Target and Wal-Mart.

Retired A piece that the manufacturer has decided to stop making.

Retoned A coin that has been dipped or cleaned and then reacquires color, whether naturally or artificially.

Retool An action figure whose design recycles many parts from a pre-viously-released item but represents a new character or version of a character.

Reverse (1) The back side of a coin. (2) The back side of a card.

Revival A comic book character that becomes active after a period of dormancy.

Rice Paper A thin, transparent paper commonly used by restorers to repair tears and replace small pieces on covers and pages of comic books.

Riddler A machine, used by minting facilities, that screens out planchets of the wrong size and shape. This procedure is completed prior to striking.

Rim The raised area around the edges of the obverse and reverse of a coin.

Rim Nick The term for a mark or indentation on the rim of a coin or other metallic numismatic item.

Roll A set number of coins rolled up in a coin wrapper.

Roll Friction Minor displacement of metal, mainly on the high points, seen on coins stored in rolls.

Rolled Edge Also known as a rim.

Rolled Edge Ten Also known as the Indian Head Eagle coin, which was struck and minted as a regular issue coin with a mintage of only 31,550 units.

Rolled Spine A condition where the left edge of a comic book curves toward the front or back. Also see *Progressive Rolled Spine.*

Roller Marks A term that refers to the mostly parallel incuse lines seen on some coins after striking.

Rookie Card (RC) The first sports trading card produced of a player or athlete, that is a part of a nationally distributed, fully licensed sports card trading set.

Roosevelt Dime The official U.S. ten-cent coin picturing President Theodore Roosevelt. The Roosevelt dime was first minted in 1946 and carries a value of ten cents or ten one-hundredths (10/100) of a dollar. Also known as a dime.

Rosette   A circular-shaped, floral ornament.

Rotisserie Restoration   When someone totally dissembles a car and the body is taken off the vehicle's frame. The body of the vehicle is then placed on a rotisserie, which can be turned to show any area on the car.

Roundel   A circular ornament, which may or may not incorporate some applied or inlaid decorative moulding or carving.

Rub   The slight wear and tear on a coin.

Rust Migration   When rust stains have moved from the staples in a comic to the paper.

Rust Stain   (1) A red brown stain caused by a comic's proximity to a rusty object. (2) A stain associated with rusty staples.

S

S Mint   Refers to coins struck and minted at the San Francisco, California branch mint. This mint uses the S mintmark.

Sacagawea Dollar   One of the United States of America's official dollar coins picturing a Shoshone woman named Sacagawea. The Sacagawea dollar coin was first minted in 2000 and carries a value of one dollar or one hundred cents. The Sacagawea dollar coin consists of a gold tone or color. Also called a Sac.

Saint   A slang term used to describe the Saint Gaudens–inspired Double Eagle which was struck and minted between 1907 and 1933.

Saint Gaudens   Refers to the name of Augustus Saint Gaudens. The Saint Gaudens coin is also known as the Liberty Head Double Eagle or Saint.

Satin Finish   An experimental proof surface used on United States gold coins after 1907.

Satin Luster   A fine, silky luster seen on many business strike coins.

Satinwood   A pale yellowish West Indian wood with a satin finish that first gained popularity in Britain in the late 18th century, replacing mahogany for small scale furniture. Due to its rarity and cost, it is typically reserved for veneer and inlays.

Scale   The size of a collectible, relative to its prototype.

Scraped Staple   A staple that has had rust or other discoloration removed by scraping the surface.

Screw Press   The first type of coining press used at the U.S. Mint.

Sea Salvage Coin   A coin that has been retrieved from the ocean, usually from a shipwreck.

Sealed Bid   An auction method where confidential bids are submitted and are to be opened at a predetermined place and time.

Seated Coinage   A term commonly used for the Liberty Seated coinage.

Second Toning   Any toning that occurs after a coin is dipped or cleaned.

Second-Year Card   The card of a player for that player's second year in his or her professional sport.

Secondary Market   Collectibles or items sold by private collectors.

Seller   The person, business or governmental entity which has legal ownership of any interests, benefits or rights inherent to the real or personal property.

Semi-Exclusive   Collectibles similar to exclusives, but often offered to more than one store.

Semi-Mechanical Bank   A toy bank that performs a mechanical function, but is independent of coin activation.

Semi-Monthly   A comic that is published twice a month.

Semi-Numismatic   A term that indicates whether a coin has a significant bullion value or some other numismatic value.

Semi-Prooflike   A term used to describe a coin that has some mirror-like surface qualities, mixed with a satin or frosty luster.

Set   (1) A complete run of a given comic book title. (2) A grouping of comics for sale. (3) A collection of coins in a particular series.

Set Registry   The listing of registered Professional Coin Grading Service (PCGS)–graded sets of coins.

Shallow Staple   A staple which has not penetrated all of the pages and is not visible at the centerfold. Also called a deformed staple.

Shield   The emblem used on certain issues that has horizontal and vertical lines in a shield shape.

Shield Nickel   The common name for the Shield five cent coin, which was struck between 1866 and 1883.

Shilling   Auction bids made to artificially raise the price of an item by the seller or persons not intending to purchase the item.

Shiny Spots   The areas on matte, roman and satin proof coins where the surface has been disturbed.

Short Print (SP)   A sports trading card which is printed in a smaller quantity than other cards in its set or subset.

Shortpack   An action figure included in a pack in limited quantities and there are less per case of this one item than the rest of its companions. Shortpacking causes YDD syndrome, the artificially inflated desire for an otherwise unpopular figure. Opposite of a heavypack.

Shotgun Rolls   (1) Rolls of coins that contain double the normal number of coins in a roll. (2) Paper-wrapped rolls which are machine crimped.

Shoulder Head   A doll's head and shoulders molded together in one piece.

Shoulder Plate   A doll's shoulder portion of a shoulder head.

Siamese Pages   A bindery defect in which pages are trimmed long and are not separated at right-hand corners or along the right edge. Also known as joined pages or bound short.

Sig or Sigs   Short for signature.

Sight Seen   A term to indicate when a buyer of a particular coin or numismatic item in a particular grade wants to view the coin before he/she buys the item.

Sight Unseen   A term used to indicate when the buyer of a particular coin or numismatic item in a particular grade will pay a certain price without examining the item.

Signature Duplicated   A rare bindery defect in which a group of comic book pages are inadvertently duplicated.

Signature Out Of Order   A rare bindery defect in which signatures of comic book pages are bound in the wrong sequence. For example: a 32-page comic book with this defect usually has pages in the following order: 9, 16, 1, 8, 25, 32, 17 and 24.

Signature Reversed   A rare bindery defect of comics in which the orientation of one of the signatures is reversed and appears upside down and backwards.

Signed Edition   A book which the author has personally signed.

Signed-In-The-Presence   An autograph that was signed in the presence of the seller or a representative of a third-party authentication service.

Silver   A term referring to coins struck mostly with silver metals. Silver coins usually consist of 90% silver.

Silver Dollar   A coin with a face value of one dollar which has a silver and copper composition.

Silver Nickel   Also known as a wartime nickel.

Silver Plug   On some early American coins, a silver plug was inserted into a hole in the center of the coin to add weight or value to the coin and to bring it into proper specifications for that time period.

Silver Proof   A black and white (B&W) actual size print on thick glossy paper hand painted by an artist to indicate colors to the engraver.

Sizing   The glaze applied to newsprint at the end of the manufacturing process.

Skirt Lines   The lines representing the folds on Miss Liberty's flowing gown on Walking Liberty half dollars.

Slab   Also known as the holder in which a coin is encased by a grading service.

Slabbed   The process of sending a coin to a third-party grading service to have it authenticated, graded and encased in a properly sealed holder.

Sleep Eyes   A doll's eyes that open when the doll is in an upright position and close when the doll is laid down.

Slug   A slang term used to describe the octagonal and round fifty dollar gold coins struck during the California gold rush.

Small Cent   Cents of a reduced size that replaced the large cent in 1857.

Small Date (SD)   The small size of the digits of the date on a coin.

Small Letters (SL)   The small size of the lettering of the date on a coin.

Small Motto (SM)   The common name for the particular variety of two cent coin of 1864 which included small letters in the motto.

Small Size   A term which refers to the particular diameter of a coin in a series.

Smoke Damage   A grey or black discoloration of a comic which is caused by smoke.

Sniperware   A computer program used to strategically outbid other auction participants at the last possible moment of an online auction to win the auction.

Sniping   The practice of bidding at the very last moment before an online auction ends to win the auction. Sniping can be done manually or through the use of computer software programs. See *Sniperware.*

Soft Sleeve   A thin, transparent plastic holder used to protect a single sports trading card from smudges, spills or anything that could damage the card.

Spare   A derogatory slang term used to describe any undesirable sports trading card, especially a rookie card, memorabilia card or autograph of an athlete who is not a top name in his/her sport.

Spark Erosion Die   A die of a coin made by an electrolytic deposition method.

Spark Erosion Strike   A coin made from spark erosion dies.

Specimen/Specimen Strike (SP)   The term used to indicate special coins struck at the mint from between 1792 and 1816.

Spine   The left-hand edge of an unopened comic book.

Spine Chip   A small piece missing from the area of the spine of a comic book.

Spine Roll   A defect of a comic book caused by improper storage which results in uneven pages and the bowing of the spine.

Spine Split   An even separation at the spine fold of a comic, commonly above or below the staple. Also known as split spine.

Spine Stress   A small fold on a comic book, usually less than a quarter-inch in length. A spine stress is perpendicular to the spine.

Splash Panel   (1) The first panel of a comic book story, usually larger than other panels and usually containing the title of the story. (2) An oversized interior panel.

Splotchy Toning   The color of a coin that is uneven in both composition and shade.

Spoofing   The unethical act of sending an e-mail which is sent to trick the e-mail recipient into thinking the e-mail is coming from a legitimate e-mail address.

Standing Liberty   A coin design with Miss Liberty in an upright, front-facing position.

Standing Liberty Quarter   The common name of a quarter struck and minted between 1917 and 1930.

Staple Extenders   (1) The portion of the staple on a comic book that actually penetrates the paper and can be seen at the centerfold. (2) The portion of the staple that is bent either upwards or downwards towards the center of staple.

State Quarters Program   Specific Washington quarters struck with unique reverse designs for each state, issued in the order of admittance to the United States of America. All 50 state quarters were issued from 1999 to 2008.

Steel Cents   The common name for cents struck in steel and plated in zinc. Steel cents were struck and issued in 1943 and 1944.

Sterling   The term used to describe the standard metal mix in the United States and England which is 92.5% silver and 7.5% copper or another metal.

Sticker on Cover   A price sticker or other sticker attached to the cover of a comic.

Stoneware   A heavy, nonporous, opaque pottery that is fired at a high temperature. It originated in China and was exported to Europe in the 17th century where it was imitated by many factories in Germany, England and the Netherlands.

Stress Lines   Very light, tiny wrinkles occurring along and projecting from the spine of a comic.

Stretche   A stabilizing rail that runs horizontally between furniture legs.

Striations   The term for the incuse polish lines on the die which result in raised lines on coins.

Strike   The act of minting a coin.

Strip   The flat metal rolled to proper thickness from which planchets are cut.

Struck   A term used to describe a coin produced from dies and a coining press.

Struck Copy   A replica of a particular coin made from dies not necessarily meant to deceive.

Struck Counterfeit   A fake coin produced from false dies.

Style Period   The furniture fashionable in a particular time period.

Subscription Center Crease   A large crease found down the center of a comic book caused by the folding of a comic book for mailing.

Subscription Copy   A comic that is sent through the mail direct from the publisher or publisher's agent.

Successful Bidder   The buyer of a particular lot from an auction.

Surface   Coating on the image of a baseball card as well as, but to a lesser degree, the printing on the back of the card.

Surfaces   Both the obverse and reverse of a coin.

Susan B. Anthony Dollar   One of the official U.S. dollar coins picturing woman's suffrage campaigner Susan B. Anthony. The Susan B. Anthony dollar coin was minted from 1979 to 1981 and once again in 1999. This coin carries a value of one dollar or one hundred cents.

Swatch Cards   Insert trading cards that feature a mounted swatch of cloth, such as from a sports player's jersey or an actor's screen-used costume.

Sweating   A procedure in which coins are placed in a bag and shaken vigorously to dislodge or knock off small pieces of metal.

T

Tab Toning   The toning often seen on commemorative coins that were sold in cardboard holders with a round tab.

Tall Chest   A one-part case piece with five, six or seven layers of drawers.

Tanning Line   A brownish stain line of tannin that occurs when wet comic paper dries.

Tape Residue   The adhesive substance from cellophane tape which has penetrated paper fibers.

Target Toning   Coins with circles of color, deeper colors on the periphery often fading to white or cream color at the center.

Tax Sale   The public sale of an individual's personal property at an auction initiated by governmental authority due to nonpayment of property taxes.

Teaser One Sheet   Also known as an advance one sheet poster.

Tear Sealed   A tear that has been glued together.

Teddy's Coin   Also known as the 1907 Indian Head Double Eagle.

Telephone Auction Bids   Bids placed over the telephone during a sale of coins.

Tensor Light   A small, direct light source used by numismatists to examine and grade coins.

Terms and Conditions   The printed rules of an auction house, read and/or distributed to potential bidders prior to an auction.

Territorial Gold   Coins and bars privately struck during the various gold rushes.

Three Cent Nickel   A nickel three cent coin with Liberty Head design. This coin was struck from 1865 to 1889.

Thumbed   A coin that has been doctored in a specific way to cover coin flaws, marks or hairlines.

Tie Bids   When two or more bidders bid exactly the same amount at the same time. When this occurs, the auctioneer must resolve the situation.

Tins   A factory metal can typically filled with trading cards or packs, often with inserts.

Tintype   A photograph made by creating a direct positive on a sheet of iron metal that is blackened by painting, lacquering or enameling. Tintype evolved from the ambrotype process of creating a positive image on a sheet of glass, except that a tintype was produced on iron rather than glass. The iron negatives were coated with black paint or lacquer. Tintypes were extremely popular during the Civil War period and thousands were produced because they could be safely sent by mail. By the 1950s, tintypes were replaced by another instant photographic method, the Polaroid.

Tissue Toning   Color, often vibrant, acquired by coins stored in original mint paper.

Tobacco Card   Cards from the early 1900s that were issued with tobacco products.

Token   A replacement for a coin. For example, bus tokens and phone tokens can be used in place of actual coinage.

Toning   The color seen on many coins.

Tooling Mark   A small and fine line that is found on both authentic and counterfeit coins.

Top Loader   A plastic holder used to protect a single sports or trading card from bending and tearing as well as from edge and corner damage.

Topps Company Inc.   One of the most famous of all sports and entertainment trading card manufacturers. Also known for their manufacturing of confections, stickers and strategy games. Founded in 1938, Topps also manufactures the popular lollipop brands marketed as Ring Pops, Push Pops, Baby Bottle Pops and other novelty candy and gum products. www.topps.com

Trade Dollar   A U.S. silver coin which is slightly heavier than the regular silver dollar. A trade dollar is specifically intended to promote trade in the Far East.

Transfer Die   A die created by relinquishing a coin for a model.

Transfer Stain   The ink from the first page of a comic that rubs off onto the inside front cover causing certain portions to appear to have a yellow color.

Transparent Cover   The printing on the inside front cover of a comic that is visible to varying degrees from the front cover. Also see *print through*.

Trigate   A political item, such as a button or pin, which includes three images. A trigate pin may have images of the presidential and vice-presidential candidates, as well as the candidates' party symbol or flags. Trigate images are also found on postcards, pennants and posters. See also *Jugate*.

Triple Struck   The condition which results when a coin is not ejected from the dies and is struck three times.

Troy Weight   A method of weighing gold and silver or the coins made from those metals.

Trustee's Sale   A sale at an auction held by a trustee.

Tudor   The style period in England from 1485 to 1600.

Two and a Half   Also known as a Quarter Eagle or two-and-one-half-dollar gold coin.

Two Cent Piece   Also known as a Shield two cent coin.

U

Ultra High Relief   A term for an extremely high relief design on a coin.

Ultra Rarity   A coin or other numismatic item that is represented by only a few examples.

Uncirculated (Unc)   (1) A coin or numismatic item that has never been in circulation. (2) A coin without wear.

Uncut Sheets   Sheets of uncut base, insert, promo or other cards.

Underglaze   Any porcelain or china decoration that is applied under, rather than over its glazed finish.

Unreleased Cards   Trading cards printed by the manufacturer but not officially distributed for a variety of reasons.

Upholder   A term used to describe an upholsterer in the 18th century.

Upper Deck, The   A major sports trading card manufacturer which was founded in 1989. The Upper Deck manufactures cards from each of the four major professional American sports: football, basketball, baseball and hockey. www.upperdeck.com

Upsetting Mill   The machine which raises the outer rim on a planchet prior to striking.

V

V nickel   Also known as a liberty head five cent coin.

Variant Cover   Refers to instances when a different cover image is used on the same issue of a comic title.

Veneer   A furniture-making process in which a thin layer of a more beautiful or valuable wood is affixed to a more inferior wood base.

Verifier   A grader at PCGS who looks at graded coins and makes the decision whether the grade indicated is the proper one.

Very Rare   When only one to ten copies of a comic are estimated to be in existence.

Vexillologist   Someone who studies and collects flags.

Vinegar Smell   The effect that occurs when the smell of acetic acid in newsprint starts deteriorating.

Vintage Cars Cars manufactured between 1915 and 1942.

Vintage Cards Cards issued prior to 1979; most commonly between 1930 and 1973.

Voice Box A mechanism used in a doll to make a doll speak or make sounds.

W

Walker Also known as a Walking Liberty half dollar.

Walking Liberty Also known as a Walking Liberty half dollar.

Walking Liberty Half Dollar A particular type of half dollars which were struck between 1916 and 1947.

Watch-List A list of auctions in which someone is interested.

Wartime Nickel A specific type of five cent coin that was struck during World War II.

Washington Quarter The official U.S. twenty-five cent coin picturing President George Washington. The Washington quarter was first minted in 1932 and carries a value of twenty-five cents or twenty-five one-hundredths (25/100) of a dollar. Also known as a quarter.

Watermark A design that is embossed into an item, usually paper, during its production and is used for identification of the paper and paper-maker. A watermark can be seen when the paper is held up directly to a light. Many times currency (paper money) will have a water-mark embossed into each bill to prove the item is authentic and not counterfeited.

Watery Look A look seen on the surfaces of most close collar proof coins.

Wax A universal collecting term for factory-sealed packs or boxes.

Wax Pack An unopened pack of cards named for its traditional form of wax packaging.

Weak Edge Lettering Indicates the edge lettering has a portion of a let-ter, star or inscription missing.

Weak Strike A coin which does not show intended detail because of improper striking pressure or improperly aligned dies.

White Label A promotional vinyl record pressing with a completely blank label denoting it is only a promotional record. This type of record may also have unique black on white printed labels with only the artist and title information or A and B symbols on the record.

White Pages A term used to describe interior pages of a comic book in the best state of preservation.

Whiteness or Whiteness Level   The whiteness of interior pages of a comic compared against a whiteness grading standard.

Wind-Ups   Describes clockwork and spring-driven toys.

Wire Edge   The thin, knife-like projection seen on some coin rims, created when metal flows between the collar and the dies.

Working Die   A die prepared from a working hub used to strike coins.

Working Hub   A hub created from a master die used to create the many working dies required for coinage.

Worm Hole   The small holes eaten into comic paper caused by a variety of termites, insects, mites and worms.

Worn Die   The die of a coin which has lost detail from extended use.

Wrappers   The original trading card pack cover, often with collectible variations.

X

Xylonite   An early and rare form of plastic invented in 1868 which was created to simulate wood.

Y

Yankee Auction   An auction with multiple bids up for sale in which the winner pays the actual price bid.

Yatate   A Japanese brush and ink holder which resembles an antique fountain pen.

Z

Zoëtrope   A large revolving cylinder which produces an illusion of action from a rapid succession of static pictures; used in early animation.

About the Authors

Aaron LaPedis

Long considered one of the world's great collectors and treasure hunters, successful television personality, fine art and memorabilia gallery owner, expert for the FBI and award-winning author of *The Garage Sale Millionaire*, Aaron LaPedis unlocks many of the highly guarded secrets of consistently successful and profitable treasure hunters. Aaron is also an esteemed lecturer at Colorado Free University in Denver, Colorado, and has been interviewed by network television, radio, cable TV and satellite radio. He has been featured in numerous magazines and newspapers.

Aaron LaPedis was the host of the highly rated PBS show in Denver, Colorado, called *Collect This!* In its last four years the show reached 1.5 million national viewers monthly as well as 100,000 viewers per weekend within the state of Colorado.

Besides being seen in many Colorado television markets, *Collect This!* also aired in several Florida markets. Earlier versions of *Collect This!* entitled *Collectibles with Aaron* and *The Collectibles Show* first began airing in May of 2001 on PBS. Aaron successfully taped more than fifty half-hour segments focusing on the diverse world of collectors and collecting. A few of the varied topics covered included coins, wine, art, animation and sports. His expertise on these subjects has made him an extremely popular and highly- sought-after public speaker. Aaron's thoroughly personable and informative style entertains while teaching his audience how they can become better collectors and treasure hunters.

Aaron's expert credentials do not end with hosting his own TV show. The Discovery Channel has featured him in their special "What's America Worth," hosted by Donald Trump, while *Entrepreneur* magazine wrote an article based on his success as a master collector and successful entrepreneur. Aaron has also guest-hosted a collectibles show on Dish Network, written articles for *Denver Magazine* and the *Denver Business Journal* and is a regular columnist for *The Denver Post*. He has also hosted a weekly four-minute segment on the local Denver ABC affiliate, KMGH, called *The Collectibles Guy.*

Aaron LaPedis is the owner of Fascination Street Fine Art Gallery in Denver, Colorado.

Jeffrey D. Kern

Co-author Jeffrey D. Kern has over thirty years of serious treasure-hunting experience to his credit. Like many children who begin the hunt for collectible treasures early in life, Jeffrey discovered his passion for treasure hunting at an early by collecting coins. This helped him develop and hone his interests and abilities, allowing him to grow into the successful collector he is today. Jeffrey actively seeks out and collects movie and television memorabilia, autographed books, coins, art, antiques, action figures, toys, magazines, finisher medals from athletic events, sports collectibles and memorabilia and anything that may be of value to resell at a profit!

Jeffrey has worked professionally as a writer since 2000. Jeffrey has also held the position of senior associate editor for *Widescreen Review,* a monthly national home theater magazine. Throughout his professional writing career, Jeffrey has amassed a portfolio consisting of more than 500 writing clips. In addition to co-authoring *The Garage Sale Millionaire,* Jeffrey has written on many different subjects including consumer electronics, home theater, computers, travel and various human interest topics.

When he isn't writing or collecting, Jeffrey is an Ironman Triathlete.